Hearing the Call across Traditions

Hearing the Call across Traditions
Readings on Faith and Service

Edited by Adam Davis · Foreword by Eboo Patel

Editorial team: Dimitra Tasiouras, Elizabeth Lynn, and Noah Silverman

A co-production of the Project on Civic Reflection,
Illinois Humanities Council, and Interfaith Youth Core

Walking Together, Finding the Way®
SKYLIGHT PATHS®
PUBLISHING
Woodstock, Vermont

Hearing the Call across Traditions: Readings on Faith and Service

2009 Hardcover Edition, First Printing

© 2009 by the Project on Civic Reflection

Foreword © 2009 by Eboo Patel

Library of Congress Cataloging-in-Publication Data

Hearing the call across traditions : readings on faith and service / edited by Adam Davis ; foreword by Eboo Patel.

    p. cm.

  Includes index.

  ISBN-13: 978-1-59473-264-5 (hardcover)

  ISBN-10: 1-59473-264-7 (hardcover)

 1. Religions. 2. Faith. 3. Service (Theology) I. Davis, Adam, 1970–

BL85.H34 2009

204'.4—dc22

                                          2009011818

10 9 8 7 6 5 4 3 2 1

Manufactured in the United States of America

Jacket design: Melanie Robinson

SkyLight Paths is creating a place where people of different spiritual traditions come together for challenge and inspiration, a place where we can help each other understand the mystery that lies at the heart of our existence.

SkyLight Paths sees both believers and seekers as a community that increasingly transcends traditional boundaries of religion and denomination—people wanting to learn from each other, *walking together, finding the way*.

SkyLight Paths, "Walking Together, Finding the Way," and colophon are trademarks of LongHill Partners, Inc., registered in the U.S. Patent and Trademark Office.

Walking Together, Finding the Way®

Published by SkyLight Paths Publishing

A Division of Longhill Partners, Inc.

Sunset Farm Offices, Route 4, P.O. Box 237

Woodstock, VT 05091

Tel: (802) 457-4000   Fax: (802) 457-4004

www.skylightpaths.com

CONTENTS

THE HEAVENS OF FAITH, THE HARLEM OF LIFE

By Eboo Patel

Perhaps the most well-known story in the tradition of Islam, the tradition I belong to, is Muhammad's pilgrimage to a cave on Mount Hira in the year 610 CE. It was there one night, during a period of intense prayer, that Muhammad was gripped three times by the angel Gabriel and, just before he was totally overwhelmed by fear, found a message from God emerging from his lips. It was the first verse of a revelation that would continue, on and off, for the next twenty-three years, and that would ultimately be compiled into the Holy Qur'an.

I remember hearing this story many times when I was young, and one point in particular was always impressed upon me: Muhammad was a regular on that mountain. In fact, he made an annual pilgrimage to the cave of Mount Hira, where he would fast and pray and give alms to the poor. In other words, Muhammad was selected by God to be a prophet precisely because he removed himself from the world to focus on worship.

That felt difficult for me. Ever since I can remember, I have wanted nothing more than to know and love the world, in all its jazz and war. To travel, to taste, to experiment, to see, to serve. And while I felt a longing for God throughout my adolescence, if connecting to the Divine meant removing myself from real life, I wasn't quite ready to make that commitment. I chose the world.

But there was something about that decision that also left me half full. However hard I danced, however far I traveled, however many I served, I felt a hunger for the cosmic. It was a gnawing need I couldn't ignore, and it sent me on a quest that ultimately led me back to a more serious study of Islam. In my reading one night I discovered a story that I was not taught in my Muslim Sunday school.

After receiving revelation, Muhammad never returned up the mountain.

Once he was touched by the Heavens of Faith, Muhammad lived the rest of his years in the Harlem of Life. He married and had children. He preached and he counseled. He brokered peace between warring clans and prepared for battle when he had to. He loved the world, and he lived his life in it, and he did it on the command of God.

In fact, in the Holy Qur'an, God makes it clear that this was His intention for all human beings. We were made to be His servant and representative on Earth. One of our primary duties is to manifest His mercy here. As God tells Muhammad in one of His revelations, "You were sent to be nothing but a special mercy upon all the worlds."

When I read those words, I felt like the curtains had lifted, like faith and life were no longer separate, like there was a bridge between Heaven and Harlem—the bridge of service.

But that wasn't the only bridge I discovered in this insight.

I was coming of age at a time of religious conflict. The grand theory of the post–Cold War era was Samuel Huntington's clash of civilizations; the American political scientist predicted an inevitable cosmic battle between the world's great faiths based on their inherent differences. The evening news seemed like one long commercial for Huntington's theory. From Northern Ireland to South Asia, the Middle East to West Africa, the fighting, the killing, and the dying were being done to the soundtrack of prayer.

It was common to hear educated people say things like, "People from different religions have always killed each other, and they always will. That's just the way religion is."

As my mind started to wrap itself around the connection between faith and service in Islam, I discovered a similar connection in other traditions. Baptist minister Martin Luther King Jr. said, "Any religion that professes to be concerned with the souls of men and is not concerned with the slums that damn them, the economic conditions that strangle them, and the social conditions that cripple them is a dry-as-dust religion." After marching with King in the civil rights march at Selma, Alabama, scholar and teacher Rabbi Abraham Joshua Heschel observed that he felt like his "legs were praying."

Service is not only a bridge between the cosmic and the concrete, but also between Islam and Judaism, Christianity and Buddhism, secular humanism and Hinduism. The diverse community that is humanity is not fated to be divided by the clash of civilizations. We can just as easily be united on the common ground of service. All we have to do is cross the bridge.

The readings that follow give glimpses of this possibility. I hope you find them as beautiful, illuminating, and inspiring as I do. But more than anything, I hope you do more than stare at the possibility of what humanity, in all our diversity, *can be*. I hope you roll up your sleeves, hold out your hand, and cross to the other side.

Two Calls

This book is a response to two calls: the call of faith and the call to service. Across the world's diverse traditions of belief, these two calls are often heard together. Called by faith, we are called to serve—to improve the world in specific ways and to care for those who share the world with us.

And yet, even as the world's religious and philosophical traditions affirm the value of service, each brings its own unique perspective and insight to service and to its manifestation. In short, just as there are many different faiths, there are many different understandings of service.

This book does not insist that we should agree about what we believe or how we serve. Instead, it is intended to help us think and talk about our own and others' commitments, and to do so with the degree of depth and consideration appropriate to the subjects at hand.

We think service is, in a word, deep—deeply meaningful, deeply complex, and deeply wonderful. But if it can be wonderful, it can also be wondered about: what exactly is service, and how is it different from other forms of action and commitment? What gives service its depth, its complexity, its meaning? And why is it that what we think about service is so often linked to what we believe about the larger order or disorder that surrounds us?

Rich Readings, Deep Questions

There are two premises behind *Hearing the Call across Traditions: Readings on Faith and Service.* The first premise is that it is good for people within and across religious and philosophical traditions to

1

reflect on and discuss connections between service and faith. The second premise is that reflection and discussion are deepened and improved when they revolve around rich readings and the questions such readings engender.

We have, in this anthology, collected a wide range of provocative readings that respond to the call to service and the call of faith. In gathering these readings and providing discussion questions and other surrounding materials, we are not hoping to create a textbook that definitively settles any historical, theological, or sociological questions. In fact, we are not hoping this book definitively settles any questions at all. Instead, we are hoping that this anthology will raise new questions and deepen old questions, and we hope that it will help people consider questions that are already close to them—so close, perhaps, that they are often overlooked.

All the readings collected here raise deep questions about service and its real or potential roots in faith. They make for rich conversation because they are wise and complex, open to a range of interpretations. They include short stories, memoirs, philosophy, poetry, sermons, scripture, and essays. The authors are Buddhist, Christian, Hindu, Jewish, Muslim, Taoist, and more. They are young and old, contemporary and ancient, Eastern and Western. They are male and female, though this sort of diversity is a little harder to ensure given the other kinds of diversity we have also pursued. These readings offer perspectives that are all over the conceptual map, but each of them helps us understand the map—our map—more fully.

What, for example, does Gerard Manley Hopkins, a Jesuit, mean when he writes in his poem, "God's Grandeur," that "all is seared with trade; bleared, smeared with toil," and yet "the world is charged with grandeur of God"? Why does Gandhi, a Hindu, write in a 1930 letter that "a life of sacrifice is the pinnacle of art and is full of true joy"? Why does Rumi, an Islamic mystic, suggest in a short poem that "if you've opened your loving to God's love, you're helping people you don't know and have never seen"? What does Chuang-Tzu, a Taoist, mean when he writes that the level of heaven and earth is the "perfect Tao"? Why, for Maimonides, a Jew, does the highest level of giving involve taking the hand of another? How might we follow what poet Mary Oliver calls "The Buddha's Last Instruction," namely, to "make of yourself a light"?

We have collected readings that give rise to questions like these because we believe that there is great value in reflecting on the varied ways we seek to improve our world and on the equally varied commitments behind these efforts. Each of the selected readings invites reflection about service, faith, and the connections between them. Together, these readings encourage us to consider how individuals belonging to different communities and believing in distinct creeds might live and serve together in mutual trust.

The readings are organized thematically to provoke reflection on three key questions:

1. Why do I serve?

2. Whom do I serve?

3. How do I serve?

These are certainly not the only questions relevant to discussing faith and service, but we believe they illuminate many of the obstacles and the joys that accompany lives devoted to faith and service. These questions also correspond to three components central to a vibrant, pluralist community:

1. Respect for particular *identities* (religious and other) of different persons and groups;

2. Intentional, mutually appreciative and enriching *relationships* between diverse individuals and communities; and

3. Active partnerships across lines of difference that promote common *action* for the common good of all groups.

The introductions to each of the three sections offer preliminary thoughts about the theme in question and some general remarks about the readings that follow. Each reading selection is accompanied by a very brief account of its author or source; these short paragraphs are meant to provide basic contextual information but are not intended to interfere with each reader's direct confrontation with the selections themselves.

There are also three appendices at the end of *Hearing the Call across Traditions: Readings on Faith and Service.* Appendix I offers a guide to planning and leading interfaith groups in service and reflection based on the texts in the anthology, as well as information about networks and campaigns of young people engaged in similar work around the world.

Appendix II consists of discussion questions for each selection in the anthology. These questions start with the meaning of the selection itself and then broaden in scope to consider the reader's own opinions, experience, and involvement in service and the inspiration behind it.

We have included these discussion questions here because our chief hope for this book is that it will help people talk with each other about the principles and beliefs that motivate and give shape to the service they do. Each of the organizations that have collaborated on this book is committed to the idea that what we do is linked closely with what we say, think, and believe, and each organization has a good deal of experience helping people talk about challenging and important matters in respectful, productive, illuminating ways. So while we want this book to be read, we also want it to be discussed, and we want it to be discussed not simply as a scholarly exercise but as a way of coming to understand our and others' choices more deeply. The discussion questions provided in appendix II are meant to assist discussion leaders and participants in thinking in fresh and constructive ways about each selection and in drawing connections between the reading and their own lives.

Appendix III organizes the readings by genre (poem, short story, and so on), by religious tradition, and by length so that readers with different uses in mind can get a quick overview of the contents.

WHO IS THIS BOOK FOR?

We have designed the anthology so that different readers can approach it differently—either start to finish, or section by section, or by handpicking readings, or by starting with the discussion questions in appendix II and working back, or some other way. Our hope is that the material we have collected and arranged helps people think and talk with each other about their important work and the commitments behind it.

Even as we have sought to create a collection that appeals to a wide range of potential readers, we have also designed it with a few broad audiences in mind: faith-based communities, service-based communities, and learning-based communities. We imagine that, in many cases, these audiences will overlap.

First, we hope that this book will be used by volunteer and discussion groups at churches, mosques, temples, and other houses of worship. Houses of worship may be the place in our society with the most strongly developed traditions of engaging both in service and in reading and discussion as a means of understanding ourselves. We anticipate that this book will fit within and provide a spark to both kinds of practice.

We hope, second, that this book will serve as a resource for youth advisors, campus chaplains, student-run interfaith youth groups, service organizations, and youth conferences and organizations, and that it will thereby prove useful to youth of diverse religious or philosophical perspectives.

Third, we hope that this book will find a place in educational institutions, from campus organizations to college classes to religious, public, and private high schools. This collection of accessible and complex texts with user-friendly surrounding material will make it an engaging and easy fit for semester-long and yearlong courses. It will also assist groups that gather outside of the classroom to engage in service or explore the many kinds of diversity that animate their communities.

Fourth, we hope that this book will be used by the growing number of civic and service-based organizations engaged in helping their staff, volunteers, and board members explore the values at the heart of their giving and serving through the practice of civic reflection. These include social service agencies, community organizations, charitable foundations, and others.

Fifth, we imagine that this book will be a helpful resource for public humanities organizations that foster humanities-based discussion on questions of individual value and community concern in a wide variety of settings across America.

Finally, we also imagine this collection resonating with individual readers interested in considering literature that addresses ethical questions from a variety of perspectives. We would like people to talk with others about what they read in here, and we would especially like people to talk about these readings in order to think more about the work they do in the world. But this book, like every book, belongs to each reader to use and enjoy. We won't put up a fight if some readers simply want to read it and think about what it contains.

REFLECTING ON SERVICE

With *Hearing the Call across Traditions: Readings on Faith and Service*, we aim to provide a collection of readings and surrounding materials that will help diverse groups of people discuss and reflect on how their different traditions define and understand service. There are a few reasons we think such an anthology is needed. First, this sort of anchored reflection and discussion helps us gain greater insight into how our own traditions articulate the call to service. Second, in talking through selections such as those included here, we gain a greater appreciation of and respect for the religious and philosophical traditions of our neighbors and fellow citizens. Third, we become more likely to engage in service, not just within our own religious or cultural group but in diverse settings with the people and traditions we have come to understand better. This, in turn, strengthens the trust and understanding between individuals and across communities.

In short, we gather this range of readings here because we believe that there is a deep yearning among the vast majority of people of all religious and philosophical traditions to make real their most enduring shared principles—to care for creation, to serve others with compassion, and to protect and enhance the gift of life—and because we believe that reflecting on these principles strengthens our capacity to embody them.

In closing, a few words of acknowledgement: this anthology benefited from the gifts, large and small, of several organizations and individuals. In particular, we would like to thank the Lake Institute on Faith and Giving for a very generous grant in support of permissions for the volume, and the Lilly Endowment for its founding support of the Project on Civic Reflection. We would also like to thank several advisors along the way, among them Scott Alexander, Dorothy Bass, Martin E. Marty, Sandy Sasso, and Robert V. Thompson. We are also grateful to many colleagues at our own organizations who offered key ideas and invaluable support: Mary Ellen Geiss, Heather Greenwell, Hafsa Kanjwal, April Kunze, Cassie Meyer, and Eboo Patel of the Interfaith Youth Core; Kelli Covey, Debbie Garbukas, Beth Marco, Susie Quern Pratt, Andy Schwich, and Catherine Tufariello of the Project on Civic Reflection; and Maggie Berndt, Amy Thomas Elder, Ryan Lewis, Maureen McCarthy, and Kristina Valaitis of the Illinois Humanities Council. Finally, thanks to Emily Wichland and Michaela Powell, and especially to Jason A. Smith, for making it possible to present these readings here.

PART I

Why Do I Serve?

I ought to be at joyous ease,
but I can't help thinking of the people in the world.

Shih Te

Two months before his death, Martin Luther King Jr. delivered a sermon in which he asked to be remembered as one who "tried to give his life serving others." Many of us might hope to be remembered similarly—as if we, too, had tried to give our lives serving others.

But King's formulation points to some challenges embedded in the endeavor to realize these hopes. First, King had to *ask* that he be remembered in this way, which suggests that he suspected he will be remembered chiefly for other things. Second, King asked to be remembered as one who *tried* to give his life serving others, which points to his awareness of some distance between his attempt to serve others and the service he actually provided. Third, King talked of "giving his life" to serve others, and this has the sound of something like sacrifice, as if the endeavor to serve others required that King give up his own life.

Even if we agree, then, with the sentiment King expressed, we might wonder why it is that King wanted to be remembered in this way and why we ourselves are likely to want something similar and similarly difficult. We might wonder why we, or anyone, would want to give our lives—or even only to live our lives—serving others. It's my life, after all—why live it for others, why live it for anyone but myself?

Now, some might say that there is nothing here to wonder about, that there is nothing more obvious than the goodness of serving others. But even if we agree that serving others is good, we are likely to have very different reasons for finding it good—reasons relating to our most fundamental beliefs. Some may consider service to be worthwhile because of a particular orientation toward the afterlife, some may consider service to be a fundamental duty, some may see others as part of the self, some may have learned that service is the surest road to happiness, some may do service because they always have, and so on. Most of us have probably internalized some combination of reasons for thinking service to be worthwhile.

This opening part of *Hearing the Call across Traditions: Readings on Faith and Service* contains readings that help us think about the many reasons and beliefs behind our endeavor to serve others— the many reasons and beliefs in many people and traditions and also the many reasons and beliefs within each of us.

For all the differences these readings illuminate, there is also at least one point on which the readings collected in this section agree, namely, that whatever the particular combination of reasons and beliefs there might be within each of us, our desire to serve is linked closely to our sense of who we are. In short, what we think and believe about serving others is a fundamental part of our identity. It is only one small further step to say that what we think and believe about serving others has a lot to do with the communities and traditions that have formed us.

Again, let's consider the example of Martin Luther King Jr.: when King asked to be remembered as one who tried to give his life serving others, he was asking to be remembered as the self he most wanted to be. This request points to the question that frames this opening section: why do I serve? Why is this self—the self that serves others—the self that I most want to be? In King's case, the desire to serve was explicitly tied to his religious community and his religious tradition: King began his sermon with references to scripture and ended it with a story about Jesus. King's attitude toward service was steeped in his beliefs about the larger order and his place within it.

In some of the other readings collected in this section, we see a similarly explicit relationship between beliefs about service and an orientation toward a faith tradition: Sunni Islamic scholar Hamza Yusuf's condemnation of miserliness is at the same time an interpretation of Islamic doctrine; the Dalai Lama explains in his essay on compassion that the Buddhist faith considers "the lives of all beings [to be] just as precious as our own"; and Jane Addams, cofounder of the settlement house Hull House, challenges her readers to express their religion through "the social organism itself."

Poet Walt Whitman and Rabbi Harold M. Schulweis, human rights activist and leading figure in Reconstructionist Judaism, also have the social organism in mind when they point to something beneath or common to religion writ large. And fourth-century Taoist philosopher Chuang-Tzu, like Whitman, moves back from specific actions to consider the underlying conditions or causes of action. In some of the foundational scriptural passages included here—from the Book of Isaiah, the Rig Veda, the Qur'an, the Bhagavad Gita, and the Book of Luke—acting with generosity contains the capacity to ripple out from the specific action, even to carry the potential for repair broadly understood.

But there are other readings in this section that explore the link between service and faith in less explicit ways: Sudanese author Tayeb Salih features a narrator who grows up loving the Qur'an and then finds himself disturbed by what he perceives as injustice within his community and his family; Abraham Joshua Heschel, a leading Jewish theologian, treats solidarity, reciprocity, and sanctity in broad existential terms; and the short Shih Te poems seem to be driven by a belief about connections between people that should be expressed but not necessarily elaborated upon.

Then, too, there are a few readings here that raise troubling questions about the relationship between service and faith, most obviously American author Flannery O'Connor's story about a babysitter who takes it upon herself to have a child baptized, American fiction writer Tim O'Brien's story about soldiers interacting with monks at a temple in Vietnam, Indian author Rabindranath Tagore's narrative poem about a beggar turned giver, and philosopher Friedrich Nietzsche's argument about "the happiness of slight superiority."

Every reading in this section, we think, helps us consider the important and complex question of why we serve. When we ask this question—why?—about service, we are reckoning with ourselves and the world around us in some deeply human way. We are also taking steps to ensure that our service is the gift it is meant to be.

But even as we encourage asking the question, Why do I serve?, we recognize that there are at least two difficulties with taking the question seriously. The first difficulty is that this is a hard—and sometimes impossible—question to answer in a fully satisfying way. When someone asks why, we see that we ourselves may not know why. *Why* can point to wobbles or gaps in our own understanding.

The second difficulty is that *why* can seem to get in the way of whatever we are trying to do. *Why* is a question that seems to back us up, or point us too far forward, or both. We sometimes become impatient with those who ask *why* because it can feel like a kind of sabotage, an obstacle to action. *Why* demands a look back to origins—why are things this way and not some other way?—or a look forward to outcomes—why is this worth doing, what might it lead to?—and thereby makes us step back from whatever we might be doing.

The opening section of this anthology rests on the belief that these difficulties with asking *why* are also invaluable opportunities—opportunities to look back and forward and also to look around at what others see when they look back and forward. Asking *why* we serve—and considering why others serve—is an indispensable part of the service we do and who we are. Without considering where our service comes from and where it is headed, our goals and our methods for reaching them, we risk creating unintended consequences and failing to achieve the difference we are trying to make.

So we hope that the readings collected here, and the discussion questions that can be found in appendix II, will help you and your communities of faith and service ask why in productive, provocative, and enjoyable ways.

◈

Martin Luther King Jr.

THE DRUM MAJOR INSTINCT

~~~

This morning I would like to use as a subject from which to preach "the drum major instinct." And our text for the morning is taken from a very familiar passage in the tenth chapter as recorded by Saint Mark; beginning with the thirty-fifth verse of that chapter, we read these words: "And James and John the sons of Zebedee came unto him saying, 'Master, we would that thou shouldest do for us whatsoever we shall desire.' And he said unto them, 'What would ye that I should do for you?' And they said unto him, 'Grant unto us that we may sit one on thy right hand, and the other on thy left hand in thy glory.' But Jesus said unto them, 'Ye know not what ye ask. Can ye drink of the cup that I drink of and be baptized with the baptism that I am baptized with?' And they said unto him, 'We can.' And Jesus said unto them, 'Ye shall indeed drink of the cup that I drink of, and with the baptism that I am baptized with all shall ye be baptized. But to sit on my right hand and on my left hand is not mine to give, but it shall be given to them for whom it is prepared.'"

Martin Luther King Jr. was born in Atlanta in 1929, graduated from Morehouse College at the age of nineteen, and was ordained a Baptist minister. King went on to become the leading figure of the civil rights movement in America, and he is revered around the world as a martyr for racial equality, social justice, and nonviolence. In 1964, King was awarded the Nobel Peace Prize. King delivered this sermon in Ebenezer Baptist Church on February 4, 1968, two months before his assassination in Memphis, Tennessee.

And then, Jesus goes on toward the end of that passage to say, "But so shall it not be among you, but whosoever will be great among you, shall be your servant; and whosoever of you will be the chiefest shall be servant of all." The setting is clear. James and John are making a specific request of the master. They had dreamed, as most Hebrews dreamed, of a coming king of Israel who would set Jerusalem free. And establish his kingdom on Mount Zion, and in righteousness rule the world. And they thought of Jesus as this kind of king, and they were thinking of that day when Jesus would reign supreme as this new king of Israel. And they were saying now, "when you establish your kingdom, let one of us sit on the right hand, and the other on the left hand of your throne."

Now very quickly, we would automatically condemn James and John, and we would say they were selfish. Why would they make such a selfish request? But before we condemn them too quickly, let us look calmly and honestly at ourselves, and we will discover that we too have those same basic desires for recognition, for importance, that same desire for attention, that same desire to be first. Of course the other disciples got mad with James and John, and you could under-stand why, but we must understand that we have some of the same James and John qualities. And there is, deep down within all of us, an instinct. It's a kind of drum major instinct—a desire to be out front, a desire to lead the parade, a desire to be first. And it is something that runs a whole gamut of life.

And so before we condemn them, let us see that we all have the drum major instinct. We all want to be important, to surpass others, to achieve distinction, to lead the parade. Alfred Adler, the great psy-choanalyst, contends that this is the dominant impulse. Sigmund Freud used to contend that sex was the dominant impulse, and Adler came with a new argument saying that this quest for recognition, this desire for attention, this desire for distinction is the basic impulse, the basic drive of human life—this drum major instinct.

And you know, we begin early to ask life to put us first. Our first cry as a baby was a bid for attention. And all through childhood the drum major impulse or instinct is a major obsession. Children ask life to grant them first place. They are a little bundle of ego. And they have innately the drum major impulse, or the drum major instinct.

Now in adult life, we still have it, and we really never get by it. We like to do something good. And you know, we like to be praised for it. Now if you don't believe that, you just go on living life, and you will discover very soon that you like to be praised. Everybody likes it, as a matter of fact. And somehow this warm glow we feel when we are praised, or when our name is in print, is something of the vitamin A to our ego. Nobody is unhappy when they are praised, even if they know they don't deserve it, and even if they don't believe it. The only unhappy people about praise is when that praise is going too much toward somebody else. But everybody likes to be praised because of this real drum major instinct.

Now the presence of the drum major instinct is why so many people are joiners. You know there are some people who just join everything. And it's really a quest for attention, and recognition, and importance. And they get names that give them that impression. So you get your groups, and they become the grand patron, and the little fellow who is henpecked at home needs a chance to be the "Most Worthy of the Most Worthy" of something. It is the drum major impulse and longing that runs the gamut of human life. And so we see it everywhere, this quest for recognition. And we join things, overjoin really, that we think that we will find that recognition in.

Now the presence of this instinct explains why we are so often taken by advertisers. You know those gentlemen of massive verbal persuasion. And they have a way of saying things to you that kind of gets you into buying. In order to be a man of distinction, you must drink this whiskey. In order to make your neighbors envious, you must drive this type of car. In order to be lovely to love, you must wear this kind of lipstick or this kind of perfume. And you know, before you know it you're just buying that stuff. That's the way the advertisers do it.

I got a letter the other day. It was a new magazine coming out. And it opened up, "Dear Dr. King. As you know, you are on many mailing lists. And you are categorized as highly intelligent, progressive, a lover of the arts and the sciences, and I know you will want to read what I have to say." Of course I did. After you said all of that and explained me so exactly, of course I wanted to read it.

But very seriously, it goes through life, the drum major instinct is real. And you know what else it causes to happen? It often causes us to live above our means. It's nothing but the drum major instinct. Do you ever see people buy cars that they can't even begin to buy in terms of their income? You've seen people riding around in Cadillacs and Chryslers who don't earn enough to have a good Model-T Ford. But it feeds a repressed ego.

You know economists tell us that your automobiles should not cost more than half of your annual income. So if you're making an income of five thousand dollars, your car shouldn't cost more than about twenty-five hundred. That's just good economics. And if it's a family of two, and both members of the family make ten thousand dollars, they would have to make out with one car. That would be good economics, although it's often inconvenient. But so often … haven't you seen people making five thousand dollars a year and driving a car that costs six thousand? And they wonder why their ends never meet. That's a fact.

Now the economists also say that your house shouldn't cost, if you're buying a house, it shouldn't cost more than twice your income. That's based on the economy, and how you would make ends meet. So, if you have an income of five thousand dollars, it's kind of difficult in this society. But say it's a family with an income of ten thousand dollars, the house shouldn't cost more than twenty thousand. But I've seen folk making ten thousand dollars, living in a forty- and fifty-thousand-dollar house. And you know they just barely make it. They get a check every month somewhere, and they owe all of that out before it comes in; never have anything to put away for rainy days.

But now the problem is, it is the drum major instinct. And you know, you see people over and over again with the drum major instinct taking them over. And they just live their lives trying to outdo the Joneses. They got to get this coat because this particular coat is a little better and a little better-looking than Mary's coat. And I got to drive this car because it's something about this car that makes my car a little better than my neighbor's car. I know a man who used to live in a thirty-five-thousand-dollar house. And other people started building thirty-five-thousand-dollar houses, so he built a seventy-thousand-dollar house, and he built a hundred-thousand-dollar house. And I don't know where he's going to end up if he's going to live his life trying to keep up with the Joneses.

There comes a time that the drum major instinct can become destructive. And that's where I want to move now. I want to move to the point of saying that if this instinct is not harnessed, it becomes a very dangerous, pernicious instinct. For instance, if it isn't harnessed, it causes one's personality to become distorted. I guess that's the most damaging aspect of it—what it does to the personality. If it isn't harnessed, you will end up day in and day out trying to deal with your ego problem by boasting.

Have you ever heard people that—you know, and I'm sure you've met them—that really become sickening because they just sit up all the time talking about themselves. And they just boast, and boast, and boast, and that's the person who has not harnessed the drum major instinct.

And then it does other things to the personality. It causes you to lie about who you know sometimes. There are some people who are influence peddlers. And in their attempt to deal with the drum major instinct, they have to try to identify with the so-called big-name people. And if you're not careful, they will make you think they know somebody that they don't really know. They know them well, they sip tea with them. And they ... this and that. That ... that happens to people.

And the other thing is that it causes one to engage ultimately in activities that are merely used to get attention. Criminologists tell us that some people are driven to crime because of this drum major instinct. They don't feel that they are getting enough attention through the normal channels of social behavior, and others turn to antisocial behavior in order to get attention, in order to feel important. And so they get that gun. And before they know it they rob the bank in a quest for recognition, in a quest for importance.

And then the final great tragedy of the distorted personality is the fact that when one fails to harness this instinct, he ends by trying to push others down in order to push himself up. And whenever you do that, you engage in some of the most vicious activities. You will spread evil, vicious, lying gossip on people, because you are trying to pull them down in order to push yourself up.

And the great issue of life is to harness the drum major instinct.

Now the other problem is when you don't harness the drum major instinct, this uncontrolled aspect of it, is that it leads to snobbish exclusivism. Now you know, this is the danger of social clubs and fraternities. I'm in a fraternity; I'm in two or three. For sororities, and all of these, I'm not talking against them; I'm saying it's the danger. The danger is that they can become forces of classism and exclusivism where somehow you get a degree of satisfaction because you are in something exclusive, and that's fulfilling something, you know. And I'm in this fraternity, and it's the best fraternity in the world and everybody can't get fraternity. So it ends up, you know, a very exclusive kind of thing.

And you know, that can happen with the church. I've known churches get in that bind sometimes. I've been to churches you know, and they say, "We have so many doctors and so many schoolteachers, and so many lawyers, and so many businessmen in our church." And that's fine, because doctors need to go to church, and lawyers, and businessmen, teachers—they ought to be in church. But they say that, even the preacher sometimes will go on through it, they say that as if the other people don't count. And the church is the one place where a doctor ought to forget that he's a doctor. The church is the one place where a PhD ought to forget that he's a PhD. The church is the one place that a schoolteacher ought to forget the degree she has behind her name. The church is the one place where the lawyer ought to forget that he's a lawyer. And any church that violates the "whosoever will, let him come" doctrine is a dead, cold church, and nothing but a little social club with a thin veneer of religiosity.

When the church is true to its nature, it says, "Whosoever will, let him come." And it does not propose to satisfy the perverted uses of the drum major instinct. It's the one place where everybody should be the same standing before a common master and savior. And a recognition grows out of this—that all men are brothers because they are children of a common father.

The drum major instinct can lead to exclusivism in one's think-ing and can lead one to feel that because he has some training, he's a little better than that person that doesn't have it, or because he has some economic security, that he's a little better than the person who doesn't have it. And that's the uncontrolled, perverted use of the drum major instinct.

Now the other thing is that it leads to tragic—and we've seen it happen so often—tragic race prejudice. Many have written about this problem—Lillian Smith used to say it beautifully in some of her books. And she would say it to the point of getting men and women to see the source of the problem. Do you know that a lot of the race problem grows out of the drum major instinct? A need that some people have to feel superior. A need that some people have to feel that they are first and to feel that their white skin ordained them to be first. And they have said it over and over again in ways that we see with our own eyes. In fact, not too long ago, a man down in Mississippi said that God was a charter member of the White Citizens Council. And so God being the charter member means that every-body who's in that has a kind of divinity, a kind of superiority.

And think of what has happened in history as a result of this perverted use of the drum major instinct. It has led to the most tragic prejudice, the most tragic expressions of man's inhumanity to man.

I always try to do a little converting when I'm in jail. And when we were in jail in Birmingham the other day, the white wardens all enjoyed coming around to the cell to talk about the race problem. And they were showing us where we were so wrong demonstrating. And they were showing us where segregation was so right. And they were showing us where intermarriage was so wrong. So I would get to preaching, and we would get to talking—calmly, because they wanted to talk about it. And then we got down one day to the point—that was the second or third day—to talk about where they lived, and how much they were earning. And when those brothers told me what they were earning, I said now, "You know what? You ought to be marching with us. You're just as poor as Negroes." And I said, "You are put in the position of supporting your oppressor. Because through prejudice and blindness, you fail to see that the same forces that oppress Negroes in American society oppress poor white people. And all you are living on is the satisfaction of your skin being white, and the drum major instinct of thinking that you are somebody big because you are white. And you're so poor you can't send your children to school. You ought to be out here marching with every one of us every time we have a march."

Now that's a fact. That the poor white has been put into this position—where through blindness and prejudice, he is forced to support his oppressors, and the only thing he has going for him is the false feeling that he is superior because his skin is white. And can't hardly eat and make his ends meet week in and week out.

And not only does this thing go into the racial struggle, it goes into the struggle between nations. And I would submit to you this morning that what is wrong in the world today is that the nations of the world are engaged in a bitter, colossal contest for supremacy. And if something doesn't happen to stop this trend I'm sorely afraid that we won't be here to talk about Jesus Christ and about God and about brotherhood too many more years. If somebody doesn't bring an end to this suicidal thrust that we see in the world today, none of us are going to be around, because somebody's going to make the mistake through our senseless blundering of dropping a nuclear bomb some-where, and then another one is going to drop. And don't let anybody fool you; this can happen within a matter of seconds. They have twenty-megaton bombs in Russia right now that can destroy a city as big as New York in three seconds with everybody wiped away and every building. And we can do the same thing to Russia and China.

But this is where we are drifting, and we are drifting there, because nations are caught up with the drum major instinct. I must be first. I must be supreme. Our nation must rule the world. And I am sad to say that the nation in which we live is the supreme culprit. And I'm going to continue to say it to America, because I love this country too much to see the drift that it has taken.

God didn't call America to do what she's doing in the world now. God didn't call America to engage in a senseless, unjust war,

[such] as the war in Vietnam. And we are criminals in that war. We have committed more war crimes almost than any nation in the world, and I'm going to continue to say it. And we won't stop it because of our pride and our arrogance as a nation.

But God has a way of even putting nations in their place. The God that I worship has a way of saying, "Don't play with me." He has a way of saying, as the God of the Old Testament used to say to the Hebrews, "Don't play with me, Israel. Don't play with me, Babylon. Be still and know that I'm God. And if you don't stop your reckless course, I'll rise up and break the backbone of your power." And that can happen to America. Every now and then I go back and read Gibbon's *Decline and Fall of the Roman Empire.* And when I come and look at America, I say to myself, the parallels are frightening.

And we have perverted the drum major instinct. But let me rush on to my conclusion, because I want you to see what Jesus was really saying. What was the answer that Jesus gave these men? It's very interesting. One would have thought that Jesus would have said, "You are out of your place. You are selfish. Why would you raise such a question?"

But that isn't what Jesus did. He did something altogether different. He said in substance, "Oh, I see, you want to be first. You want to be great. You want to be important. You want to be significant. Well you ought to be. If you're going to be my disciple, you must be." But he reordered priorities. And he said, "Yes, don't give up this instinct. It's a good instinct if you use it right. It's a good instinct if you don't distort it and pervert it. Don't give it up. Keep feeling the need for being important. Keep feeling the need for being first. But I want you to be first in love. I want you to be first in moral excellence. I want you to be first in generosity. That is what I want you to do."

And he transformed the situation by giving a new definition of greatness. And you know how he said it? He said now, "Brethren, I can't give you greatness. And really, I can't make you first." This is what Jesus said to James and John. You must earn it. True greatness comes not by favoritism but by fitness. And the right hand and the left are not mine to give; they belong to those who are prepared.

And so Jesus gave us a new norm of greatness. If you want to be important—wonderful. If you want to be recognized—wonderful. If you want to be great—wonderful. But recognize that he who is greatest among you shall be your servant. That's your new definition of greatness. And this morning, the thing that I like about it ... by giving that definition of greatness, it means that everybody can be great. Because everybody can serve. You don't have to have a college degree to serve. You don't have to make your subject and your verb agree to serve. You don't have to know about Plato and Aristotle to serve. You don't have to know Einstein's theory of relativity to serve. You don't have to know the second theory of thermodynamics in physics to serve. You only need a heart full of grace. A soul generated by love. And you can be that servant.

I know a man, and I just want to talk about him a minute, and maybe you will discover who I'm talking about as I go down the way, because he was a great one. And he just went about serving. He was born in an obscure village, the child of a poor peasant woman. And then he grew up in still another obscure village, where he worked as a carpenter until he was thirty years old. Then for three years, he just got on his feet, and he was an itinerant preacher. And then he went about doing some things. He didn't have much. He never wrote a book. He never held an office. He never had a family. He never owned a house. He never went to college. He never visited a big city. He never went two hundred miles from where he was born. He did none of the usual things that the world would associate with greatness. He had no credentials but himself.

He was thirty-three when the tide of public opinion turned against him. They called him a rabble-rouser. They called him a troublemaker. They said he was an agitator. He practiced civil disobedience; he broke injunctions. And so he was turned over to his enemies and went through the mockery of a trial. And the irony of it all is that his friends turned him over to them. One of his closest friends denied him. Another of his friends turned him over to his enemies. And while he was dying, the people who killed him gambled for his clothing, the only possession that he had in the world. When he was dead, he was buried in a borrowed tomb, through the pity of a friend.

Nineteen centuries have come and gone, and today, he stands as the most influential figure that ever entered human history. All of the armies that ever marched, all the navies that ever sailed, all the parliaments that ever sat, and all the kings that ever reigned put together have not affected the life of man on this earth as much as that one solitary life. His name may be a familiar one. But today I can hear them talking about him. Every now and then somebody says, "He's king of kings." And again I can hear somebody saying, "He's lord of lords." Somewhere else I can hear somebody saying, "In Christ there is no east or west." And they go on and talk about.... "In him there's no north and south but one great fellowship of love throughout the whole wide world." He didn't have anything. He just went around serving and doing good.

This morning, you can be on his right hand and his left hand if you serve. It's the only way in.

Every now and then I guess we all think realistically about that day when we will be victimized with what is life's final common denominator—that something we call death. We all think about it. And every now and then I think about my own death, and I think about my own funeral.

And I don't think of it in a morbid sense. Every now and then I ask myself, "What is it that I would want said?" And I leave the word to you this morning.

If any of you are around when I have to meet my day, I don't want a long funeral. And if you get somebody to deliver the eulogy, tell them not to talk too long. Every now and then I wonder what I want them to say. Tell them not to mention that I have a Nobel Peace Prize; that isn't important. Tell them not to mention that I have three or four hundred other awards; that's not important. Tell him not to mention where I went to school.

I'd like somebody to mention that day that Martin Luther King Jr. tried to give his life serving others. I'd like for somebody to say that day that Martin Luther King Jr. tried to love somebody. I want you to say that day that I tried to be right on the war question. I want you to be able to say that day that I did try to feed the hungry. And I want you to be able to say that day that I did try, in my life, to clothe those who were naked. I want you to say, on that day, that I did try, in my life, to visit those who were in prison. I want you to say that I tried to love and serve humanity.

Yes, if you want to say that I was a drum major, say that I was a drum major for justice; say that I was a drum major for peace; I was a drum major for righteousness. And all of the other shallow things will not matter. I won't have any money to leave behind. I won't have the fine and luxurious things of life to leave behind. But I just want to leave a committed life behind.

And that's all I want to say … if I can help somebody as I pass alone, if I can cheer somebody with a word or song, if I can show somebody he's traveling wrong, then my living will not be in vain. If I can do my duty as a Christian ought, if I can bring salvation to a world once wrought, if I can spread the message as the master taught, then my living will not be in vain.

Yes, Jesus, I want to be on your right side or your left side, not for any selfish reason. I want to be on your right or your best side, not in terms of some political kingdom or ambition, but I just want to be there in love and in justice and in truth and in commitment to others, so that we can make of this old world a new world.

WHY THE BUDDHA HAD GOOD DIGESTION

from *Avadānaśataka*

～～～

T he Blessed Buddha was respected, venerated, esteemed and adored by kings, ministers, wealthy people, citizens, merchants, traders, *devas, nāgas, yaksas, asuras, garudas, kimnaras* and *mahoragas.* Thus honoured by all such beings, the Blessed Buddha—well-known, of great merit, rich in the personal belongings of a monk [robe, alms-bowl, furnishings and medicine]—was dwelling in Śrāvastī with an assembly of disciples, at prince Jeta's grove, in Anāthapindada's garden.

At the time of the autumn season, the monks were stricken by illness. They were yellow and pale, their bodies emaciated and their limbs weak. But the Blessed One was free from disease, free from illness, healthy and strong. Seeing this, the monks addressed the Blessed One:

"Look, Venerable One, these monks are stricken by an autumnal illness. They are yellow and pale, their bodies emaciated and their limbs weak. But the Blessed One is free from disease, free from illness,

The *Avadānaśataka* (*One Hundred Legends*) is a collection of *avadāna*, a genre of Buddhist stories in which an initial question about the way things are opens the door for the Buddha to tell a story about something remembered from a prior life. The *Avadānaśataka* is a work of the Sarvāstivādin school. It was written, in Sanskrit, around 100 CE. The legend included here was translated by Reiko Ohnuma in Padmakāvadāna as part of J. S. Speyer's *Avadānaśataka: A Century of Edifying Tales Belonging to the Hīnayāna.*

strong and healthy by nature, endowed with a stomach whose digestion is regular."

The Blessed One said: "Formerly, monks, in other births, the
Tathāgata alone performed certain acts. These acts have accumulated,
their necessary requirements have been met, their conditions have
ripened, they rush towards one like a rapid flow, their consequences
are inevitable. I am the one who performed and accumulated these
acts—who else would experience their fruits? The acts that a person
performs and accumulates, monks, do not bear fruit outside of that
person—not in the earth, not in the water, not in fire and not in the
air. Rather, the acts that a person performs, whether pure or impure,
bear fruit in the body and mind that he receives."

> Deeds do not perish, even after hundreds of aeons.
>
> When completeness is achieved and time has arrived,
>
> they inevitably bear fruit for embodied beings.

And with that, he launched into a story of the past.

Formerly, monks, long ago, in the city of Vārānasī, a king named
Padmaka ruled over his kingdom. It was prosperous, flourishing and
safe; abundant in food and well-populated; tranquil and free of quar-
rels, fights, riots, or tumults; free of thievery and disease; rich in rice,
sugar cane, cows and buffalo; self-contained and free of enemies;
ruled over like an only son.

Now, this king was faithful and good. He had a virtuous disposition and worked for the welfare of himself and others. He was compassionate and magnanimous, loved virtue and was affectionate
towards living beings. He was a giver of everything, a renouncer of
everything, one who gave without attachment and engaged in great
generosity.

Now, at that time in Vārānasī, because of a disturbance in the
weather or the elements, an epidemic arose and most of the people
in Vārānasī became ill. Seeing them, the king gave rise to compassion.
"I must attend to them medically and save their lives," he thought.

So the king gathered together all of the doctors residing within
his territories; observed the cause, basis and effects of the people's ill-

ness; and himself began to assemble all kinds of medicines and care for the sick. But although the people were treated for a long time and furnished with doctors, medicines, herbs and attendants, they failed to be cured.

So the king summoned all of the doctors again and respectfully asked them: "Why am I having such a hard time curing these people?"

The doctors, having considered his question and come to one opinion, told him both the good news and the bad news. "Lord," they said, "we believe the illness is a result of a disturbance in the weather or in the elements. However, Lord, there is one cure—the type of fish called a Rohita. If you can catch it, they can be cured."

So the king began the search for the Rohita fish. But even though many of the king's men searched for it, the king was soon informed that the fish could not be caught.

Later on, when the king went out for an excursion, the sick assembled together and said to the king: "Save us from this disease, Great King! Give us life!" Hearing their suffering voices and their miserable, sad and depressed words, the king's heart trembled out of compassion and his face was tearful and gloomy.

He thought to himself: "Of what use to me is a life such as this? Of what use to me are kingship, sovereignty and supremacy? For I am unable to comfort others who are afflicted by suffering!"

Having reflected thus, the king made a great gift of all his wealth and established his eldest son in the kingship, sovereignty and supremacy. He begged for the pardon of his relatives, citizens and ministers, and consoled those who were miserable. He undertook a vow consisting of eight parts. Then he ascended to the roof of his palace, threw down incense, flowers, perfumes, garlands and unguents and, facing towards the east, began to take a vow:

"Seeing beings who have fallen into great misfortune and are tormented by disease, I will sacrifice my own cherished life. By these true words of truth, may I appear as a great Rohita fish in this sandy river!"

Having spoken thus, he threw himself from the roof of the palace. As soon as he fell, he died and reappeared as a great Rohita fish in the sandy river. And the gods let loose a cry throughout the whole country:

"This great Rohita fish has appeared like ambrosia in the sandy river for beings long tormented by great illness!"

As soon as they heard this, a great crowd of people carrying baskets and gripping weapons in their hands came out, and, with various types of sharp weapons, they began to cut up the flesh of the fish while he was still alive. But even as his body was being carved up, the *bodhisattva* suffused those beings with love, and with his face flowing with tears, thought to himself:

"My capture is a wonderful thing, since by means of my flesh and blood, these beings will be put at ease."

Thus, in this way, he satiated those beings with his own flesh and blood for twelve years, and he never turned his mind away from unsurpassed perfect awakening.

When he had fully cured the people's illness, the Rohita fish said these words:

"Listen, you beings! I am King Padmaka! I have acquired this type of body for your sake through the sacrifice of my own life. Let your minds be appeased in my presence. When I have awakened to unsurpassed perfect awakening, I will liberate you from the supreme illness of *samsāra* and establish you in the supreme end of *nirvāna*!"

Upon hearing this, the crowd of people felt serene, and the king, ministers and citizens—honouring him with flowers, incense, garlands and unguents—undertook a vow:

"O you who accomplish extremely difficult deeds, when you have awakened to unsurpassed perfect awakening, may we be your disciples!"

The Blessed One concluded: "What do you think, monks? He who was, at that time, in that epoch, the king named Padmaka—I am he. It is because I made such sacrifices that I experienced perpetual well-being in *samsāra*, and even now—having awoken to unsurpassed, perfect awakening—am endowed with a stomach whose digestion is regular, by means of which everything I eat, drink, chew and enjoy is digested with perfect ease, and I am free of disease and have left illness behind.

"Therefore, monks, this is the lesson to be learned: You must show compassion for all beings. This, monks, is the lesson to be learned."

Thus spoke the Blessed One. And the monks, delighted in mind, rejoiced at what the Blessed One had said.

IN PRAISE OF GENEROSITY

from the Rig Veda

The gods surely did not ordain hunger alone for
slaughter; various deaths reach the man who is
well-fed. The riches of the man who gives fully do
not run out, but the miser finds no one with
sympathy.
The man with food who hardens his heart against
the poor man who comes to him suffering and
searching for nourishment—though in the past he
had made use of him—he surely finds no one with
sympathy.
The man who is truly generous gives to the beggar
who approaches him thin and in search for food.
He puts himself at the service of the man who calls
to him from the road, and makes him a friend for
times to come.
That man is no friend who does not give of his
own nourishment to his friend, the companion at

The Rig Veda, one of the four sacred texts of Hinduism known as Vedas, is
an Indian collection of more than one thousand Sanskrit hymns dedicated
to the gods. Evidence suggests that the Rig Veda was composed in the
northwestern region of the Indian subcontinent between 1700 and 1100
BCE (the early Vedic period), making it among the world's oldest religious
texts in continued use, and the oldest in Sanskrit or any Indo-European
language. The hymns are dedicated to several deities, among them Indra, a
heroic god praised for slaying his enemy Vrtra; Agni, the sacrificial fire; and
Soma, the sacred potion or the plant from which it is made. This translation is by Wendy Doniger.

his side. Let the friend turn away from him; this is not his dwelling place. Let him find another man who gives freely, even if he be a stranger.

Let the stronger man give to the man whose need is greater; let him gaze upon the lengthening path. For riches roll like the wheels of a chariot, turning from one to another.

The man without foresight gets food in vain; I speak the truth: it will be his death. He cultivates neither a patron nor a friend. The man who eats alone brings trouble on himself alone.

The plough that works the soil makes a man well-fed; the legs that walk put the road behind them. The priest who speaks is better than the one who does not speak. The friend who gives freely surpasses the one who does not.

One-foot surpasses Two-foot; and Two-foot leaves Three-foot behind. Four-foot comes at the call of Two-foot, watching over his herd and serving him. The two hands, though the same, do not give the same thing. Two cows from the same mother do not give the same amount of milk. The powers of two twins are not the same. Two kinsmen do not give with the same generosity.

Abraham Joshua Heschel

SOLIDARITY, RECIPROCITY, AND SANCTITY

three selections from *Who Is Man?*

~~~

SOLITUDE AND SOLIDARITY

Self-sufficiency, independence, the capacity to stand apart, to differ, to resist, and to defy—all are modes of being human. There is no dignity without the ability to stand alone. One must withdraw and be still in order to hear. Solitude is a necessary protest to the incursions and the false alarms of society's hysteria, a period of cure and recovery.

The truth, however, is that man is never alone. It is together with all my contemporaries that I live, suffer, and rejoice, even while living in seclusion. Genuine solitude is not discarding but distilling humanity. Genuine solitude is a search for genuine solidarity. Man

Abraham Joshua Heschel was born in Poland in 1907, received his early education from a *yeshiva* (a school for Talmudic or rabbinical study), and earned his doctorate from the University of Berlin. In 1939, six weeks before the Nazi invasion of Poland, he left for London and then for the United States, where he taught at the Jewish Theological Seminary in New York City from 1945 until his death in 1972. An activist as well as a scholar and a teacher, Heschel was deeply engaged in social movements for peace, civil rights, and interfaith understanding. The following three selections are excerpted from his 1965 work, *Who Is Man?*

alone is a conceit. He is for the sake of, by the strength of, unknowingly and even knowingly involved in the community of man.

Man in his being is derived from, attended by, and directed to the being of community. For man *to* be means *to* be *with* other human beings. His existence *is* coexistence. He can never attain fulfillment, or sense meaning, unless it is shared, unless it pertains to other human beings.

Although it is true that in order to grasp the meaning of being human we analyze the human individual rather than the human species, any analysis that disregards social involvement, man's interdependence and correlativity, will miss the heart of being human.

Human solidarity is not the product of being human; being human is the product of human solidarity. Indeed, even the most personal concern, the search for meaning, is utterly meaningless as a pursuit of personal salvation. Its integrity discloses compassion, a hope or intuition of meaning in which all men may share.

Even preoccupation with the self, self-defense and self-aggrandizement, typical of all men, includes in its consciousness acknowledgment of the existence and dignity of other men. The prestige a person seeks involves respect for others whose recognition is desired. All achievements are born in the conviction that what is good for me will prove to be good for others.

"To be" is an intransitive verb; to be human, I repeat, is more than just to be. Man reflects about his being, and his reflection discloses to him that in order to be he must continually accept what is not his own, since being is never self-sufficient.

RECIPROCITY

Science is a way of interpreting experiences. For the self-understanding of man it is important to realize that experiences interpret and elucidate man.

The primary experience with which we begin in our infancy and continue in our childhood is *obtaining and seizing* things we care for. Developing and entering maturity we become involved in *giving and providing* for those we care for.

These are fundamental facts and must be recognized as primary data in the make-up of living, independent of motivations that may affect their intensity.

We receive continually; our very being is a gift in the form of an enigma; a breath of fresh air is inhalation of grace. Fullness of existence, personal being is achieved by what we offer in return. "How shall I ever repay to the Lord all the bounty He has given to me!" (Psalm 116:12) is a genuine question of man. *The dignity of human existence is in the power of reciprocity.*

For every new insight we must pay a new deed. We must strive to maintain a balance of power and mercy, of truth and generosity. Knowledge is a debt, not a private property. To be a person is to reciprocate, to offer in return for what one receives. Reciprocity involves appreciation. Biologically we all take in and give off. I become a person by knowing the meaning of receiving and giving. I become a person when I begin to reciprocate.

The degree to which one is sensitive to other people's suffering, to other men's humanity, is the index of one's own humanity. It is the root not only for social living but also of the study of humanities. The vital presupposition of the philosopher's question about man is his care for man.

The opposite of humanity is brutality, the failure to acknowledge the humanity of one's fellow man, the failure to be sensitive to his needs, to his situation. Brutality is often due to a failure of imagination as well as to the tendency to treat a person as a generality, to regard a person as an average man.

Man achieves fullness of being in fellowship, in care for others. He expands his existence by "bearing his fellow-man's burden." As we have said, animals are concerned for their own needs; the degree of our being human stands in direct proportion to the degree in which we care for others.

The central problem in terms of biblical thinking is not: "What is 'to be'?" but rather: "How to be and how not to be?"

The issue we face is not the dichotomy of being and misbeing, but that of righteous and unrighteous being. The tension is not between existence and essence but between existence and performance. For animals as well as for human beings when in peril and anguish the problem is to be or not to be. What distinguishes a human being is that his problem is *how* to be and *how* not to be. Indeed, man alone is motivated by the awareness of the insufficiency of sheer being, of sheer living. Man alone is open to the problem of how to be and how not to be on all levels of his existence. Our first theme, then, is not what man is but how he is, not human being but being human, which is the sum of many relationships in which a human being is involved.

In the actual human situation "to be" is inseparable from "how to be." Thus on the level of his being human the process of his being stands over against him as a question: How should I live the existence that I am? Thus we see that the implied intent of the question, *Who is man?* is really, *How is man?*

SANCTITY

As said above, man is the only entity in nature with which sanctity is associated. Sanctity of human life is not something we know conceptually, established on the basis of premises; it is an underived insight. It is not a quality that man can bestow upon himself; it is either bestowed upon us or spurious. We come upon it first in pondering the mystery of another person's life, and subsequently in the realization that one's own life is not something acquired or owned. Life is something *I* am. What I have is mine; what I am is not mine. Life is not my property.

Being human involves being sensitive to the sacred. The objects regarded as sacred may differ from country to country, yet sensitivity to the sacred is universal.

The acceptance of the sacred is an existential paradox: it is saying "yes" to a no; it is the antithesis of the will to power; it may contradict interests and stand in the way of satisfying inner drives.

To our sense of power the world is at our disposal, to be exploited to our advantage. To accept the sacred is an acknowledgment that certain things are not available to us, are not at our disposal. However, it is a profound misunderstanding to think of the sacred in terms of negativity. Its negativity and separateness is but a protective screen for the positive aspect of the sacred. For accepting the sacred means not only giving up claims, but also facing a unique dimension of reality.

What is the positive aspect of the sacred? Being a unique quality, it is not capable of being described in terms of any other quality, just as beauty cannot be described in terms of goodness. The sacred is perceptible to the sense of the sacred. The beauty of a beautiful object is inherent in the object, whereas the sanctity of a sacred object transcends the object. Beauty is given with the nature of a thing, sanctity is imposed on things. Beauty is in the form of an object, sanctity in its status.

There are degrees of sanctity, but they all share one aspect: ultimate preciousness. To sense the sacred is to sense what is dear to God. Its mode of being differs from the modes of being of other qualities.

It is true that sacred objects are objects set apart from the rest of reality, but it is a mistake to regard the sacred and the profane as absolute contrasts. For some parts of reality to be endowed with sanctity, all of reality must be a reflection of sanctity. Reality embraces the actually sacred and the potentially sacred.

علم

Tayeb Salih

A HANDFUL OF DATES

in *The Wedding of Zein and Other Stories*

~~~

I must have been very young at the time. While I don't remember exactly how old I was, I do remember that when people saw me with my grandfather they would pat me on the head and give my cheek a pinch—things they didn't do to my grandfather. The strange thing was that I never used to go out with my father, rather it was my grandfather who would take me with him wherever he went, except for the mornings, when I would go to the mosque to learn the Koran. The mosque, the river, and the fields—these were the landmarks in our life. While most of the children of my age grumbled at having to go to the mosque to learn the Koran, I used to love it. The reason was, no doubt, that I was quick at learning by heart and the Sheik always asked me to stand up and recite the Chapter of the Merciful whenever we had visitors, who would pat me on my head and cheek just as people did when they saw me with my grandfather.

Yes, I used to love the mosque, and I loved the river, too. Directly we finished our Koran reading in the morning I would

Tayeb Salih was born in the Northern Province of Sudan in 1929. After studying at a qur'anic elementary school, the University of Khartoum, and the University of London, Salih became a journalist and fiction writer. His writing draws on Islamic, Sufi, and Western literary traditions. "A Handful of Dates" first appeared in his 1964 collection, *The Wedding of Zein and Other Stories*. This translation is by Denys Johnson-Davies.

throw down my wooden slate and dart off, quick as a genie, to my mother, hurriedly swallow down my breakfast, and run off for a plunge in the river. When tired of swimming about, I would sit on the bank and gaze at the strip of water that wound away eastwards, and hid behind a thick wood of acacia trees. I loved to give rein to my imagination and picture myself a tribe of giants living behind that wood, a people tall and thin with white beards and sharp noses, like my grandfather. Before my grandfather ever replied to my many questions, he would rub the tip of his nose with his forefinger; as for his beard, it was soft and luxuriant and as white as cotton wool— never in my life have I seen anything of a purer whiteness or greater beauty. My grandfather must also have been extremely tall, for I never saw anyone in the whole area address him without having to look up at him, nor did I see him enter a house without having to bend so low that I was put in mind of the way the river wound round behind the wood of acacia trees. I loved him and would imagine myself, when I grew to be a man, tall and slender like him, walking along with great strides. I believe I was his favorite grandchild: no wonder, for my cousins were a stupid bunch and I—so they say—was an intelligent child. I used to know when my grandfather wanted me to laugh, when to be silent; also I would remember the times for his prayers and would bring him his prayer rug and fill the ewer for his ablutions without his having to ask me. When he had nothing else to do he enjoyed listening to me reciting to him from the Koran in a lilting voice, and I could tell from his face that he was moved.

One day I asked him about our neighbor Masood. I said to my grandfather: I fancy you don't like our neighbor Masood?

To which he answered, having rubbed the tip of his nose: He's an indolent man and I don't like such people.

I said to him: What's an indolent man?

My grandfather lowered his head for a moment; then, looking across the wide expanse of field, he said: Do you see it stretching out from the edge of the desert up to the Nile bank? A hundred feddans. Do you see all those date palms? And those trees—sant, acacia, and sayal? All this fell into Masood's lap, was inherited by him from his father.

Taking advantage of the silence that had descended on my grandfather, I turned my gaze from him to the vast area defined by words. I don't care, I told myself, who owns those date palms, those trees or this black, cracked earth—all I know is that it's the arena for my dreams and my playground.

My grandfather then continued: Yes, my boy, forty years ago all this belonged to Masood—two-thirds of it is now mine.

This was news for me, for I had imagined that the land had belonged to my grandfather ever since God's Creation.

I didn't own a single feddan when I first set foot in this village. Masood was then the owner of all these riches. The position has changed now, though, and I think that before Allah calls me to Him I shall have bought the remaining third as well.

I do not know why it was I felt fear at my grandfather's words—and pity for our neighbor Masood. How I wished my grandfather wouldn't do what he'd said! I remembered Masood's singing, his beautiful voice and powerful laugh that resembled the gurgling of water. My grandfather never laughed.

I asked my grandfather why Masood had sold his land.

Women, and from the way my grandfather pronounced the word I felt that women was something terrible. Masood, my boy, was a much-married man. Each time he married he sold me a feddan or two. I made the quick calculation that Masood must have married some ninety women. Then I remembered his three wives, his shabby appearance, his lame donkey and its dilapidated saddle, his galabia with the torn sleeves. I had all but rid my mind of the thoughts that jostled in it when I saw the man approaching us, and my grandfather and I exchanged glances.

We'll be harvesting the dates today, said Masood. Don't you want to be there?

I felt, though, that he did not really want my grandfather to attend. My grandfather, however, jumped to his feet and I saw that his eyes sparkled momentarily with an intense brightness. He pulled me by the hand and we went off to the harvesting of Masood's dates.

Someone brought my grandfather a stool covered with an oxhide, while I remained standing. There was a vast number of people there, but though I knew them all, I found myself for some reason watching Masood: aloof from that great gathering of people he stood as though it were no concern of his, despite the fact that the date palms to be harvested were his own. Sometimes his attention would be caught by the sound of a huge clump of dates crashing down from on high. Once he shouted up at the boy perched on the very summit of the date palm who had begun hacking at a clump with his long, sharp sickle: Be careful you don't cut the heart of the palm.

No one paid any attention to what he said and the boy seated at the very summit of the date palm continued, quickly and energetically, to work away at the branch with his sickle till the clump of dates began to drop like something descending from the heavens.

I, however, had begun to think about Masood's phrase, the heart of the palm. I pictured the palm tree as something with feeling, something possessed of a heart that throbbed. I remembered Masood's remark to me when he had once seen me playing with the branch of a young palm tree: Palm trees, my boy, like humans, experience joy and suffering. And I had felt an inward and unreasoned embarrassment.

When I again looked at the expanse of ground stretching before me I saw my young companions swarming like ants around the trunks of the palm trees, gathering up dates and eating most of them. The dates were collected into high mounds. I saw people coming along and weighing them into measuring bins and pouring them into sacks, of which I counted thirty. The crowd of people broke up, except for Hussein the merchant, Mousa the owner of the field next to ours on the east, and two men I'd never seen before.

I heard a low whistling sound and saw that my grandfather had fallen asleep. Then I noticed that Masood had not changed his stance, except that he had placed a stalk in his mouth and was munching at it like someone sated with food who doesn't know what to do with the mouthful he still has.

Suddenly my grandfather woke up, jumped to his feet, and walked toward the sacks of dates. He was followed by Hussein the merchant, Mousa the owner of the field next to ours and two strangers. I glanced at Masood and saw that he was making his way toward us with extreme slowness, like a man who wants to retreat but whose feet insist on going forward. They formed a circle around the sacks of dates and began examining them, some taking a date or two to eat. My grandfather gave me a fistful, which I began munching. I saw Masood filling the palms of both hands with dates and bringing them up close to his nose, then returning them.

Then I saw them dividing up the sacks between them. Hussein the merchant took ten; each of the strangers took five. Mousa the owner of the field next to ours on the eastern side took five, and my grandfather took five. Understanding nothing, I looked at Masood and saw that his eyes were darting to left and right like two mice that have lost their way home.

You're still fifty pounds in debt to me, said my grandfather to Masood. We'll talk about it later.

Hussein called his assistants and they brought along the donkeys, the two strangers produced camels, and the sacks of dates were loaded onto them. One of the donkeys let out a braying which set the camels frothing at the mouth and complaining noisily. I felt myself drawing close to Masood, felt my hand stretch out toward him as though I wanted to touch the hem of his garment. I heard him make a noise in his throat like the rasping of a sheep being slaughtered. For some unknown reason, I experienced a sharp sensation of pain in my chest.

I ran off into the distance. Hearing my grandfather call after me, I hesitated a little, then continued on my way. I felt at that moment that I hated him. Quickening my pace, it was as though I carried within me a secret I wanted to rid myself of. I reached the riverbank near the bend it made behind the wood of acacia trees. Then, without knowing why, I put my finger into my throat and spewed up the dates I'd eaten.

علم

Jane Addams

THE SUBJECTIVE NECESSITY OF SOCIAL SETTLEMENTS

in *Twenty Years at Hull-House*

~~~

This paper is an attempt to analyze the motives that underlie a movement based not only upon conviction but upon genuine emotion, wherever educated young people are seeking an outlet for that sentiment of universal brotherhood, which the best spirit of our times is forcing from an emotion into a motive. These young people accomplish little toward the solution of this social problem and bear the brunt of being cultivated into unnourished, oversensitive lives. They have been shut off from the common labor by which they live that is a great source of moral and physical health. They feel a fatal want of harmony between their theory and their lives, a lack of coordination between thought and action. I think it is hard for us to realize how seriously many of them are taking to the notion of human brotherhood, how eagerly they long to give tangible expression to the

Jane Addams was born in 1860 and raised in Cedarville, Illinois. After graduating from Rockford Seminary in 1881, Addams spent several years traveling, studying, and searching for a future direction in life. In 1889, inspired by the English example of Toynbee Hall, Addams and her friend Ellen Starr founded Hull House, a settlement house on the west side of Chicago. Addams died in 1935. The following lecture was presented at the School of Applied Ethics in Plymouth, Massachusetts, in 1892, and published in her autobiographical masterpiece, *Twenty Years at Hull-House*, in 1910.

democratic ideal. These young men and women, longing to socialize their democracy, are animated by certain hopes that may be thus loosely formulated; that if in a democratic country nothing can be permanently achieved save through the masses of the people, it will be impossible to establish a higher political life than the people themselves crave; that it is difficult to see how the notion of a higher civic life can be fostered save through common intercourse; that the blessings that we associate with a life of refinement and cultivation can be made universal and must be made universal if they are to be permanent; that the good we secure for ourselves is precarious and uncertain, is floating in midair, until it is secured for all of us and incorporated into our common life. It is easier to state these hopes than to formulate the line of motives, which I believe to constitute the trend of the subjective pressure toward the settlement. There is something primordial about these motives, but I am perhaps overbold in designating them as a great desire to share the race life. We all bear traces of the starvation struggle that for so long made up the life of the race. Our very organism holds memories and glimpses of that long life of our ancestors that still goes on among so many of our contemporaries. Nothing so deadens the sympathies and shrivels the power of enjoyment as the persistent keeping away from the great opportunities for helpfulness and a continual ignoring of the starvation struggle that makes up the life of at least half the race. To shut one's self away from that half of the race life is to shut one's self away from the most vital part of it; it is to live out but half the humanity to which we have been born heir and to use but half our faculties. We have all had longings for a fuller life that should include the use of these faculties. These longings are the physical complement of the "intimations of immortality," on which no ode has yet been written. To portray these would be the work of a poet, and it is hazardous for any but a poet to attempt it.

You may remember the forlorn feeling that occasionally seizes you when you arrive early in the morning a stranger in a great city: the stream of laboring people goes past you as you gaze through the plate-glass window of your hotel; you see hard working men lifting great burdens; you hear the driving and jostling of huge carts and your heart sinks with a sudden sense of futility. The door opens behind you and you turn to the man who brings in your breakfast with a quick sense of human fellowship. You find yourself praying that you may never lose your hold on it all. A more poetic prayer would be that the great mother breasts of our common humanity, with its labor and suffering and its homely comforts, may never be withheld from you. You turn helplessly to the waiter and feel that it would be almost grotesque to claim from him the sympathy you crave because civilization has placed you apart, but you resent your position with a sudden sense of snobbery. Literature is full of portrayals of these glimpses: they come to shipwrecked men on rafts; they overcome the differences of an incongruous multitude when in the presence of a great danger or when moved by a common enthusiasm. They are not, however, confined to such moments, and if we were in the habit of telling them to each other, the recital would be as long as the tales of children are, when they sit down on the green grass and confide to each other how many times they have remembered that they lived once before. If these childish tales are the stirring of inherited impressions, just so surely is the other the striving of inherited powers.

"It is true that there is nothing after disease, indigence, and a sense of guilt, so fatal to health and to life itself as the want of a proper outlet for active faculties." I have seen young girls suffer and grow sensibly lowered in vitality in the first years after they leave school. In our attempt then to give a girl pleasure and freedom from care we succeed, for the most part, in making her pitifully miserable. She finds "life" so different from what she expected it to be. She is besotted with innocent little ambitions and does not understand this apparent waste of herself, this elaborate preparation, if no work is provided for her. There is a heritage of noble obligation that young people accept and long to perpetuate. The desire for action, the wish to right wrong and alleviate suffering, haunts them daily. Society smiles at it indulgently instead of making it of value to itself. The wrong to them begins even farther back, when we restrain the first childish desires for "doing good" and tell them that they must wait until they are older and better fitted. We intimate that social obligation begins at a fixed date, forgetting that it begins with birth itself. We treat them as children who, with strong-growing limbs, are allowed to use their legs but not their arms, or whose legs are daily carefully exercised that after a while their arms may be put to high use. We do this in spite of the protest of the best educators, Locke and Pestalozzi. We are fortunate in the meantime if their unused members do not weaken and disappear. They do sometimes. There are a few girls who, by the time they are "educated," forget their old childish desires to help the world and to play with poor little girls "who haven't play-things." Parents are often inconsistent: they deliberately expose their daughters to knowledge of the distress in the world; they send them to hear missionary addresses on famines in India and China; they accompany them to lectures on the suffering in Siberia; they agitate together over the forgotten region of East London. In addition to this, from babyhood the altruistic tendencies of these daughters are persistently cultivated. They are taught to be self-forgetting and self-sacrificing, to consider the good of the whole before the good of the ego. But when all this information and culture show results, when the daughter comes back from college and begins to recognize her social claim to the "submerged tenth," and to evince a disposition to fulfill it, the family claim is strenuously asserted; she is told that she is unjustified, ill advised in her efforts. If she persists, the family too often are injured and unhappy unless the efforts are called mission-ary and the religious zeal of the family carry them over their sense of abuse. When this zeal does not exist, the result is perplexing. It is a curious violation of what we would fain believe a fundamental law—that the final return of the deed is upon the head of the doer. The deed is that of exclusiveness and caution, but the return, instead of falling upon the head of the exclusive and cautious, falls upon a young head full of generous and unselfish plans. The girl loses some-thing vital out of her life to which she is entitled. She is restricted and unhappy; her elders, meanwhile, are unconscious of the situation and we have all the elements of a tragedy.

We have in America a fast-growing number of cultivated young people who have no recognized outlet for their active faculties. They hear constantly of the great social maladjustment, but no way is pro-vided for them to change it, and their uselessness hangs about them heavily. Huxley declares that the sense of uselessness is the severest shock that the human system can sustain, and that if persistently sustained, it results in atrophy of function. These young people have had advantages of college, of European travel, and of economic study, but they are sustaining this shock of inaction. They have pet phrases, and they tell you that the things that make us all alike are stronger than the things that make us different. They say that all men are united by needs and sympathies far more permanent and radical than anything that temporarily divides them and sets them in opposition to each other. If they affect art, they say that the decay in artistic expression is due to the decay in ethics, that art when shut away from the human interests and from the great mass of humanity is self-destructive. They tell their elders with all the bitterness of youth that if they expect success from them in business or politics or in whatever lines their ambition for them has run, they must let them consult all of humanity; that they must let them find out what the people want and how they want it. It is only the stronger young people, however, who formulate this. Many of them dissipate their energies in so-called enjoyment. Others not content with that go on studying and go back to college for their second degrees; not that they are especially fond of study, but because they want something definite to do, and their powers have been trained in the direction of mental accumulation. Many are buried beneath this mental accumulation that lowered vitality and discontent. Walter Besant says they have had the vision that Peter had when he saw the great sheet let down from heaven, wherein was neither clean nor unclean. He calls it the sense of humanity. It is not philanthropy nor benevolence but a thing fuller and wider than either of these.

This young life, so sincere in its emotion and good phrase and yet so undirected, seems to me as pitiful as the other great mass of destitute lives. One is supplementary to the other, and some method of communication can surely be devised. Mr. Barnett, who urged the first settlement—Toynbee Hall, in East London—recognized this need of outlet for the young men of Oxford and Cambridge and hoped that the settlement would supply the communication. It is easy to see why the settlement movement originated in England, where the years of education are more constrained and definite than they are here, where class distinctions are more rigid. The necessity of it was greater there, but we are fast feeling the pressure of the need and meeting the necessity for settlements in America. Our young people feel nervously the need of putting theory into action and respond quickly to the settlement form of activity.

Other motives that I believe make toward the settlement are the result of a certain renaissance going forward in Christianity. The impulse to share the lives of the poor, the desire to make social service, irrespective of propaganda, express the spirit of Christ is as old as Christianity itself. We have no proof from the records themselves that the early Roman Christians, who strained their simple art to the point of grotesqueness in their eagerness to record a "good news" on the walls of the catacombs, considered this good news a religion. Jesus had no set of truths labeled religious. On the contrary, his doctrine was that all truth is one, that the appropriation of it is freedom. His teaching had no dogma to mark it off from truth and action in general. He himself called it a revelation—a life. These early Roman Christians received the Gospel message, a command to love all men, with a certain joyous simplicity. The image of the Good Shepherd is blithe and gay beyond the gentlest shepherd of Greek mythology; the heart no longer pants but rushes to the water brooks. The Christians looked for the continuous revelation but believed what Jesus said, that this revelation, to be retained and made manifest, must be put into terms of action; that action is the only medium man has for receiving and appropriating truth; that the doctrine must be known through the will.

That Christianity has to be revealed and embodied in the line of social progress is a corollary to the simple proposition that man's action is found in his social relationships in the way in which he connects with his fellows; that his motives for action are the zeal and affection with which he regards his fellows. By this simple process was created a deep enthusiasm for humanity, which regarded man as at once the organ and the object of revelation; and by this process came about the wonderful fellowship, the true democracy of the early church, that so captivates the imagination. The early Christians were preeminently nonresistant. They believed in love as a cosmic force. There was no iconoclasm during the minor peace of the church. They did not yet denounce nor tear down temples, nor preach the end of the world. They grew to a mighty number, but it never occurred to them, either in their weakness or in their strength, to regard other men for an instant as their foes or as aliens. The spectacle of the Christians loving all men was the most astounding Rome had ever seen. They were eager to sacrifice themselves for the weak, for children, and for the aged; they identified themselves with slaves and did not avoid the plague; they longed to share the common lot that they might receive the constant revelation. It was a new treasure that the early Christians added to the sum of all treasures, a joy hitherto unknown in the world—the joy of finding the Christ who lieth in each man but who no man can unfold save in fellowship. A happiness ranging from the heroic to the pastoral enveloped them. They were to possess a revelation as long as life had new meaning to unfold, new action to propose.

I believe that there is a distinct turning among many young men and women toward this simple acceptance of Christ's message. They resent the assumption that Christianity is a set of ideas that belong to the religious consciousness, whatever that may be. They insist that it cannot be proclaimed and instituted apart from the social life of the community and that it must seek a simple and natural expression in the social organism itself. The settlement movement is only one manifestation of that wider humanitarian movement that throughout Christendom, but preeminently in England, is endeavoring to embody itself not in a sect but in society itself.

I believe that this turning, this renaissance of the early Christian humanitarianism, is going on in America, in Chicago, if you please, without leaders who write or philosophize, without much speaking, but with a bent to express in social service and in terms of action the spirit of Christ. Certain it is that spiritual force is found in the settlement movement, and it is also true that this force must be evoked and must be called into play before the success of any settlement is assured. There must be the overmastering belief that all that is noblest in life is common to men as men, in order to accentuate the likenesses and ignore the differences that are found among the people whom the settlement constantly brings into juxtaposition. It may be true, as the positivists insist, that the very religious fervor of man can be turned into love for his race, and his desire for a future life into content to live in the echo of his deeds; Paul's formula of seeking for the Christ who lieth in each man and founding our likenesses on him seems a simpler formula to many of us.

In a thousand voices singing the Hallelujah Chorus in Handel's *Messiah*, it is possible to distinguish the leading voices, but the differences of training and cultivation between them and the voices of the chorus are lost in the unity of purpose and in the fact that they are all human voices lifted by a high motive. This is a weak illustration of what a settlement attempts to do. It aims, in a measure, to develop whatever of social life its neighborhood may afford, to focus and give form to that life, to bring to bear upon it the results of cultivation and training; but it receives in exchange for the music of isolated voices the volume and strength of the chorus. It is quite impossible for me to say in what proportion or degree the subjective necessity that led to the opening of Hull-House combined the three trends: first, the desire to interpret democracy in social terms; second, the impulse beating at the very source of our lives, urging us to aid in the race progress; and, third, the Christian movement toward humanitarianism. It is difficult to analyze a living thing; the analysis is at best imperfect. Many more motives may blend with the three trends; possibly the desire for a new form of social success due to the nicety of imagination, which refuses worldly pleasures unmixed with the joys of self-sacrifice; possibly a love of approbation, so vast that it is not content with the treble clapping of delicate hands but wishes also to hear the brass notes from toughened palms, may mingle with these.

The settlement, then, is an experimental effort to aid in the solution of the social and industrial problems that are engendered by the modern conditions of life in a great city. It insists that these problems are not confined to any one portion of a city. It is an attempt to relieve, at the same time, the overaccumulation at one end of society and the destitution at the other; but it assumes that this overaccumulation and destitution is most sorely felt in the things that pertain to social and educational privileges. From its very nature it can stand for no political or social propaganda. It must, in a sense, give the warm welcome of an inn to all such propaganda, if perchance one of them be found an angel. The one thing to be dreaded in the settlement is that it lose its flexibility, its power of quick adaptation, its readiness to change its methods as its environment may demand. It must be open to conviction and must have a deep and abiding sense of tolerance. It must be hospitable and ready for experiment. It should demand from its residents a scientific patience in the accumulation of facts and the steady holding of their sympathies as one of the best instruments for that accumulation. It must be grounded in a philosophy whose foundation is on the solidarity of the human race, a philosophy that will not waver when the race happens to be represented by a drunken woman or an idiot boy. Its residents must be emptied of all conceit of opinion and all self-assertion and ready to arouse and interpret the public opinion of their neighborhood. They must be content to live quietly side by side with their neighbors, until they grow into a sense of relationship and mutual interests. Their neighbors are held apart by differences of race and language that the residents can more easily overcome. They are bound to see the needs of their neighborhood as a whole, to furnish data for legislation, and to use their influence to secure it. In short, residents are pledged to devote themselves to the duties of good citizenship and to the arousing of the social energies that too largely lie dormant in every neighborhood given over to industrialism. They are bound to regard the entire life of their city as organic, to make an effort to unify it, and to protest against its overdifferentiation.

It is always easy to make all philosophy point one particular moral and all history adorn one particular tale; but I may be forgiven the reminder that the best speculative philosophy sets forth the solidarity of the human race; that the highest moralists have taught that without the advance and improvement of the whole, no man can hope for any lasting improvement in his own moral or material individual condition; and that the subjective necessity for social settlements is therefore identical with that necessity, which urges us on toward social and individual salvation.

Chuang-Tzu

ACTION AND NON-ACTION

The non-action of the wise man is not inaction.
It is not studied. It is not shaken by anything.
The sage is quiet because he is not moved,
Not because he wills to be quiet.
Still water is like glass.
You can look in it and see the bristles on your chin.
It is a perfect level;
A carpenter could use it.
If water is so clear, so level,
How much more the spirit of man?
The heart of the wise man is tranquil.
It is the mirror of heaven and earth
The glass of everything.
Emptiness, stillness, tranquillity, tastelessness,

Chuang-Tzu was a renowned Chinese Taoist philosopher of the fourth century BCE. Little is known about his life. He is said to have been from the town of Meng, in the modern-day Henan Province, and to have lived for many years as a hermit. Traditionally it is thought that Chuang-Tzu wrote the first seven ("inner") chapters of the compilation of writings attributed to him, the "Chuang-Tzu," and that his students and other philosophers wrote the rest. His interpretation of Taoist philosophy greatly influenced the development of Zen Buddhism. This translation is by Thomas Merton.

Silence, non-action: this is the level of heaven and earth.
This is perfect Tao. Wise men find here
Their resting place.
Resting, they are empty.

From emptiness comes the unconditioned.
From this, the conditioned, the individual things.
So from the sage's emptiness, stillness arises:
From stillness, action. From action, attainment.
From their stillness comes their non-action,
    which is also action
And is, therefore, their attainment.
For stillness is joy. Joy is free from care
Fruitful in long years.
Joy does all things without concern:
For emptiness, stillness, tranquillity, tastelessness,
Silence, and non-action
Are the root of all things.

Isaiah 58:2–12

Yet day after day they seek me and delight to know my ways,

as if they were a nation that practiced righteousness and did
not forsake the ordinance of their God;

they ask of me righteous judgments, they delight to draw
near to God.

"Why do we fast, but you do not see? Why humble ourselves, but you do not notice?"

Look, you serve your own interest on your fast day, and
oppress all your workers.

Look, you fast only to quarrel and to fight and to strike with
a wicked fist.

Such fasting as you do today will not make your voice heard
on high.

Is such the fast that I choose, a day to humble oneself?

Is it to bow down the head like a bulrush, and to lie in sackcloth and ashes?

Will you call this a fast, a day acceptable to the LORD?

The Book of Isaiah is a book of the Hebrew Bible and the Christian Old
Testament found between the Song of Solomon and the Book of Jeremiah
in the King James version. It is attributed to the prophet Isaiah, who
preached in the second half of the eighth century BCE. In the book's sixty-
six chapters, Isaiah prophecies doom for a sinful Judah and for all nations
that oppose God, followed by chapters covering prophecies of the restoration of the nation under a divine king. Two manuscripts of the Book of
Isaiah have been found among the Dead Sea Scrolls. This selection comes
from the New Revised Standard Version.

Is not this the fast that I choose: to loose the bonds of injustice, to undo the thongs of the yoke,

to let the oppressed go free, and to break every yoke?

Is it not to share your bread with the hungry, and bring the homeless poor into your house;

when you see the naked, to cover them, and not to hide yourself from your own kin?

Then your light shall break forth like the dawn, and your healing shall spring up quickly;

your vindicator shall go before you, the glory of the LORD shall be your rearguard.

Then you shall call, and the LORD will answer; you shall cry for help, and he will say, Here I am.

If you remove the yoke from among you, the pointing of the finger, the speaking of evil,

if you offer your food to the hungry and satisfy the needs of the afflicted,

then your light shall rise in the darkness and your gloom be like the noonday.

The LORD will guide you continually, and satisfy your needs in parched places, and make your bones strong;

and you shall be like a watered garden, like a spring of water, whose waters never fail.

Your ancient ruins shall be rebuilt; you shall raise up the foundations of many generations;

you shall be called the repairer of the breach, the restorer of streets to live in.

Shih Te

THREE POEMS

I

You say, "If you want to be happy
there's no way, but to be a hermit.
Flowers in the grove are better than brocade,
every single season's colors new.
Just sit by a creek and turn your head
to watch the moon's ball roll."
And me? I ought to be at joyous ease,
but I can't help thinking of the people in the world.

II

You want to learn to catch a mouse?
Don't try to learn from a pampered cat.
If you want to learn the nature of the world,
don't study fine-bound books.
The True Jewel's in a coarse bag.

Shih Te is a pseudonym meaning "The Foundling" and was used by a variety of poets who wrote in the style of Han Shan, an eighth-century Zen tramp in east central China. Han Shan's poetry was direct and unpolished, and the Shih Te poems seek to reproduce this. The poems included here were translated by J. P. Seaton.

Buddha–nature stops at huts.
The whole herd of folks who clutch at looks of things
never seem to make the connection.

III

My poems are poems;
some people call them sermons.
Well, poems and sermons share one thing:
when you read them you've got to be careful.
Keep at it. Get into detail.
Don't just claim they're easy.
If you were to live your life like that,
a lot of funny things might happen.

LUKE 10:25–37

Just then a lawyer stood up to test Jesus. "Teacher," he said, "what must I do to inherit eternal life?" He said to him, "What is written in the law? What do you read there?" He answered, "You shall love the Lord your God with all your heart, and with all your soul, and with all your strength, and with all your mind; and your neighbor as yourself." And he said to him, "You have given the right answer; do this, and you will live."

But wanting to justify himself, he asked Jesus, "And who is my neighbor?" Jesus replied, "A man was going down from Jerusalem to Jericho, and fell into the hands of robbers, who stripped him, beat him, and went away, leaving him half dead. Now by chance a priest was going down that road; and when he saw him, he passed by on the other side. So likewise a Levite, when he came to the place and saw him, passed by on the other side. But a Samaritan while traveling came near him; and when he saw him, he was moved with pity. He went to him and bandaged his wounds, having poured oil and wine on them. Then he put him on his own animal, brought him to an inn, and took care of him. The next day he took out two denarii, gave

---

The Gospel of Luke is the third and longest of the four canonical Gospels that open the New Testament, which is the second part of the Christian Bible. The text of Luke narrates the life of Jesus of Nazareth, from his birth and ministry to his crucifixion and resurrection. Luke 10:25–37 presents the well-known parable of the "Good Samaritan," also sometimes known as the parable of the "Good Neighbor." It is worth noting that this parable depicts (but does not call explicit attention to) a social context in which Samaritans were not generally held in high esteem. This selection comes from the New Revised Standard Version.

them to the innkeeper, and said, 'Take care of him; and when I come back, I will repay you whatever more you spend.' Which of these three, do you think, was a neighbor to the man who fell into the hands of the robbers?" He said, "The one who showed him mercy." Jesus said to him, "Go and do likewise."

Hamza Yusuf

MISERLINESS

from *Purification of the Heart*

~~~

Poem Verses 16–25

Now then: the refusal to give what is obliged according
to Sacred Law or to virtuous merit is the essence of
miserliness, which is mentioned [among the diseases of the
heart].

As for the obligations of Sacred Law, they are such things
as *Zakāt*, supporting one's dependents, and rights due to
others, and relieving the distressed. Examples of [virtuous
merit] include not nitpicking over trivialities.

Avoiding this is even more important with respect to a
neighbor, a relative, or a wealthy person;

Hamza Yusuf is a Sunni Islamic scholar and founder of the Zaytuna Institute
and Academy, a nonprofit organization dedicated to the traditional study of
the core sciences of Islam. Born Mark Hanson in 1960 in Washington State,
he became a Muslim in 1977 and studied for ten years in the United Arab
Emirates, Saudi Arabia, and North and West Africa. He was the first
American scholar to teach in Morocco's oldest and most prestigious
university, Al-Karaouine in Fes. Yusuf has translated several classical Arabic
traditional texts and poems into modern English, including *The Creed of
Imām al-Tahawi* and *Purification of the Heart*.

59

or when hosting guests; or concerning something in which such behavior is inappropriate, such as purchasing a burial shroud or a sacrificial animal, or purchasing something you intend to donate to the needy.

Thus one who makes matters difficult for one whose rights clearly render this inappropriate to do so, such as a neighbor, has indeed torn away the veils of dignity. This is as the majestic and guiding sages have stated.

This is comparable to one who fulfills his obligations without good cheer or who spends from the least of what he possesses.

Its root is love of this world for its own sake,
or so that the self can acquire some of its fleeting pleasures.

DEFINITION AND CAUSES

Imām Mawlūd brings to the fore the definitions of these diseases, their etiology (origins and causes), and how to cure them. The first disease he speaks of is miserliness (*bukhl*). It is first not because it is the worst of characters but because of alphabetical ordering in Arabic.

He mentions two aspects of miserliness. One relates to the Sacred Law, *Sharī'a*, that is, rights due to God and to His creation. The other pertains to *muru'a*, which is an important Arabic concept that connotes *manliness* and *valor*. In pre-Islamic Arab culture, *valor* was a defining concept. It is similar to Western ideals of *chivalry* and *virtue*. (The Latin word *vir* means *man*. Similarly, the Arabic root for *virtue*, *murū'a*, is a cognate of the word for *man*—though scholars state that it refers both to manliness and humanity.)

Regarding the first aspect, the Sacred Law obliges payment of *Zakāt*—charity distributed to the needy. Miserliness in the form of not giving *Zakāt* is explicitly forbidden. The same is true with one's obligation to support his wife and children. Even if a couple suffers a divorce, the man must still pay child support. Miserliness, when it comes to the obligations of Sacred Law, is the most virulent form.

In terms of valor, the Imām goes into some detail. One should never create difficulty over paltry matters, he says. When it come to debt, it is far better for the creditor to be flexible and magnanimous than demanding and unbearable. This is especially true when the creditor is not in need of repayment, while the debtor faces hardship. An understanding and compassionate creditor is one who has valor. Having this quality of magnanimity is not an obligation in Sacred Law because the creditor has the right to what is owed to him. But if he is apathetic to the needs of the debtor and insists on his payment, this is considered reprehensible.

It is an Islamic ethic that a wealthy person have magnanimity, generosity, and the demeanor of lenience. A hadith speaks of a wealthy man who would instruct his servants when collecting money on his behalf, "If [the debtors] do not have the means, tell them their debts are absolved." When this wealthy man died without any good deeds save his largesse with debtors, according to the hadith, God said to His angels, "This man was forgiving of people's transgressions against him, and I'm more worthy of forgiving transgressions. Therefore, I forgive him." When hosting guests, one should not be persnickety, says Imām Mawlūd. If a guest, for example, spills something on the carpet, the host should not display anger or, worse yet, scold the guest. It is far better humanity and valor to make one's guests feel no consternation at all. The Imām mentions buying a funeral shroud, saying there should be no haggling over the cost, for the funeral shroud should remind one of death and not worldly matters. Also, when buying livestock in order to give meat to the needy, one should not haggle over the price. (This applies to purchasing other goods that are intended for charity as well.)

A person who doles out difficulty without cause strips away the veils of dignity; this is what the "wise guides" (that is, the scholars) have said. It is equally regrettable when one discharges an obligation or fulfills a trust without good cheer. When paying charity, for example, one should smile and be humble, allowing the hand of the indigent to be above the giver's hand. It is a privilege to be in the position to give charity and an honor to fulfill a divine obligation.

In Islam, it is an anathema to give away in charity what is shoddy and inferior. There is parsimony and miserliness in this. The Muslim tradition is to give away from what one loves; God blesses this charity and extends its goodness. *O you who believe, spend from the good things you have earned and from what We brought out for you from the earth. And do not seek what is inferior in order to spend from it, though you yourselves would not take it unless your eyes were closed to it. And know that God is ever-rich and worthy of praise* (Qur'an 2:267); and *You will not attain to righteousness until you spend of what you love* (Qur'an 3:92).

Generosity is one of the highest virtues of Islam and one of the manifest qualities of the Prophet Muhammad, who was known as the most generous of people. The word for *generosity* here is derived from *karam*, which also means *nobility*. In fact, one of the most excellent names of God is *al-Karīm*, the Generous. It is better to go beyond the minimum of what the Sacred Law demands when giving charity. This generosity is an expression of gratitude to God, who is the Provider of all wealth and provision.

The etiology of miserliness comes down to loving the fleeting stuff of this world. The miser ardently *clings* to his wealth and hoards it up. The word for *cling* in Arabic is *masak*, which is derived from another Arabic word that means *constipation*. Miserly people are those who are unable to let go of something that otherwise poisons them. The Prophet said, "God has made what is excreted from the son of Adam a metaphor for the world [*dunya*]." When one is hungry, he seeks out food, eats, and is pleased. But when it leaves the body, it is the most odious of things. Giving *Zakāt* is letting go of a portion of one's wealth to purify all of one's other assets and, ultimately, one's soul. It is possible that someone's earning may have some impurity in it, some doubtful source. By giving *Zakāt,* one purifies one's provision from whatever unknown impurities that may have entered.

Imām 'Alī said, "The worst person is the miser. In this world he is deprived of his own wealth, and in the Hereafter he is punished."

The ultimate casualty of miserliness is the miser himself. Many wealthy people in our society live impoverished lives, though they have millions in the bank. Their choice of living is not inspired by spiritual austerity. Rather, it causes them great discomfort to spend their money even on themselves and their families, let alone on others. The nature of the miser is that he does not benefit from his wealth in this world; and in the Hereafter he is bankrupt and debased for refusing to give to the needy—refusing to purify his wealth and preventing it from being a cause of light and relief in the Hereafter. The miser would argue that he hoards wealth to alleviate his fear of poverty. What is remarkable about this mindset is that the miser never truly feels relieved of anxiety; a miser is constantly worried about money and devoted to servicing his worry. The Prophet once asked some clansmen about their leader. They mentioned his name and said, "But he is a bit of a miser." The Prophet said, "A leader should never be a miser." And then he added, "Do you know of any disease that is worse than miserliness?"

PURIFICATION OF THE HEART

Poem Verses 26–29

Treat this by realizing that those who achieved [affluence] did so only by exhausting themselves over long periods of time, thus finally accumulating what they sought.

Meanwhile, just as they approach the heights of [earthly] splendor, death suddenly assails them.

[Treat miserliness by also recognizing] the disdain shown to misers, and the hatred people have for them—even [hatred] amongst [misers] themselves.
With this same treatment, treat the person
whose heart's ailment is love of wealth.

TREATMENT

The treatment for miserliness is *realizing* that those who achieve wealth usually do so only after exhausting themselves over long periods of time, working for it day and night. Meanwhile, life passes on and time runs out. The culture of wanting more simply for more's sake can occupy a person for an entire lifetime. And in the end, life is over. It terminates for the beggar and the affluent just the same, whether one is old or young, rich or poor, happy or sad.

This is Imām Mawlūd's counsel: reflect long and hard on the fact that just as people climb to the heights of affluence and start to achieve what they have worn themselves out for, death assails them without invitation. When death takes us and moves us on, our wealth stays behind for others to wrangle over and spend.

One must also realize the level of disdain shown to misers. Nobody likes a miser. Even misers loathe each other. Realizing the hatred people have for misers is enough to turn one away from their disease.

عِلم

Flannery O'Connor

THE RIVER

in *A Good Man Is Hard to Find and Other Stories.*

~~~

The child stood glum and limp in the middle of the dark living room while his father pulled him into a plaid coat. His right arm was hung in the sleeve but the father buttoned the coat anyway and pushed him forward toward a pale spotted hand that stuck through the half-open door.

"He ain't fixed right," a loud voice said from the hall.

"Well then for Christ's sake fix him," the father muttered. "It's six o'clock in the morning." He was in his bathrobe and barefooted. When he got the child to the door and tried to shut it, he found her looming in it, a speckled skeleton in a long pea-green coat and felt helmet.

"And his and my carfare," she said. "It'll be twict we have to ride the car."

He went in the bedroom again to get the money and when he came back, she and the boy were both standing in the middle of the room. She was taking stock. "I couldn't smell those dead cigarette

---

Mary Flannery O'Connor was born in Savannah, Georgia, in 1925. She was diagnosed with lupus in 1950 and died of the disease at the age of thirty-nine. Cared for by her mother at their family's dairy farm in Milledgeville, Georgia, O'Connor wrote novels and short stories between bouts of the illness. O'Connor was raised Roman Catholic but often featured Protestant fundamentalist characters in her stories. "The River" is from the collection *A Good Man Is Hard to Find and Other Stories.*

butts long if I was ever to come sit with you," she said, shaking him down in his coat.

"Here's the change," the father said. He went to the door and opened it wide and waited.

After she had counted the money she slipped it somewhere inside her coat and walked over to a watercolor hanging near the phonograph. "I know what time it is," she said, peering closely at the black lines crossing into broken planes of violent color. "I ought to. My shift goes on at 10 P.M. and don't get off till 5 and it takes me one hour to ride the Vine Street car."

"Oh, I see," he said; "well, we'll expect him back tonight, about eight or nine?"

"Maybe later," she said. "We're going to the river to a healing. This particular preacher don't get around this way often. I wouldn't have paid for that," she said, nodding at the painting, "I would have drew it myself."

"All right, Mrs. Connin, we'll see you then," he said, drumming on the door.

A toneless voice called from the bedroom, "Bring me an icepack."

"Too bad his mamma's sick," Mrs. Connin said. "What's her trouble?"

"We don't know," he muttered.

"We'll ask the preacher to pray for her. He's healed a lot of folks. The Reverend Bevel Summers. Maybe she ought to see him some-time."

"Maybe so," he said. "We'll see you tonight," and he disappeared into the bedroom and left them to go.

The little boy stared at her silently, his nose and eyes running. He was four or five. He had a long face and bulging chin and half-shut eyes set far apart. He seemed mute and patient, like an old sheep waiting to be let out.

"You'll like this preacher," she said. "The Reverend Bevel Summers. You ought to hear him sing."

The bedroom door opened suddenly and the father stuck his head out and said, "Good-by, old man. Have a good time."

"Good-by," the little boy said and jumped as if he had been shot.

Mrs. Connin gave the watercolor another look. Then they went out into the hall and rang for the elevator. "I wouldn't have drew it," she said.

Outside the gray morning was blocked off on either side by the unlit empty buildings. "It's going to fair up later," she said, "but this is the last time we'll be able to have any preaching at the river this year. Wipe your nose, Sugar Boy."

He began rubbing his sleeve across it but she stopped him. "That ain't nice," she said. "Where's your handkerchief?"

He put his hands in his pockets and pretended to look for it while she waited. "Some people don't care how they send one off," she murmured to her reflection in the coffee shop window. "You pervide." She took a red and blue flowered handkerchief out of her pocket and stooped down and began to work on his nose. "Now blow," she said and he blew. "You can borry it. Put it in your pocket."

He folded it up and put it in his pocket carefully and they walked on to the corner and leaned against the side of a closed drugstore to wait for the car. Mrs. Connin turned up her coat collar so that it met her hat in the back. Her eyelids began to droop and she looked as if she might go to sleep against the wall. The little boy put a slight pressure on her hand.

"What's your name?" she asked in a drowsy voice. "I don't know but only your last name. I should have found out your first name."

His name was Harry Ashfield and he had never thought at any time before of changing it. "Bevel," he said.

Mrs. Connin raised herself from the wall. "Why ain't that a coincident!" she said. "I told you that's the name of this preacher!"

"Bevel," he repeated.

She stood looking down at him as if he had become a marvel to her. "I'll have to see you meet him today," she said. "He's no ordinary preacher. He's a healer. He couldn't do nothing for Mr. Connin though. Mr. Connin didn't have the faith but he said he would try anything once. He had this griping in his gut."

The trolley appeared as a yellow spot at the end of the deserted street.

"He's gone to the government hospital now," she said, "and they taken one-third of his stomach. I tell him he better thank Jesus for what he's got left but he says he ain't thanking nobody. Well I declare," she murmured, "Bevel!"

They walked out to the tracks to wait. "Will he heal me?" Bevel asked.

"What you got?"

"I'm hungry," he decided finally.

"Didn't you have your breakfast?"

"I didn't have time to be hungry yet then," he said.

"Well when we get home we'll both have us something," she said. "I'm ready myself."

They got on the car and sat down a few seats behind the driver and Mrs. Connin took Bevel on her knees. "Now you be a good boy," she said, "and let me get some sleep. Just don't get off my lap." She lay her head back and as he watched, gradually her eyes closed and her mouth fell open to show a few long scattered teeth, some gold and some darker than her face; she began to whistle and blow like a musical skeleton. There was no one in the car but themselves and the driver and when he saw she was asleep, he took out the flowered handkerchief and unfolded it and examined it carefully. Then he folded it up again and unzipped a place in the innerlining of his coat and hid it in there and shortly he went to sleep himself.

Her house was a half-mile from the end of the car line, set back a little from the road. It was tan paper brick with a porch across the front of it and a tin top. On the porch there were three little boys of different sizes with identical speckled faces and one tall girl who had her hair up in so many aluminum curlers that it glared like the roof. The three boys followed them inside and closed in on Bevel. They looked at him silently, not smiling.

"That's Bevel," Mrs. Connin said, taking off her coat. "It's a coincident he's named the same as the preacher. These boys are J. C., Spivey, and Sinclair, and that's Sarah Mildred on the porch. Take off that coat and hang it on the bed post, Bevel."

The three boys watched him while he unbuttoned the coat and took it off. Then they watched him hang it on the bed post and then they stood, watching the coat. They turned abruptly and went out the door and had a conference on the porch.

Bevel stood looking around him at the room. It was part kitchen and part bedroom. The entire house was two rooms and two porches. Close to his foot the tail of a light-colored dog moved up and down between two floor boards as he scratched his back on the underside of the house. Bevel jumped on it but the hound was experienced and had already withdrawn when his feet hit the spot.

The walls were filled with pictures and calendars. There were two round photographs of an old man and woman with collapsed mouths and another picture of a man whose eyebrows dashed out of two bushes of hair and clashed in a heap on the bridge of his nose; the rest of his face stuck out like a bare cliff to fall from. "That's Mr. Connin," Mrs. Connin said, standing back from the stove for a second to admire the face with him, "but it don't favor him any more." Bevel turned from Mr. Connin to a colored picture over the bed of a man wearing a white sheet. He had long hair and a gold circle around his head and he was sawing on a board while some children stood watching him. He was going to ask who that was when the three boys came in again and motioned for him to follow them. He thought of crawling under the bed and hanging onto one of the legs but the three boys only stood there, speckled and silent, waiting, and after a second he followed them at a little distance out on the porch and around the corner of the house. They started off through a field of rough yellow weeds to the hog pen, a five-foot boarded square full of shoats, which they intended to ease him over into. When they reached it, they turned and waited silently, leaning against the side.

He was coming very slowly, deliberately bumping his feet together as if he had trouble walking. Once he had been beaten up in the park by some strange boys when his sitter forgot him, but he hadn't known anything was going to happen that time until it was over. He began to smell a strong odor of garbage and to hear the noises of a wild animal. He stopped a few feet from the pen and waited, pale but dogged.

The three boys didn't move. Something seemed to have happened to them. They stared over his head as if they saw something coming behind him but he was afraid to turn his own head and look. Their speckles were pale and their eyes were still and gray as glass. Only their ears twitched slightly. Nothing happened. Finally, the one in the middle said, "She'd kill us," and turned, dejected and hacked, and climbed up on the pen and hung over, staring in.

Bevel sat down on the ground, dazed with relief, and grinned up at them.

The one sitting on the pen glanced at him severely. "Hey you," he said after a second, "if you can't climb up and see these pigs you can lift that bottom board off and look in thataway." He appeared to offer this as a kindness.

Bevel had never seen a real pig but he had seen a pig in a book and knew they were small fat pink animals with curly tails and round grinning faces and bow ties. He leaned forward and pulled eagerly at the board.

"Pull harder," the littlest boy said. "It's nice and rotten. Just lift out thet nail."

He eased a long reddish nail out of the soft wood.

"Now you can lift up the board and put your face to the …" a quiet voice began.

He had already done it and another face, gray, wet and sour, was pushing into his, knocking him down and back as it scraped out under the plank. Something snorted over him and charged back again, rolling him over and pushing him up from behind and then sending him forward, screaming through the yellow field, while it bounded behind.

The three Connins watched from where they were. The one sitting on the pen held the loose board back with his dangling foot. Their stern faces didn't brighten any but they seemed to become less taut, as if some great need had been partly satisfied. "Maw ain't going to like him letting out thet hawg," the smallest one said.

Mrs. Connin was on the back porch and caught Bevel up as he reached the steps. The hog ran under the house and subsided, panting, but the child screamed for five minutes. When she had finally calmed him down, she gave him his breakfast and let him sit on her lap while he ate it. The shoat climbed the two steps onto the back porch and stood outside the screen door, looking in with his head lowered sullenly. He was long-legged and hump-backed and part of one of his ears had been bitten off.

"Git away!" Mrs. Connin shouted. "That one yonder favors Mr. Paradise that has the gas station," she said. "You'll see him today at the healing. He's got the cancer over his ear. He always comes to show he ain't been healed."

The shoat stood squinting a few seconds longer and then moved off slowly. "I don't want to see him," Bevel said.

They walked to the river, Mrs. Connin in front with him and the three boys strung out behind and Sarah Mildred, the tall girl, at the end to holler if one of them ran out on the road. They looked like the skeleton of an old boat with two pointed ends, sailing slowly on the edge of the highway. The white Sunday sun followed at a little distance, climbing fast through a scum of gray cloud as if it meant to overtake them. Bevel walked on the outside edge, holding Mrs. Connin's hand and looking down into the orange and purple gulley that dropped off from the concrete.

It occurred to him that he was lucky this time that they had found Mrs. Connin who would take you away for the day instead of an ordinary sitter who only sat where you lived or went to the park. You found out more when you left where you lived. He had found out already this morning that he had been made by a carpenter named Jesus Christ. Before he had thought it had been a doctor named Sladewall, a fat man with a yellow mustache who gave him shots and thought his name was Herbert, but this must have been a joke. They joked a lot where he lived. If he had thought about it before, he would have thought Jesus Christ was a word like "oh" or "damm" or "God," or maybe somebody who had cheated them out of something sometime. When he had asked Mrs. Connin who the man in the sheet in the picture over her bed was, she had looked at him a while with her mouth open. Then she had said, "That's Jesus," and she had kept on looking at him.

In a few minutes she had got up and got a book out of the other room. "See here," she said, turning over the cover, "this belonged to my great grandmamma. I wouldn't part with it for nothing on earth." She ran her finger under some brown writing on a spotted page. "Emma Stevens Oakley, 1832," she said. "Ain't that something to have? And every word of it the gospel truth." She turned the next page and read him the name: "The Life of Jesus Christ for Readers Under Twelve." Then she read him the book.

It was a small book, pale brown on the outside with gold edges and a smell like old putty. It was full of pictures, one of the carpenter driving a crowd of pigs out of a man. They were real pigs, gray and sour-looking, and Mrs. Connin said Jesus had driven them all out of this one man. When she finished reading, she let him sit on the floor and look at the pictures again.

Just before they left for the healing, he had managed to get the book inside his innerlining without her seeing him. Now it made his coat hang down a little farther on one side than the other. His mind was dreamy and serene as they walked along and when they turned off the highway onto a long red clay road winding between banks of honeysuckle, he began to make wild leaps and pull forward on her hand as if he wanted to dash off and snatch the sun which was rolling away ahead of them now.

They walked on the dirt road for a while and then they crossed a field stippled with purple weeds and entered the shadows of a wood where the ground was covered with thick pine needles. He had never been in woods before and he walked carefully, looking from side to side as if he were entering a strange country. They moved along a bridle path that twisted downhill through crackling red leaves, and once, catching at a branch to keep himself from slipping, he looked into two frozen green-gold eyes enclosed in the darkness of a tree hold. At the bottom of the hill, the woods opened suddenly onto a pasture dotted here and there with black and white cows and sloping down, tier after tier, to a broad orange stream where the reflection of the sun was set like a diamond.

There were people standing on the near bank in a group, singing. Long tables were set up behind them and a few cars and trucks were parked in a road that came up by the river. They crossed the pasture, hurrying, because Mrs. Connin, using her hand for a shed over her eyes, saw the preacher already standing out in the water. She dropped her basket on one of the tables and pushed the three boys in front of her into the knot of people so that they wouldn't linger by the food. She kept Bevel by the hand and eased her way up to the front.

The preacher was standing about ten feet out in the stream where the water came up to his knees. He was a tall youth in khaki trousers that he had rolled up higher than the water. He had on a blue shirt and a red scarf around his neck but no hat and his light colored hair was cut in sideburns that curved into the hollows of his cheeks. His face was all bone and red light reflected from the river. He looked as if he might have been nineteen years old. He was singing in a high twangy voice, above the singing on the bank, and he kept his hands behind him and his head tilted back.

He ended the hymn on a high note and stood silent, looking down at the water and shifting his feet in it. Then he looked up at the people on the bank. They stood close together, waiting; their faces were solemn but expectant and every eye was on him. He shifted his feet again.

"Maybe I know why you come," he said in the twangy voice, "maybe I don't.

"If you ain't come for Jesus, you ain't come for me. If you just come to see can you leave your pain in the river, you ain't come for Jesus. You can't leave your pain in the river," he said. "I never told nobody that." He stopped and looked down at his knees.

"I seen you cure a woman oncet!" a sudden high voice shouted from the hump of people. "Seen that woman git up and walk out straight where she had limped in!"

The preacher lifted one foot and then the other. He seemed almost but not quite to smile. "You might as well go home if that's what you come for," he said.

Then he lifted his head and arms and shouted, "Listen to what I got to say, you people! There ain't but one river and that's the River of Life, made out of Jesus' Blood. That's the river you have to lay your pain in, in the River of Faith, in the River of Life, in the River of Love, in the rich red river of Jesus' Blood, you people!"

His voice grew soft and musical. "All the rivers come from that one River and go back to it like it was the ocean sea and if you believe, you can lay your pain in that River and get rid of it because that's the River that was made to carry sin. It's a River full of pain itself, pain itself, moving toward the Kingdom of Christ, to be washed away, slow, you people, slow as this here old red water river round my feet.

"Listen," he sang, "I read in Mark about an unclean man, I read in Luke about a blind man, I read in John about a dead man! Oh you people hear! The same blood that makes this River red, made that leper clean, made that blind man stare, made that dead man leap! You people with trouble," he cried, "lay it in that River of Blood, lay it in that River of Pain, and watch it move away toward the Kingdom of Christ."

While he preached, Bevel's eyes followed drowsily the slow circles of two silent birds revolving high in the air. Across the river there was a low red and gold grove of sassafras with hills of dark blue trees behind it and an occasional pine jutting over the skyline. Behind, in the distance, the city rose like a cluster of warts on the side of the mountain. The birds revolved downward and dropped lightly in the top of the highest pine and sat hunch-shouldered as if they were supporting the sky.

"If it's this River of Life you want to lay your pain in, then come up," the preacher said, "and lay your sorrow here. But don't be thinking this is the last of it because this old red river don't end here. This old red suffering stream goes on, you people, slow to the Kingdom of Christ. This old red river is good to Baptize in, good to lay your faith in, good to lay your pain in, but it ain't this muddy water here that saves you. I been all up and down this river this week," he said. "Tuesday I was in Fortune Lake, next day in Ideal, Friday me and my wife drove to Lulawillow to see a sick man there. Them people didn't see no healing," he said and his face burned redder for a second. "I never said they would."

While he was talking a fluttering figure had begun to move forward with a kind of butterfly movement—an old woman with flapping arms whose head wobbled as if it might fall off any second. She managed to lower herself at the edge of the bank and let her arms churn in the water. Then she bent farther and pushed her face down in it and raised herself up finally, streaming wet; and still flapping, she turned a time or two in a blind circle until someone reached out and pulled her back into the group.

"She's been that way for thirteen years," a rough voice shouted. "Pass the hat and give this kid his money. That's what he's here for." The shout, directed out to the boy in the river, came from a huge old man who sat like a humped stone on the bumper of a long ancient gray automobile. He had on a gray hat that was turned down over one ear and up over the other to expose a purple bulge on his left temple. He sat bent forward with his hands hanging between his knees and his small eyes half closed.

Bevel stared at him once and then moved into the folds of Mrs. Connin's coat and hid himself.

The boy in the river glanced at the old man quickly and raised his fist. "Believe Jesus or the devil!" he cried. "Testify to one or the other!"

"I know from my own self-experience," a woman's mysterious voice called from the knot of people, "I know from it that this preacher can heal. My eyes have been opened! I testify to Jesus!"

The preacher lifted his arms quickly and began to repeat all that he had said before about the River and the Kingdom of Christ and the old man sat on the bumper, fixing him with a narrow squint. From time to time Bevel stared at him again from around Mrs. Connin.

A man in overalls and a brown coat leaned forward and dipped his hand in the water quickly and shook it and leaned back, and a woman held a baby over the edge of the bank and splashed its feet with water. One man moved a little distance away and sat down on the bank and took off his shoes and waded out into the stream; he stood there for a few minutes with his face tilted as far back as it would go, then he waded back and put on his shoes. All this time, the preacher sang and did not appear to watch what went on.

As soon as he stopped singing, Mrs. Connin lifted Bevel up and said, "Listen here, preacher, I got a boy from town today that I'm keeping. His mamma's sick and he wants you to pray for her. And this is a coincident—his name is Bevel! Bevel," she said, turning to look at the people behind her, "same as his. Ain't that a coincident, though?"

There were some murmurs and Bevel turned and grinned over her shoulder at the faces looking at him. "Bevel," he said in a loud jaunty voice.

"Listen," Mrs. Connin said, "have you ever been Baptized, Bevel?" He only grinned.

"I suspect he ain't ever been Baptized," Mrs. Connin said, raising her eyebrows at the preacher.

"Swang him over here," the preacher said and took a stride forward and caught him.

He held him in the crook of his arm and looked at the grinning face. Bevel rolled his eyes in a comical way and thrust his face forward, close to the preacher's. "My name is Bevvvuuuuul," he said in a loud deep voice and let the tip of his tongue slide across his mouth.

The preacher didn't smile. His bony face was rigid and his narrow gray eyes reflected the almost colorless sky. There was a loud laugh from the old man sitting on the car bumper and Bevel grasped the back of the preacher's collar and held it tightly. The grin had already disappeared from his face. He had the sudden feeling that this was not a joke. Where he lived everything was a joke. From the preacher's face, he knew immediately that nothing the preacher said or did was a joke. "My mother named me that," he said quickly.

"Have you ever been Baptized?" the preacher asked.

"What's that?" he murmured.

"If I Baptize you," the preacher said, "you'll be able to go to the Kingdom of Christ. You'll be washed in the river of suffering, son, and you'll go by the deep river of life. Do you want that?"

"Yes," the child said, and thought, I won't go back to the apartment then, I'll go under the river.

"You won't be the same again," the preacher said. "You'll count." Then he turned his face to the people and began to preach and Bevel looked over his shoulder at the pieces of the white sun scattered in the river. Suddenly the preacher said, "All right, I'm going to Baptize you now," and without more warning, he tightened his hold and swung him upside down and plunged his head into the

76

water. He held him under while he said the words of Baptism and then he jerked him up again and looked sternly at the gasping child. Bevel's eyes were dark and dilated. "You count now," the preacher said. "You didn't even count before."

The little boy was too shocked to cry. He spit out the muddy water and rubbed his wet sleeve into his eyes and over his face.

"Don't forget his mamma," Mrs. Connin called. "He wants you to pray for his mamma. She's sick."

"Lord," the preacher said, "we pray for somebody in affliction who isn't here to testify. Is your mother sick in the hospital?" he asked. "Is she in pain?"

The child stared at him. "She hasn't got up yet," he said in a high dazed voice. "She has a hangover." The air was so quiet he could hear the broken pieces of the sun knocking in the water.

The preacher looked angry and startled. The red drained out of his face and the sky appeared to darken in his eyes. There was a loud guffaw from the bank and Mr. Paradise shouted, "Haw! Cure the afflicted woman with the hangover!" and began to beat his knee with his fist.

"He's had a long day," Mrs. Connin said, standing with him in the door of the apartment and looking sharply into the room where the party was going on. "I reckon it's past his regular bedtime." One of Bevel's eyes was closed and the other half closed; his nose was running and he kept his mouth open and breathed through it. The damp plaid coat dragged down on one side.

That would be her, Mrs. Connin decided, in the black britches—long black satin britches and barefoot sandals and red toenails. She was lying on half the sofa, with her knees crossed in the air and her head propped on the arm. She didn't get up.

"Hello Harry," she said. "Did you have a big day?" She had a long pale face, smooth and blank, and straight sweet-potato-colored hair, pulled back.

The father went off to get the money. There were two other couples. One of the men, blond with little violet-blue eyes, leaned out of his chair and said, "Well Harry, old man, have a big day?"

"His name ain't Harry. It's Bevel," Mrs. Connin said.

"His name is Harry," *she* said from the sofa. "Whoever heard of anybody named Bevel?"

The little boy had seemed to be going to sleep on his feet, his head drooping farther and farther forward; he pulled it back suddenly and opened one eye; the other was stuck.

"He told me this morning his name was Bevel," Mrs. Connin said in a shocked voice. "The same as our preacher. We been all day at a preaching and healing at the river. He said his name was Bevel, the same as the preacher's. That's what he told me."

"Bevel!" his mother said. "My God! what a name."

"This preacher is name Bevel and there's no better preacher around," Mrs. Connin said. "And further more," she added in a defiant tone, "he Baptized this child this morning!"

His mother sat straight up. "Well the nerve!" she muttered.

"Furthermore," Mrs. Connin said, "he's a healer and he prayed for you to be healed."

"Healed!" she almost shouted. "Healed of what for Christ's sake?"

"Of your affliction," Mrs. Connin said icily.

The father had returned with the money and was standing near Mrs. Connin waiting to give it to her. His eyes were lined with red threads. "Go on, go on," he said, "I want to hear more about her affliction. The exact nature of it has escaped …" He waved the bill and his voice trailed off. "Healing by prayer is mighty inexpensive," he muttered.

Mrs. Connin stood a second, staring into the room, with a skeleton's appearance of seeing everything. Then, without taking the money, she turned and shut the door behind her. The father swung around, smiling vaguely, and shrugged. The rest of them were looking at Harry. The little boy began to shamble toward the bedroom.

"Come here, Harry," his mother said. He automatically shifted his direction toward her without opening his eye any farther. "Tell me what happened today," she said when he reached her. She began to pull off his coat.

"I don't know," he muttered.

"Yes you do know," she said, feeling the coat heavier on one side. She unzipped the innerlining and caught the book and a dirty handkerchief as they fell out. "Where did you get these?"

"I don't know," he said and grabbed for them. "They're mine. She gave them to me."

She threw the handkerchief down and held the book too high for him to reach and began to read it, her face after a second assuming an exaggerated comical expression. The others moved around and looked at it over her shoulder. "My God," somebody said.

One of the men peered at it sharply from behind a thick pair of glasses. "That's valuable," he said. "That's a collector's item," and he took it away from the rest of them and retired to another chair.

"Don't let George go off with that," his girl said.

"I tell you it's valuable," George said. "1832."

Bevel shifted his direction again toward the room where he slept. He shut the door behind him and moved slowly in the darkness to the bed and sat down and took off his shoes and got under the cover. After a minute a shaft of light let in the tall silhouette of his mother. She tiptoed lightly across the room and sat down on the edge of his bed. "What did that dolt of a preacher say about me?" she whispered. "What lies have you been telling today, honey?"

He shut his eye and heard her voice from a long way away, as if he were under the river and she on top of it. She shook his shoulder. "Harry," she said, leaning down and putting her mouth to his ear, "tell me what he said." She pulled him into a sitting position and he felt as if he had been drawn up from under the river. "Tell me," she whispered and her bitter breath covered his face.

He saw the pale oval close to him in the dark. "He said I'm not the same now," he muttered. "I count."

After a second, she lowered him by his shirt front onto the pillow. She hung over him an instant and brushed her lips against his forehead. Then she got up and moved away, swaying her hips lightly through the shaft of light.

He didn't wake up early but the apartment was still dark and close when he did. For a while he lay there, picking his nose and eyes. Then he sat up in bed and looked out the window. The sun came in palely, stained gray by the glass. Across the street at the Empire Hotel, a colored cleaning woman was looking down from an upper window, resting her face on her folded arms. He got up and put on his shoes and went to the bathroom and then into the front room. He ate two crackers spread with anchovy paste, that he found on the coffee table, and drank some ginger ale left in a bottle and looked around for his book but it was not there.

The apartment was silent except for the faint humming of the refrigerator. He went into the kitchen and found some raisin bread heels and spread a half jar of peanut butter between them and climbed up on the tall kitchen stool and sat chewing the sandwich slowly, wiping his nose every now and then on his shoulder. When he finished he found some chocolate milk and drank that. He would rather have had the ginger ale he saw but they left the bottle openers where he couldn't reach them. He studied what was left in the refrigerator for a while—some shriveled vegetables that she had forgot were there and a lot of brown oranges that she bought and didn't squeeze; there were three or four kinds of cheese and something fishy in a paper bag; the rest was a pork bone. He left the refrigerator door open and wandered back into the dark living room and sat down on the sofa.

He decided they would be out cold until one o'clock and that they would all have to go to a restaurant for lunch. He wasn't high enough for the table yet and the waiter would bring a highchair and he was too big for a highchair. He sat in the middle of the sofa, kicking it with his heels. Then he got up and wandered around the room, looking into the ashtrays at the butts as if this might be a habit. In his own room he had picture books and blocks but they were for the most part torn up; he found the way to get new ones was to tear up the ones he had. There was very little to do at any time but eat; however, he was not a fat boy.

He decided he would empty a few of the ashtrays on the floor. If he only emptied a few, she would think they had fallen. He emptied two, rubbing the ashes carefully into the rug with his finger. Then he lay on the floor for a while, studying his feet which he held up in the air. His shoes were still damp and he began to think about the river.

Very slowly, his expression changed as if he were gradually seeing appear what he didn't know he'd been looking for. Then all of a sudden he knew what he wanted to do.

He got up and tiptoed into their bedroom and stood in the dim light there, looking for her pocketbook. His glance passed her long pale arm hanging off the edge of the bed down to the floor, and across the white mound his father made, and past the crowded bureau, until it rested on the pocketbook hung on the back of a chair. He took a car-token out of it and half a package of Life Savers. Then he left the apartment and caught the car at the corner. He hadn't taken a suitcase because there was nothing from there he wanted to keep.

He got off the car at the end of the line and started down the road he and Mrs. Connin had taken the day before. He knew there wouldn't be anybody at her house because the three boys and the girl went to school and Mrs. Connin had told him she went out to clean. He passed her yard and walked on the way they had gone to the river. The paper brick houses were far apart and after a while the dirt place to walk on ended and he had to walk on the edge of the highway. The sun was pale yellow and high and hot.

He passed a shack with an orange gas pump in front of it but he didn't see the old man looking out at nothing in particular from the doorway. Mr. Paradise was having an orange drink. He finished it slowly, squinting over the bottle at the small plaid-coated figure disappearing down the road. Then he set the empty bottle on a bench and, still squinting, wiped his sleeve over his mouth. He went in the shack and picked out a peppermint stick, a foot long and two inches thick, from the candy shelf, and stuck it in his hip pocket. Then he got in his car and drove slowly down the highway after the boy.

By the time Bevel came to the field speckled with purple weeds, he was dusty and sweating and he crossed it at a trot to get into the woods as fast as he could. Once inside, he wandered from tree to tree, trying to find the path they had taken yesterday. Finally he found a line worn in the pine needles and followed it until he saw the steep trail twisting down through the trees.

Mr. Paradise had left his automobile back some way on the road and had walked to the place where he was accustomed to sit almost every day, holding an unbaited fishline in the water while he stared at the river passing in front of him. Anyone looking at him from a distance would have seen an old boulder half hidden in the bushes.

Bevel didn't see him at all. He only saw the river, shimmering reddish yellow, and bounded into it with his shoes and his coat on and took a gulp. He swallowed some and spit the rest out and then he stood there in water up to his chest and looked around him. The sky was a clear pale blue, all in one piece—except for the hole the sun made—and fringed around the bottom with treetops. His coat floated to the surface and surrounded him like a strange gay lily pad and he stood grinning in the sun. He intended not to fool with preachers any more but to Baptize himself and to keep on going this time until he found the Kingdom of Christ in the river. He didn't mean to waste any more time. He put his head under the water at once and pushed forward.

In a second he began to gasp and sputter and his head reappeared on the surface; he started under again and the same thing happened. The river wouldn't have him. He tried again and came up, choking. This was the way it had been when the preacher held him under—he had had to fight with something that pushed him back in the face. He stopped and thought suddenly: it's another joke, it's just another joke! He thought how far he had come for nothing and he began to hit and splash and kick the filthy river. His feet were already treading on nothing. He gave one low cry of pain and indignation. Then he heard a sound and turned his head and saw something like a giant pig bounding after him, shaking a red and white club and shouting. He plunged under once and this time, the waiting current caught him like a long gentle hand and pulled him swiftly forward and down. For an instant he was overcome with surprise; then since he was moving quickly and knew that he was getting somewhere, all his fury and his fear left him.

Mr. Paradise's head appeared from time to time on the surface of the water. Finally, far downstream, the old man rose like some ancient water monster and stood empty-handed, staring with his dull eyes as far down the river line as he could see.

ہللہ

The Dalai Lama

COMPASSION

from *The Essential Dalai Lama: His Important Teachings*

~~~

Ithink that every human being has an innate sense of "I." We cannot explain why that feeling is there, but it is. Along with it comes a desire for happiness and a wish to overcome suffering. This is quite justified, we have a natural right to achieve as much happiness as possible, and we also have the right to overcome suffering.

The whole of human history has developed on the basis of this feeling. In fact it is not limited to human beings; from the Buddhist point of view, even the tiniest insect has this feeling and, according to its capacity, is trying to gain some happiness and avoid unhappy situations.

However, there are some major differences between human beings and other animal species. They stem from human intelligence. On account of our intelligence, we are much more advanced and have

The XIVth Dalai Lama, Tenzin Gyatso, was born Lhamo Thondup in 1935 to a poor family in the northeastern Tibetan village of Takster. At the age of two, he was recognized by the Tibetan government as the reincarnation of the XIIIth Dalai Lama. At the age of five, he was installed as Tibet's spiritual leader, and at the age of fifteen he assumed full political authority. In 1959, the Dalai Lama fled from Lhasa, the capital of Tibet, under pressure from the Chinese, and established the Tibetan government in exile in India. The Dalai Lama received the Nobel Peace Prize in 1989, and he has, for much of his life, been a spiritual guide to people from all over the world. This selection appears in *The Essential Dalai Lama: His Important Teachings* edited by Rajiv Mehrotra.

a greater capacity. We are able to think much further into the future, and our memory is powerful enough to take us back many years. Furthermore, we have oral and written traditions which remind us of events many centuries ago. Now, thanks to scientific methods, we can even examine events which occurred millions of years ago.

So our intelligence makes us very smart, but at the same time, precisely because of that fact, we also have more doubts and suspicions, and hence more fears. I think the imagination of fear is much more developed in humans than in other animals. In addition, the many conflicts within the human family and within one's own family, not to mention the conflicts within the community and between nations, as well as the internal conflicts within the individual—all conflicts and contradictions arise from the different ideas and views our intelligence brings. So unfortunately, intelligence can sometimes create a quite unhappy state of mind. In this sense, it becomes another source of human misery. Yet, at the same time, I think that ultimately intelligence is the tool with which we can overcome all these conflicts and differences.

From this point of view, of all the various species of animal on the planet, human beings are the biggest troublemakers. That is clear. I imagine that if there were no longer any humans on the planet, the planet itself would be safer! Certainly millions of fish, chicken and other small animals might enjoy some sort of genuine liberation!

It is therefore important that human intelligence be utilized in a constructive way. That is the key. If we utilize its capacity properly, then not only human beings would become less harmful to each other, and to the planet, but also individual human beings would be happier in themselves. It is in our hands. Whether we utilize our intelligence in the right way or the wrong way is up to us. Nobody can impose their values on us. How can we learn to use our capacity constructively? First, we need to recognize our nature and then, if we have the determination, there is a real possibility of transforming the human heart.

On this basis, I will speak today on how a human being can find happiness as an individual, because I believe the individual is the key to all the rest. For change to happen in any community, the initiative must come from the individual. If the individual can become a good, calm, peaceful person, this automatically brings a positive atmosphere to the family around him or her. When parents are warm-hearted, peaceful and calm people, generally speaking their children will also develop that attitude and behavior.

The way our attitude works is such that it is often troubled by outside factors, so one side of the issue is to eliminate the existence of trouble around you. The environment, meaning the surrounding situation, is a very important factor for establishing a happy frame of mind. However, even more important is the other side of the issue, which is one's own mental attitude.

The surrounding situation may not be so friendly, it may even be hostile, but if your inner mental attitude is right, then the situation will not disturb your inner peace. On the other hand, if your attitude is not right, then even if you are surrounded by good friends and the best facilities, you cannot be happy. This is why mental attitude is more important than external conditions. Despite this, it seems to me that many people are more concerned about their external conditions and neglect the inner attitude of mind. I suggest that we should pay more attention to our inner qualities.

There are a number of qualities which are important for mental peace, but from the little experience I have, I believe that one of the most important factors is human compassion and affection, a sense of caring.

Let me explain what we mean by compassion. Usually, our concept of compassion or love refers to the feeling of closeness we have with our friends and loved ones. Sometimes compassion also carries a sense of pity. This is wrong—any love or compassion which entails looking down on the other is not genuine compassion. To be genuine, compassion must be based on respect for the other, and on the realization that others have the right to be happy and overcome suffering just as much as you. On this basis, since you can see that others are suffering, you develop a genuine sense of concern for them.

As for the closeness we feel toward our friends, this is usually more like attachment than compassion. Genuine compassion should be unbiased. If we only feel close to our friends, and not to our enemies, or to the countless people who are unknown to us personally and toward whom we are indifferent, then our compassion is only partial or biased.

85

Compassion also brings us a certain inner strength. Once it is developed, it naturally opens an inner door, through which we can communicate with other fellow human beings, and even other sentient beings, with ease, and heart to heart. On the other hand, if you feel hatred and ill feeling toward others, they may feel similarly toward you, and as a result suspicion and fear will automatically create a distance between you and make communication difficult. You will then feel lonely and isolated.

Compassion naturally creates a positive atmosphere, and as a result you feel peaceful and content. Wherever there lives a compassionate person, there is always a pleasant atmosphere. Even dogs and birds approach the person easily. Almost fifty years ago, I used to keep some birds in the Norbulinga Summer Palace, in Lhasa. Among them was a small parrot. At that time I had an elderly attendant whose appearance was somewhat unfriendly—he had very round, stern eyes—but he was always feeding this parrot with nuts and so on. So whenever the attendant would appear, just the sound of his footsteps or his coughing would mean the parrot would show some excitement. The attendant had an extraordinarily friendly manner with that small bird, and the parrot also had an amazing response to him. On a few occasions I fed him some nuts but he never showed such friendliness to me, so I started to poke him with a stick, hoping he might react differently; the result was totally negative. I was using more force than the bird had, so it reacted accordingly.

Therefore, if you want a genuine friend, first you must create a positive atmosphere around you. We are social animals, after all, and friends are very important. How can you bring a smile to people's faces? If you remain stony and suspicious, it is very difficult. Perhaps if you have power or money, some people may offer you an artificial smile, but a genuine smile will only come from compassion.

The question is how to develop compassion. In fact, can we really develop this unbiased compassion at all? My answer is that we definitely can. I believe that human nature is gentle and compassionate, although many people, both in the past and now, think that human nature is basically aggressive. Let us examine this point.

At the time of conception, and while we are in our mother's womb, our mother's compassionate and peaceful mental state is a very positive factor for our development. If the mother's mind is very agitated, it is harmful for us. And that is just the beginning of life! Even the parents' state of mind at conception itself is important. If a child is conceived through rape, for example, then the child will be unwanted, which is a terrible thing. For conception to take place properly, it should come from genuine love and mutual respect, not just mad passion. It is not enough to have some casual love affair, the two partners should know each other well and respect each other as people, and this is the basis for a happy marriage. Furthermore, marriage itself should be for life, or at least should be long lasting. Life should properly start from such a situation.

Then, according to medical science, in the few weeks after birth, the child's brain is still growing. During that period, the experts claim that physical touch is a crucial factor for the proper development of the brain. This alone shows that the mere growth of our body requires another's affection.

After birth, one of the first acts on the mother's side is to give milk, and from the child's side it is to suckle. Milk is often considered a symbol of compassion. Without it, traditionally the child cannot survive. Through the process of suckling there comes a closeness between mother and child. If that closeness is not there, then the child will not seek its mother's breast, and if the mother is feeling dislike toward the child her milk may not come freely. So milk comes with affection. This means that the first act of our life, that of taking milk, is a symbol of affection. I am always reminded of this when I visit a church and see Mary carrying Jesus as a small baby; that to me is a symbol of love and affection.

It has been found that those children who grow up in homes where there is love and affection have a healthier physical development and study better at school. Conversely, those who lack human affection have more difficulty in developing physically and mentally. These children also find it difficult to show affection when they grow up, which is such a great tragedy.

Now let us look at the last moment of our lives—death. Even at the time of death, although the dying person can no longer benefit much from his friends, if he is surrounded by friends his mind may be more calm. Therefore throughout our lives, from the very beginning right up to our death, human affection plays a very important role.

An affectionate disposition not only makes the mind more peaceful and calm, but it affects our body in a positive way too. On the other hand, hatred, jealousy and fear upset our peace of mind, make us agitated and affect our body adversely. Even our body needs peace of mind and is not suited to agitation. This shows that an appreciation of peace of mind is in our blood.

Therefore, although some may disagree, I feel that although the aggressive side of our nature is part of life, the dominant force of life is human affection. This is why it is possible to strengthen that basic goodness which is our human nature.

We can also approach the importance of compassion through intelligent reasoning. If I help another person and show concern for him or her, then I myself will benefit from that. However, if I harm others, eventually I will be in trouble. I often joke, half sincerely and half seriously, saying that if we wish to be truly selfish then we should be wisely selfish rather than foolishly selfish. Our intelligence can help to adjust our attitude in this respect. If we use it well, we can gain insight as to how we can fulfill our own self-interest by leading a compassionate way of life. It would even be possible to argue that being compassionate is ultimately selfish.

In this context, I do not think that selfishness is wrong. Loving oneself is crucial. If we do not love ourselves, how can we love others? It seems that when some people talk of compassion, they have the notion that it entails a total disregard for one's own interests—a sacrificing of one's interests. This is not the case. In fact genuine love should first be directed at oneself.

There are two different senses of self. One has no hesitation in harming other people, and that is negative and leads to trouble. The other is based on determination, willpower and self-confidence, and that sense of I is very necessary. Without it, how can we develop the confidence we need to carry out any task in life? Similarly, there are two types of desire also. However, hatred is invariably negative and destructive of harmony.

How can we reduce hatred? Hatred is usually preceded by anger. Anger rises as a reactive emotion and gradually develops into a feeling of hatred. The skillful approach here is first to know that anger is negative. Often people think that as anger is part of us, it is better to express it, but I think this is misguided. You may have grievances or resentment due to your past and by expressing your anger you might be able to finish with them. That is very possible. Usually, however, it is better to check your anger, and then gradually, year by year, it diminishes. In my experience, this works best when you adopt the position that anger is negative and it is better not to feel it. That position itself will make a difference.

Whenever anger is about to come, you can train yourself to see the object of your anger in a different light. Any person or circumstance which causes anger is basically relative; seen from one angle it makes you angry, but seen from another perspective you may discover some good things in it. We lost our country, for example, and became refugees. If we look at our situation from that angle, we might feel frustration and sadness, yet the same event has created new opportunities—meeting with other people from different religious traditions, and so on. Developing a more flexible way of seeing things helps us cultivate a more balanced mental attitude. This is one method.

There are other situations where you might fall sick, for example, and the more you think about your sickness the worse your frustration becomes. In such a case, it is very helpful to compare your situation with the worst case scenario related to your illness, or with what would have happened if you had caught an even more serious illness, and so on. In this way, you can console yourself by realizing that it could have been much worse. Here again, you train yourself to see the relativity of your situation. If you compare it with something that is much worse, this will immediately reduce your frustration.

Similarly, if difficulties come they may appear enormous when you look at them closely, but if you approach the same problem from a wider perspective, it appears smaller. With these methods, and by developing a larger outlook, you can reduce your frustration whenever you face problems. You can see that constant effort is needed, but if you apply it in this way, then the angry side of you will diminish. Meanwhile, you strengthen your compassionate side and increase your good potential. By combining these two approaches, a negative person can be transformed into a kind one. This is the method we use to effect that transformation.

In addition, if you have religious faith, it can be useful in extending these qualities. For example, the Gospels teach us to turn the other cheek, which clearly shows the practice of tolerance. For me, the main message of the Gospels is love for our fellow human beings, and the reason we should develop this is because we love God. I understand this in the sense of having infinite love. Such religious teachings are very powerful to increase and extend our good qualities. The Buddhist approach presents a very clear method. First, we try to consider all sentient beings as equal. Then we consider that the lives of all beings are just as precious as our own, and through this we develop a sense of concern for others.

What of the case of someone who has no religious faith? Whether we follow a religion or not is a matter of individual right. It is possible to manage without religion, and in some cases it may make life simpler! But when you no longer have any interest in religion, you should not neglect the value of good human qualities. As long as we are human beings, and members of human society, we need human compassion. Without that, you cannot be happy. Since we all want to be happy and to have a happy family and friends, we have to develop compassion and affection. It is important to recognize that there are two levels of spirituality, one with religious faith, and one without. With the latter, we simply try to be a warm-hearted person.

We should also remember that once we cultivate a compassionate attitude, nonviolence comes automatically. Nonviolence is not a diplomatic word, it is compassion in action. If you have hatred in your heart, then very often your actions will be violent, whereas if you have compassion in your heart, your actions will be nonviolent.

As I said earlier, as long as human beings remain on this earth there will always be disagreements and conflicting views. We can take that as given. If we use violence in order to reduce disagreements and conflict, then we must expect violence every day and I think the result of this is terrible. Furthermore, it is actually impossible to eliminate disagreements through violence. Violence only brings even more resentment and dissatisfaction.

Nonviolence, on the other hand, means dialogue, it means using language to communicate. And dialogue means compromise, listening to others' views, and respecting others' rights, in a spirit of reconciliation. Nobody will be 100 percent a winner, and nobody will be 100 percent a loser. That is the practical way. In fact, that is the only way. Today, as the world becomes smaller and smaller, the concept of "us" and "them" is almost outdated. If our interests existed independently of those of others, then it would be possible to have a complete winner and a complete loser, but since in reality we all depend on one another, our interests and those of others are very interconnected. So how can you gain 100 percent victory? It is impossible. You have to share, half-half, or if at all possible 60 percent this side and 40 percent the other side! Without this approach, reconciliation is impossible.

The reality of the world today means that we need to learn to think in this way. This is the basis of my own approach—the "middle way" approach. Tibetans will not be able to gain 100 percent victory, for whether we like it or not, the future of Tibet very much depends on China. Therefore, in the spirit of reconciliation, I advocate a sharing of interests so that genuine progress is possible. Compromise is the only way. Through nonviolent means we can share views, feelings and rights, and in this way we can solve the problem.

I sometimes call the twentieth century a century of bloodshed, a century of war. Over this century there have been more conflicts, more bloodshed and more weapons than ever before. Now, on the basis of the experience we have all had this century, and of what we have learned from it, I think we should look to the next century to be one of dialogue. The principle of nonviolence should be practiced everywhere. This cannot be achieved simply by sitting here and praying. It means work and effort, and yet more effort.

Friedrich Nietzsche

THE JOY OF GIVING JOY

from *On the Genealogy of Morality*

~~~

Much more frequent than this sort of hypnotic general suppression of sensitivity, of susceptibility to pain—which presupposes even rarer forces, above all courage, contempt of opinion, "intellectual stoicism,"—is the attempt at a different kind of training against conditions of depression, one that is in any case easier: *mechanical activity*. That this relieves a suffering existence to a not inconsiderable degree is beyond all doubt: today this fact is called, somewhat dishonestly, "the blessing of work." The relief consists in this: that the interest of the sufferer is thoroughly diverted from the suffering—that it is continually doing and yet again only doing that enters into consciousness and, consequently, that little room remains in it for suffering: for it is *narrow*, this chamber of human consciousness! Mechanical activity and that which belongs to it—like absolute regularity, punctual unreflected obedience, one's way of life set once and

Friedrich Nietzsche, born in 1844 in the Prussian Province of Saxony, was one of the most influential philosophers of the nineteenth century. He studied theology and philology at the University of Bonn and then, at the age of twenty-four, became professor of classical philology at the University of Basel. Nietzsche's many provocative books include *Human, All Too Human, Beyond Good and Evil, Thus Spoke Zarathustra*, and *On the Genealogy of Morality*, from which the selection below is excerpted. Nietzsche died in 1900, soon after experiencing a psychological breakdown. This translation was done by Maudemarie Clark and Alan J. Swensen.

for all, the filling up of time, a certain permission for, indeed discipline in "impersonality," in self-forgetfulness, in "*incuria sui*"—how thoroughly, how subtly the ascetic priest knew how to use these in the battle with pain! Precisely when he had to deal with sufferers of the lower social ranks, with work slaves or prisoners (or with women: who are of course usually both at the same time, work slaves and prisoners), it required little more than a small art of name-changing and rebaptizing to make them henceforth see in hated things a boon, a relative bit of good fortune:—in any case the dissatisfaction of the slave with his lot was *not* invented by priests.—A still more valued means in the battle with depression is the prescription of a *small* joy that is easily accessible and can be made a regular practice; this medication is frequently made use of in connection with the one just discussed. The most frequent form in which joy is thus prescribed as a means to a cure is the joy of *giving* joy (as doing good, giving gifts, relieving, helping, encouraging, comforting, praising, honoring); by prescribing "love of one's neighbor" the ascetic priest is basically prescribing in arousal of the strongest, most life-affirming drive, even if in the most cautious of doses—the *will to power*. The happiness of the "smallest superiority," such as accompanies all doing good, being useful, helping, honoring, is the most plentiful means of consolation that the physiologically inhibited tend to make use of, assuming they are well advised: otherwise they cause each other pain, in obedience to the same basic instinct, naturally. When one looks for the beginnings of Christianity in the Roman world, one finds associations for mutual support, pauper-, invalid-, burial-associations, which sprung up on the undermost soil of the society of that time, and in which that principal medicine against depression, the small joy, that of mutual good deeds was consciously cultivated—perhaps this was something new back then, a true discovery? In a "will to mutuality," to herd-formation, to "community," to "cenacle" elicited in this manner, the will to power thus aroused in the process—even if it is on the smallest scale—must now in turn come to a new and much fuller outburst: *herd-formation* is an essential step and victory in the battle with depression. With the growth of the community a new interest also grows strong in the individual, one that often enough lifts him above and beyond that which is most personal in his ill-humor, his aversion to *himself* (the "*despectio sui*" of Geulincx). Out of a longing to shake off the dull listlessness and the felling of weakness, all the sick, the diseased strive instinctively for a herd organization: the ascetic priest intuits this instinct and fosters it; wherever there are herds it is the instinct of weakness that willed the herds and the shrewdness of priests that organized them. For do not overlook this: the strong strive just as naturally and necessarily *away* from each other as the weak strive *toward* each other, when the former band together it occurs only with a view to an aggressive joint action and joint satisfaction of their will to power, with a great deal of resistance from the individual conscience; the latter, on the other hand, arrange themselves into groups with pleasure precisely in the arrangement into groups—their instinct is satisfied in the process just as much as the instinct of the born "lords" (that is of the solitary beast-of-prey species of human) is at the bottom irritated and disquieted by organization. Beneath every oligarchy—all of history teaches this—*tyrannical* craving always lies hidden; every oligarchy trembles constantly from the tension that every individual in it needs in order to remain lord over this craving. (Thus it was for example with the *Greeks*: Plato attests it in a hundred passages, Plato who knew his own kind—*and* himself …)

Selfless Service

from the Bhagavad Gita

ARJUNA

1. If thy thought is that vision is greater than action, why dost thou enjoin upon me the terrible action of war?

2. My mind is in confusion because in thy words I find contradictions. Tell me in truth therefore by what path may I attain the Supreme.

KRISHNA

3. In this world there are two roads of perfection, as I told thee before, O prince without sin: Jñana Yoga, the path of wisdom of the Sankhyas, and Karma Yoga, the path of action of the Yogis.

4. Not by refraining from action does man attain freedom from action. Not by mere renunciation does he attain supreme perfection.

5. For not even for a moment can a man be without action. Helplessly are all driven to action by the forces born of Nature.

The Bhagavad Gita is considered to be one of the most sacred scriptures of Hinduism. It takes the form of an extended dialogue between Vishnu, in the avatar of Krishna, and Arjuna. The dialogue occurs against the backdrop of a great battle between the forces of good and evil. The Bhagavad Gita's seven hundred verses in eighteen chapters were originally written in Sanskrit. This selection—the third chapter—directly addresses karma yoga. This is Juan Mascaro's 1962 translation from the Sanskrit.

6. He who withdraws himself from actions, but ponders on their pleasures in his heart, he is under a delusion and is a false follower of the Path.

7. But great is the man who, free from attachments, and with a mind ruling its powers in harmony, works on the path of Karma Yoga, the path of consecrated action.

8. Action is greater than inaction: perform therefore thy task in life. Even the life of the body could not be if there were no action.

9. The world is in the bonds of action, unless the action is consecration. Let thy actions then be pure, free from the bonds of desire.

10. Thus spoke the Lord of Creation when he made both man and sacrifice: "By sacrifice thou shalt multiply and obtain all thy desires.

11. "By sacrifice shalt thou honour the gods and the gods will then love thee. And thus in harmony with them shalt thou attain the supreme good.

12. "For pleased with thy sacrifice, the gods will grant to thee the joy of all thy desires. Only a thief would enjoy their gifts and not offer them in sacrifice."

13. Holy men who take as food the remains of sacrifice become free from all their sins; but the unholy who have feasts for themselves eat food that is in truth sin.

14. Food is the life of all beings, and all food comes from rain above. Sacrifice brings the rain from heaven, and sacrifice is sacred action.

15. Sacred action is described in the Vedas and these come from the Eternal, and therefore is the Eternal everpresent in a sacrifice.

16. Thus was the Wheel of the Law set in motion, and that man lives indeed in vain who in a sinful life of pleasures helps not in its revolutions.

17. But the man who has found the joy of the Spirit and in the Spirit has satisfaction, who in the Spirit has found his peace, that man is beyond the law of action.

18. He is beyond what is done and beyond what is not done, and in all his works he is beyond the help of mortal beings.

19. In liberty from the bonds of attachment, do thou therefore the work to be done: for the man whose work is pure attains indeed the Supreme.

20. King Janaka and other warriors reached perfection by the path of action: let thy aim be the good of all, and then carry on thy task in life.

21. In the actions of the best men others find their rule of action. The path that a great man follows becomes a guide to the world.

22. I have no work to do in all the worlds, Arjuna—for these are mine. I have nothing to obtain, because I have all. And yet I work.

23. If I was not bound to action, never-tiring, everlastingly, men that follow many paths would follow my path of inaction.

24. If ever my work had an end, these worlds would end in destruction, confusion would reign within all: this would be the death of all beings.

25. Even as the unwise work selfishly in the bondage of selfish work, let the wise man work unselfishly for the good of all the world.

26. Let not the wise disturb the mind of the unwise in their selfish work. Let him, working with devotion, show them the joy of good work.

27. All actions take place in time by the interweaving of the forces of Nature; but the man lost in selfish delusion thinks that he himself is the actor.

28. But the man who knows the relation between the forces of Nature and actions, sees how some forces of Nature work upon other forces of Nature, and becomes not their slave.

29. Those who are under the delusion of the forces of Nature bind themselves to the work of these forces. Let not the wise man who sees the All disturb the unwise man who sees not the All.

30. Offer to me all thy works and rest thy mind on the Supreme. Be free from vain hopes and selfish thoughts, and with inner peace fight thou thy fight.

31. Those who ever follow my doctrine and who have faith, and have a good will, find through pure work their freedom.

32. But those who follow not my doctrine, and who have ill-will, are men blind to all wisdom, confused in mind: they are lost.

33. "Even a wise man acts under the impulse of his nature: all beings follow nature. Of what use is restraint?"

34. Hate and lust for things of nature have their roots in man's lower nature. Let him not fall under their power: they are the two enemies in his path.

35. And do thy duty, even if it be humble, rather than another's, even if it be great. To die in one's duty is life: to live in another's is death.

ARJUNA

36. What power is it, Krishna, that drives man to act sinfully, even unwillingly, as if powerlessly?

KRISHNA

37. It is greedy desire and wrath, born of passion, the great evil, the sum of destruction: this is the enemy of the soul.

38. All is clouded by desire: as fire by smoke, as a mirror by dust, as an unborn babe by its covering.

39. Wisdom is clouded by desire, the everpresent enemy of the wise, desire in its innumerable forms, which like a fire cannot find satisfaction.

40. Desire has found a place in man's senses and mind and reason. Through these it blinds the soul, after having over-clouded wisdom.

41. Set thou, therefore, thy senses in harmony, and then slay thou sinful desire, the destroyer of vision and wisdom.

42. They say that the power of the senses is great. But greater than the senses is the mind. Greater than the mind is Buddhi, reason; and greater than reason is He—the Spirit in man and in all.

43. Know Him therefore who is above reason; and let his peace give thee peace. Be a warrior and kill desire, the powerful enemy of the soul.

Surahs 93 and 107

from the Qur'an

~~~

Surah 93. Ad-Duha (The Morning Hours, Morning Bright!)

In the Name of Allah, Most Gracious, Most Merciful.

1. By the Glorious Morning Light,

2. And by the Night when it is still,

3. Thy Guardian-Lord hath not forsaken thee, nor is He displeased.

4. And verily the Hereafter will be better for thee than the present.

5. And soon will thy Guardian-Lord give thee (that wherewith) thou shalt be well-pleased.

6. Did He not find thee an orphan and give thee shelter (and care)?

7. And He found thee wandering, and He gave thee guidance.

8. And He found thee in need, and made thee independent.

The Qur'an, believed by Muslims to be a record of God's words through the angel Gabriel to Muhammad, is the central religious text of Islam. Approximately fourteen centuries ago, Muhammad memorized these words and dictated them to his companions. The 114 surahs, or chapters, were then written down by scribes. The Qur'an is the prime source of Muslims' faith and guidance, and it is complemented by the Sunna (the practice and example of the Prophet) and Hadith (reliably transmitted reports of what the Prophet did, said, or approved). This is Abdullah Yusuf Ali's translation from the Arabic.

9. Therefore, treat not the orphan with harshness,

10. Nor repulse the petitioner (unheard);

11. But the bounty of the Lord—rehearse and proclaim!

SURAH 107. AL-MA'UN (SMALL KINDNESSES, ALMSGIVING, HAVE YOU SEEN?)

In the Name of Allah, Most Gracious, Most Merciful.

1. Seest thou one who denies the Judgment (to come)?

2. Then such is the (man) who repulses the orphan (with harshness),

3. And encourages not the feeding of the indigent.

4. So woe to the worshippers

5. Who are neglectful of their prayers,

6. Those who (want but) to be seen (of men),

7. But refuse (to supply) (even) neighbourly needs.

بسم

Tim O'Brien

CHURCH

in *The Things They Carried*

~~~

One afternoon, somewhere west of the Batangan Peninsula, we
came across an abandoned pagoda. Or almost abandoned,
because a pair of monks lived there in a tar paper shack, tending a
small garden and some broken shrines. They spoke almost no English
at all. When we dug our foxholes in the yard, the monks did not seem
upset or displeased, though the younger one performed a washing
motion with his hands. No one could decide what it meant. The
older monk led us into the pagoda. The place was dark and cool, I
remember, with crumbling walls and sandbagged windows and a
ceiling full of holes. "It's bad news," Kiowa said. "You don't mess with
churches." But we spent the night there, turning the pagoda into a
little fortress, and then for the next seven or eight days we used the
place as a base of operations. It was mostly a very peaceful time. Each
morning the two monks brought us buckets of water. They giggled

---

Tim O'Brien was born in 1946 in Austin, Minnesota, and grew up in
Worthington. After graduating from college, O'Brien was drafted and sent
to serve in Vietnam with the division involved in the My Lai massacre of
1968. After his return from Vietnam with a Purple Heart, O'Brien entered
graduate school, became a newspaper reporter, and turned to fiction writing. O'Brien's writing has received many awards, including the National
Book Award. The selection below comes from his 1990 work, *The Things
They Carried*.

when we stripped down to bathe; they smiled happily while we soaped up and splashed one another. On the second day the older monk carried in a cane chair for the use of Lieutenant Jimmy Cross, placing it near the altar area, bowing and gesturing for him to sit down. The old monk seemed proud of the chair, and proud that such a man as Lieutenant Cross should be sitting in it. On another occasion the younger monk presented us with four ripe watermelons from his garden. He stood watching until the watermelons were eaten down to the rinds, then he smiled and made the strange washing motion with his hands.

Though they were kind to all of us, the monks took a special liking for Henry Dobbins.

"Soldier Jesus," they'd say, "good soldier Jesus."

Squatting quietly in the cool pagoda, they would help Dobbins disassemble and clean his machine gun, carefully brushing the parts with oil. The three of them seemed to have an understanding. Nothing in words, just a quietness they shared.

"You know," Dobbins said to Kiowa one morning, "after the war maybe I'll join up with these guys."

"Join how?" Kiowa said.

"Wear robes. Take the pledge."

Kiowa thought about it. "That's a new one. I didn't know you were all that religious."

"Well, I'm not," Dobbins said. Beside him, the two monks were working on the M-60. He watched them take turns running oiled swabs through the barrel. "I mean, I'm not the churchy type. When I was a little kid, way back, I used to sit there on Sunday counting bricks in the wall. Church wasn't for me. But then in high school, I started to think how I'd like to be a minister. Free house, free car. Lots of potlucks. It looked like a pretty good life."

"You're serious?" Kiowa said.

Dobbins shrugged his shoulders. "What's serious? I was a kid. The thing is, I believed in God and all that, but it wasn't the religious part that interested me. Just being nice to people, that's all. Being decent."

"Right," Kiowa said.

"Visit sick people, stuff like that. I would've been good at it, too. Not the brainy part—not sermons and all that—but I'd be okay with the people part."

Henry Dobbins was silent for a time. He smiled at the older monk, who was now cleaning the machine gun's trigger assembly.

"But anyway," Dobbins said, "I couldn't ever be a real minister, because you have to be super sharp. Upstairs, I mean. It takes brains. You have to explain some hard stuff, like why people die, or why God invented pneumonia and all that." He shook his head. "I just didn't have the smarts for it. And there's the religious thing, too. All these years, man, I still hate church."

"Maybe you'd change," Kiowa said.

Henry Dobbins closed his eyes briefly, then laughed.

"One thing for sure, I'd look spiffy in those robes they wear— just like Friar Tuck. Maybe I'll do it. Find a monastery somewhere. Wear a robe and be nice to people."

"Sounds good," Kiowa said.

The two monks were quiet as they cleaned and oiled the machine gun. Though they spoke almost no English, they seemed to have great respect for the conversation, as if sensing that important matters were being discussed. The younger monk used a yellow cloth to wipe dirt from a belt of ammunition.

"What about you?" Dobbins said.

"How?"

"Well, you carry that Bible everywhere, you never hardly swear or anything, so you must—"

"I grew up that way," Kiowa said.

"Did you ever—you know—did you think about being a minister?"

"No. Not ever."

Dobbins laughed. "An Indian preacher. Man, that's one I'd love to see. Feathers and buffalo robes."

Kiowa lay on his back, looking up at the ceiling, and for a time he didn't speak. Then he sat up and took a drink from his canteen.

"Not a minister," he said, "but I do like churches. The way it feels inside. It feels good when you just sit there, like you're in a forest and everything's really quiet, except there's still this sound you can't hear."

"Yeah."

"You ever feel that?"

"Sort of."

Kiowa made a noise in his throat. "This is all wrong," he said.

"What?"

"Setting up here. It's wrong. I don't care what, it's still a church."

Dobbins nodded. "True."

"A church," Kiowa said. "Just wrong."

When the two monks finished cleaning the machine gun, Henry Dobbins began reassembling it, wiping off the excess oil, then he handed each of them a can of peaches and a chocolate bar. "Okay," he said, "didi mau, boys. Beat it." The monks bowed and moved out of the pagoda into the sunlight.

Henry Dobbins made the washing motion with his hands.

"You're right," he said. "All you can do is be nice. Treat them decent, you know?"

ﷺ

Rabindranath Tagore

SECTION 50
from *Gitanjali: Song Offerings*

I had gone a-begging from door to door in the village path, when thy golden chariot appeared in the distance like a gorgeous dream and I wondered who was this King of all kings!

My hopes rose high and methought my evil days were at an end, and I stood waiting for alms to be given unasked and for wealth scattered on all sides in the dust.

The chariot stopped where I stood. Thy glance fell on me and thou camest down with a smile. I felt that the luck of my life had come at last. Then of a sudden thou didst hold out thy right hand and say, "What hast thou to give to me?"

Ah, what a kingly jest was it to open thy palm to a beggar to beg! I was confused and stood undecided, and then from my wallet I slowly took out the least little grain of corn and gave it to thee.

But how great when at the day's end I emptied my bag on the floor to find at least a little grain of gold among the poor heap. I bitterly wept and wished that I had had the heart to give thee my all.

Rabindranath Tagore was born in 1861 in Calcutta (now Kolkatta), India, and became a widely successful author whose work ranged across genres and continents. In 1913, Tagore was awarded the Nobel Prize in Literature. In addition to his literary work, Tagore started an experimental school adhering to Upanishadic ideals, participated in the Indian nationalist movement, and managed his family's estates. The selection below comes from Tagore's own English translation of *Gitanjali: Song Offerings,* which first appeared in Bengali in 1912. Tagore died in 1941.

Harold M. Schulweis

BETWEEN

God is not in me
nor in you
but between us.

God is not me or mine
nor you or yours
but ours.

God is known
not alone
but in relationship.

Not as a separate, lonely power
but through our kinship, our
friendship,
through our healing and binding
and raising up of each other.

Rabbi Harold M. Schulweis, the spiritual leader of Valley Beth Shalom in Encino, California, is one of the most influential rabbis in the United States and a leading figure in Reconstructionist Judiasm. Schulweis was born in the Bronx, New York, in 1925, and was educated widely, including at the Jewish Theological Seminary. Schulweis founded the Jewish World Watch project in 2004 to combat genocide and human rights violations world-wide, with a special focus on Darfur. His many books include *For Those Who Can't Believe, Evil and the Morality of God*, and *Conscience: The Duty to Obey and the Duty to Disobey* (Jewish Lights).

To know God is to know others,
to love God is to love others,
to hear God is to hear others.

More than meditation,
more than insight,
more than feeling,
between us are
claims, obligations, commandments;
to act, to do, to behave our beliefs.

I seek God
not as if God were alone,
an isolated person, He or She,
a process, a power, a being, a thing.
I seek God
not as if I were alone,
a thinker, a mediator, a discrete entity.

I seek God in connection,
in the nexus of community.
I pray and celebrate the betweenness
which binds and holds us together.

And even when I am left alone,
I am sustained by my
memory of our betweenness
and the promise of our betweenness.

God is not in me, or in you, or in God's self,
but in betweenness
and it is there we find the evidence of
God's reality and our own.

THE BASE OF ALL METAPHYSICS

in *Leaves of Grass*

~~~

And now gentlemen,
A word I give to remain in your memories and minds,
As base and finale too for all metaphysics.

(So to the students the old professor,
At the close of his crowded course.)

Having studied the new and antique, the Greek and
    Germanic systems,
Kant having studied and stated, Fichte and Schelling and
    Hegel,
Stated the lore of Plato, and Socrates greater than Plato,

Born in 1819 in Long Island, New York, Walt Whitman was a poet, essayist, and journalist best known for *Leaves of Grass* (first published in 1855) and the poems "Song of Myself" and "I Sing the Body Electric." In the early years of the Civil War, Whitman traveled to Washington, D.C., to search for his brother, who was reported missing in action. Whitman stayed in Washington and volunteered as an aide in the hospitals, tending to sick and wounded soldiers. One of the first American poets to gain international attention, Whitman died in 1862 in Camden, New Jersey. This poem is from the 1881–82 edition of *Leaves of Grass*.

And greater than Socrates sought and stated, Christ
    divine having studied long,
I see reminiscent to-day those Greek and Germanic systems,
See the philosophies all, Christian churches and tenets see,
Yet underneath Socrates clearly see, and underneath
    Christ the divine I see,
The dear love of man for his comrade, the attraction of
    friend to friend,
Of the well-married husband and wife, of children and
    parents,
Of city for city and land for land.

PART II

Whom Do I Serve?

Reach your long hand out to another door, beyond where you go on the street.

Rumi

The Sufi poet Rumi, in a poem included in this section, exhorts us to reach our long hand out—an exhortation that may be provoked by Rumi's sense that we are better with the short hand. Even when we reach out, Rumi implies, we are more comfortable in the streets we know, giving to and among people we can reach without reaching too far.

Why should we reach out with one hand rather than another, the long hand as opposed to the short? Why, to put it differently, serve the stranger rather than the friend? Or, for that matter, why serve the friend rather than the stranger?

Polish poet Anna Swir, in another poem included in this section, recognizes upon coming across a beggar in the street that "she was the same inside as I." Swir's narrator had not been previously acquainted with the beggar woman, but she knows her instantly and deeply. When she reaches out to the beggar woman, she does not feel that she is using her long hand; she hardly feels that she is reaching out at all. Instead, she sees herself in the beggar. The other's hand is not other; it is Swir's own hand.

Swir's poem is short, though, and it may be that this sense of sameness and connection is short, too. And it may be precisely because the beggar woman is in some significant ways different from,

111

or other than, Swir's narrator that the interaction begins. She is, to take the most obvious difference, begging, whereas Swir's narrator seems to have something to give. She is standing on the street; Swir's narrator is moving past. The beggar most likely comes from one place, Swir's narrator from another. And so on.

Despite however many actual differences there may be between the two people, there is no question that a relationship is quickly established. What makes this moment exceptional in Swir's view is not what each individual is like inside but that there is a *relationship* between what each is like: on the inside, the two women are the same, and suddenly there is relationship where there might not have been.

For Swir, then, it seems we ought to serve those who are like us—not necessarily like us in a demographic or historical sense, but like us in spirit or soul, like us on the inside. Ruth, in the Book of Ruth, appears to embody a similar conception of spiritual rather than historical kinship, and Thich Nhat Hanh, a Zen Buddhist monk, in the selected chapters from *Peace Is Every Step*, also shows us how we might make the other close, or not other.

There are other works in this part, though, that push us to consider principles other than sameness, proximity, or relationship. Yiddish writer I. L. Peretz's story "If Not Higher;" cofounder of the Catholic Worker movement Dorothy Day's autobiographical chapter, "The Faces of Poverty;" American poet Linda Gregg's work "The Shopping-Bag Lady"; and American writer Valerie Martin's biographical portrait of St. Francis of Assisi are connected by their exploration of a commitment to serve the toughest cases, the most needy, simply because of where they are and the difficulties they face. Here the emphasis is on their need, not on how they are related to us or what precisely is happening inside of us. In all of these instances, however, there is something about their distance or difference from us that should or does provoke discomfort in us.

Such discomfort—or a deeper kind of unease—in some traditions seems to indicate holiness or to present an opportunity for demonstrations of piety. In poet and Sufi master Hafiz's "The Difference Between," for example, it is the intensely and offensively vulgar character who proves to be worthy of service—and who seems, in her way, to provide service as well. In "The Legend of the Lowly Devotee," from *The Tiruvaçagam*, a visitor demands to be served in unspeakably cruel ways and thereby elicits and provides the highest form of service.

No matter which tradition we consider, the question of how to treat visitors or strangers, those who are different from us, is an essential part of our understanding of the impulse to serve. This is a particularly germane question when the apparently needy stranger or outsider tests and potentially enlivens one's own tradition. In Cherokee writer John Oskison's story "The Problem of Old Harjo," Indian writer Chitra Banerjee Divakaruni's poem "The Walk," and American novelist Leslie Marmon Silko's story "The Man to Send Rain Clouds," we are pushed to think about how close to hold the outsider, especially at the most difficult times. Cesar Chavez, founder of the National Farm Workers Association, in his speech "The Mexican-American and the Church," explicitly makes the case that those who are like him should, when deciding whom and how to serve, observe and implement practices that have had more purchase in traditions other than his own.

Here, too, there are a few readings that make what appear to be very straightforward claims about whom we serve. Lao-Tzu, purported author of the *Tao Te Ching,* in "A good traveler has no fixed plans," suggests that a good man ought, quite simply, to be a bad man's teacher. In Bidpai's fable, the implication is that, no matter what we say about whom we serve, our actions reveal that we finally serve ourselves. And in Lebanese writer Mikhail Naimy's short story "His Grace," the restaurant owner serves one who demands to be served— one who asks.

Every reading in this section, as well as the readings taken together, provoke us to consider the relationship between the ideals we serve and the people we serve, between the beliefs that call us and the other beings we feel called to serve. And they provoke us to consider the relationship between those we believe we should serve and those we actually do serve.

By way of conclusion to this introduction, a word about a great open secret in the world of giving today. The secret is this: whatever we say about worthy causes and wonderful organizations, we give mainly when we are asked to give by people we know. Now, even if this is true on a broad scale, we might benefit from considering why this might be so as well as whether it is a good thing. We might think afresh about reaching out with the long hand or the short hand, if not to alter our practices, then at least to learn about other practices and to come to understand more deeply the reasons for our own.

A GOOD TRAVELER HAS NO FIXED PLANS

in the *Tao Te Ching*

⁓

A good traveler has no fixed plans
and is not intent upon arriving.
A good artist lets his intuition
lead him wherever it wants.
A good scientist has freed himself of concepts
and keeps his mind open to what is.

Thus the Master is available to all people
and doesn't reject anyone.
He is ready to use all situations

A Chinese philosopher believed to have lived during the sixth century BCE, Lao-Tzu ("old man" or "old sage") is reputedly the author of the *Tao Te Ching,* the main text of Taoist thought, and the father of Chinese Taoism. Historians have debated whether Lao-Tzu was an individual, a synthesis of multiple historical figures, a mythical figure, or even whether he existed at all. The main source of information, Ssu-ma Ch'ien's biography in his *Records of the Historian,* contains an account of not one, but three men named Lao-Tzu. The authorship of the *Tao Te Ching* has also been debated throughout history. Lao-Tzu is often associated with Confucius, another early Chinese philosopher. This translation was done by Stephen Mitchell.

and doesn't waste anything.
This is called embodying the light.

What is a good man but a bad man's teacher?
What is a bad man but a good man's job?
If you don't understand this, you will get lost,
however intelligent you are.
It is the great secret.

Dorothy Day

THE FACES OF POVERTY

in *Loaves and Fishes*

~~~~~

Poverty is a strange and elusive thing. I have tried to write about it, its joys and its sorrows, for thirty years now; and I could probably write about it for another thirty without conveying what I feel about it as well as I would like. I condemn poverty and I advocate it; poverty is simple and complex at once; it is a social phenomenon and a personal matter. Poverty is an elusive thing, and a paradoxical one.

We need always to be thinking and writing about it, for if we are not among its victims its reality fades from us. We must talk about poverty because people insulated by their own comfort lose sight of it. So many good souls who visit us tell us how they were brought up in poverty, but how, through hard work and cooperation, their parents managed to educate all the children—even raise up priests and nuns for the Church. They contend that healthful habits and a

---

Dorothy Day was born in Brooklyn, New York, in 1897, and raised in Chicago in a nominally Protestant home. Day became a writer, a radical social thinker, a pacifist and—in time—a convert to Catholicism. In the early 1930s, with Peter Maurin, she cofounded and for many years led the Catholic Worker movement in America, a movement joining Catholic tradition to social action. She published *The Catholic Worker* newspaper to promote Catholic social teaching and created "houses of hospitality" to shelter and feed the poor without financial or religious expectations in return. Day died in 1980. The following chapter on "The Faces of Poverty" appeared in *Loaves and Fishes,* Day's story of the Catholic Worker movement, first published in 1963.

stable family situation enable people to escape from the poverty class, no matter how mean the slum they may once have been forced to live in. The argument runs, so why can't everybody do it? No, these people don't know about the poor. Their concept of poverty is of something as neat and well ordered as a nun's cell.

Poverty has many faces. People can, for example, be poor in space alone. Last month I talked to a man who lives in a four-room apartment with a wife, four children, and relatives besides. He has a regular job and can feed his family, but he is poor in light and air and space. We know what this can be. Once, at the Peter Maurin Farm, every corner of the women's dormitory was occupied. When an extra visitor came she lived in the middle of the room.

Then there are those who live under outwardly decent economic circumstances but are forever on the fearful brink of financial disaster. During a visit to Georgia and South Carolina I saw the trailer camps around Augusta, near the hydrogen bomb plant. Families of construction workers who live on the move make up a considerable part of our great migrant population. They may have comfortable trailers, but they are poor in the other physical things necessary for a good life. No matter how high wages go, a sudden illness and an accumulation of doctor and hospital bills, for example, may mean a sudden plunge into destitution. Everybody so shudders at the idea of insecurity that fear of it causes people to succumb to its pressure, mentally as well as physically, until our hospitals all over the country are crowded. Here, indeed, is another face of poverty.

The merchant, counting his profits in pennies, the millionaire with his efficiency experts, have both learned how to amass wealth. By following their example, and given health of mind and body, there is no necessity for anyone, so they say, to be poor nowadays. But the fact remains that every house of hospitality is full, and we wish we had room for more. Families write us pitifully for help.

More obvious and familiar is the poverty of the slums. We live in such a slum. It is becoming ever more crowded with Puerto Ricans, who have the lowest wages in the city and do the hardest and most menial work. They have been undernourished through generations of exploitation and privation. We used to have a hard time getting rid of the small-size clothes which come in to *The Catholic Worker.* Those who eat steak and salads and keep their figures slim contribute clothes to us; and Anne Marie, who takes care of the clothes room for us, used to say, "Why is it always the poor who are fat? We never get enough clothes of a size to fit them." Some of the poor who come to us may be fat from the starches they eat, but the Puerto Rican poor are lean. The stock in the clothes room at St. Joseph's House moves more quickly now.

Not only are the Puerto Ricans underfed and underclothed; they are underhoused as well. Their families double up in vermin-ridden, dark, crowded tenements. And this problem is not confined to the Puerto Ricans, by any means. In this era of widely proclaimed prosperity, shelter, a basic need, is the hardest thing to come by in our city. When *The Catholic Worker* started back in 1933, it was possible to rent all the apartments you wanted. Anybody could have a home in the "old-law tenements," which, after all, had water and toilets, and could be heated quite well with gas or potbellied stoves. (Such heat was often more satisfactory than steam heat, which cooled off too early in the night or stayed on during warm spring or fall days.)

But housing reform has meant that thousands of the older buildings have been closed down rather than repaired and made suitable for occupancy, while the new housing has not sufficed to take care of the dispossessed people. Our municipal lodging houses are full of families, as well as single men who are unemployable or migrant; surviving old-law tenements are overcrowded as never before by the tremendous influx from those that have been torn down.

Years ago there was no problem in renting an apartment even if there were five children in the family. Now it is quite another story. Most young families we know in New York today have had to "buy" a place, seeking a down payment from bank loans, from the G.I. Bill of Rights, from relatives or friends, or in some cases, with grim self-denial cutting out all nonessentials until the money for the down payment has been saved. The fact is we are no longer a nation of homeowners and apartment renters. We are a nation of people owning debts and mortgages, and so enslaved by these and by installment buying that families do indeed live in poverty, only poverty with a new face.

In front of me as I write is Fritz Eichenberg's picture of St. Vincent De Paul (Fritz, a Quaker, does the woodcuts in *The Catholic Worker*). He holds a chubby child in his arms, and a thin, pale child is clinging to him. Yes, the poor will always be with us—Our Lord told us that—and there will always be a need for our sharing, for stripping ourselves to help others. It is—and always will be—a lifetime job. But I am sure that God did not intend that there be so many poor. The class struggle is of *our* making and by *our* consent, not His, and we must do what we can to change it. This is why we at the *Worker* urge such measures as credit unions and cooperatives, leagues for mutual aid, voluntary land reforms and farming communes.

So many sins against the poor cry out to high heaven! One of the most deadly sins is to deprive the laborer of his hire. There is another: to instill in him paltry desires so compulsive that he is willing to sell his liberty and his honor to satisfy them. We are all guilty of concupiscence, but newspapers, radio, television, and battalions of advertising men (woe to that generation) deliberately stimulate our desires, the satisfaction of which so often means the deterioration of the family. Whatever we can do to combat these widespread social evils by combating their causes we must do. But above all the responsibility is a personal one. The message we have been given comes from the Cross.

In our country, we have revolted against the poverty and hunger of the world. Our response has been characteristically American: we have tried to clean up everything, build bigger and better shelters and hospitals. Here, hopefully, misery was to be cared for in an efficient and orderly way. Yes, we have tried to do much, with Holy Mother the State taking over more and more responsibility for the poor. But charity is only as warm as those who administer it. When bedspreads may not be ruffled by the crooked limbs of age and bedside tables will not hold the clutter of those who try to make a home around them with little possessions, we know that we are falling short in our care for others.

THE DIFFERENCE BETWEEN

A saintly man and a Perfect One both resided on the
Outskirts of a beautiful city,
Though several miles apart.

One day it came to the attention
Of these two households that a visiting prince
Desired to pay his respects to the most revered spiritual
Leader in that province,
Wanting to gift a small fortune to that man
To help further God's work.

As there had for years been some question
Amongst the population who in fact was
The most spiritual of these two figures,
The prince devised something of a contest,
As he only had time to visit
One of these personages.

Hafiz was born Shams-ud-din Muhammad sometime around 1320, in
Shiraz, Persia. Hafiz lived in Shiraz most of his life and became a Sufi master. Scholars estimate that Hafiz wrote approximately five thousand poems,
several hundred of which have survived. Hafiz became famous in the West
thanks to the efforts of Goethe and Emerson, as well as Hazrat Inayat Khan.
This selection was translated by Daniel Ladinsky.

The prince sent word:
"In three days I would like to meet with,
In my quarters, the chief representative of each
Of these two renowned religious men
And after questioning them extensively
I and my ministers will then determine
Who in fact of their teachers is the
Closer to God, and thus
To whom we will gift God's own bounty."

The saint upon receiving this news met with
All his close ones. This council discussed the situation
For hours, exploring every nuance,
And considering how much this gold could mean to them.
Then, with a clear majority vote—
Ramjoo was chosen.

Ramjoo was a strikingly young handsome man,
A great hunter, a legendary warrior, a renowned artist.
His intellect was superb, his manners impeccable,
He spoke twenty different languages
And was descended from royal blood himself—
A great-aunt was a queen.
Someone in the saint's camp also knew this prince
Enjoyed the intimate company of men as well as women.
Ramjoo, they all nodded, was the right choice.

The Perfect One upon receiving this "news"
From the prince immediately called for Yasamin;
No consultation with anyone was needed.

Yasamin was a servant woman in the master's
Household.
She was nearly eighty, a famous hag,

And had worked for him all her life—
No one else in the city would hire Yasamin
As she was completely mad
(Perhaps just God-mad), nevertheless her qualifications
For this essential, delicate diplomacy were exact:

She had not combed her hair or bathed for months;
She mostly muttered unintelligible sounds
In her own secret language
That only the master knew.
She often made obscene gestures
While exposing her private regions.

She compulsively picked her nose
And threw boogers with astounding accuracy.
No one had ever known her to go five minutes
Without loudly farting at least four times.
She was psychic, too,
And would probably start beating the prince if
She "saw" he had ever gone too far romantically—
With his camels.
Yasamin, the Perfect One knew,

Was the right choice to be his envoy
Especially when she agreed with a deep enlightened laugh
To add to her already majestic-sublimely free-being
The crown of three live chickens
She would proudly drape over her head
Come the appointed
Royal minute.

The day of the prince came. The two envoys entered
The prince's quarters but were kept separate
And did not even see one another.

Ramjoo went in first
And from behind a door Yasamin could hear singing,
And light lively talk that went on for two hours.

She knew what was happening.
The prince was falling in love with his new guest.

Then Yasamin was brought in
And the prince could not believe his eyes.
He felt tremendously insulted and even became
A bit terrified when, in fact, Yasamin being
Able to "see" into the prince's past,
Started shouting things even he could understand
About that one regrettable night in the desert—

With that young, gorgeous camel,
She even hit the prince with two gigantic boogers
From twenty feet away;
Bouncing off his forehead
They both fell right into his tea.

Yasamin was ordered
Beaten and thrown out.

She returned to the master ecstatic
And has never been happier since.

That night the prince could not sleep, but
Finally dozed off for a few minutes just before dawn.
During that short sleep he had this dream:

The Prophet Muhammad
Was seated on a magnificent white horse
And behind the Prophet sat a man smiling wonderfully
At the prince for a moment, before saying,

"Why did you beat my dear Yasamin,
When she spoke only the truth to you?"

The prince bolted awake
And sat up in bed trembling with sweat.

He called for his horse to be saddled
And with ten of his soldiers rode right then
To the saintly man's house pleading to see him.

Upon seeing this man and realizing
He was not the person in the dream,
He then dismissed his soldiers and taking off his shoes,
Weeping now,
Began to walk to the Perfect One's household.

Dear ones,
Use your own storytelling abilities
To end this tale

In a way that will most
Uplift your heart.

علم

Leslie Marmon Silko

THE MAN TO SEND RAIN CLOUDS

ONE

They found him under a big cottonwood tree. His Levi jacket and pants were faded light-blue so that he had been easy to find. The big cottonwood tree stood apart from a small grove of winterbare cottonwoods which grew in the wide, sandy arroyo. He had been dead for a day or more, and the sheep had wandered and scattered up and down the arroyo. Leon and his brother-in-law, Ken, gathered the sheep and left them in the pen at the sheep camp before they returned to the cottonwood tree. Leon waited under the tree while Ken drove the truck through the deep sand to the edge of the arroyo. He squinted up at the sun and unzipped his jacket. It sure was hot for this time of year. But high and northwest the blue mountains were still deep in snow. Ken came sliding down the low, crumbling bank about fifty yards down, and he was bringing the red blanket.

Before they wrapped the old man, Leon took a piece of string out of his pocket and tied a small gray feather in the old man's long white hair. Ken gave him the paint. Across the brown wrinkled forehead he

Leslie Marmon Silko was born in Albuquerque, New Mexico, in 1948 to a family of Laguna Pueblo, Mexican, Plains Indian, and Anglo-American ancestry. Silko attended schools administered by the Bureau of Indian Affairs and then the University of New Mexico. She briefly attended law school and then devoted herself to writing literature, including the novels *Ceremony* and *Almanac of the Dead*. Silko wrote and published the short story "The Man to Send Rain Clouds"—for which she received a National Endowment for the Humanities Discovery Grant—while she was still in college.

drew a streak of white and along the high cheekbones he drew a strip of blue paint. He paused and watched Ken throw pinches of corn meal and pollen into the wind that fluttered the small gray feather. Then Leon painted with yellow under the old man's broad nose, and finally, when he had painted green across the chin, he smiled.

"Send us rain clouds, Grandfather." They laid the bundle in the back of the pickup and covered it with with a heavy tarp before they started back to the pueblo.

They turned off the highway onto the sandy pueblo road. Not long after they passed the store and post office they saw Father Paul's car coming toward them. When he recognized their faces he slowed his car and waved for them to stop. The young priest rolled down the car window.

"Did you find old Teofilo?" he asked loudly.

Leon stopped the truck. "Good morning, Father. We were just out to the sheep camp. Everything is O.K. now."

"Thank God for that. Teofilo is a very old man. You really shouldn't allow him to stay at the sheep camp alone."

"No, he won't do that any more now."

"Well, I'm glad you understand. I hope I'll be seeing you at Mass this week. We missed you last Sunday. See if you can get old Teofilo to come with you." The priest smiled and waved at them as they drove away.

Two

Louise and Teresa were waiting. The table was set for lunch, and the coffee was boiling on the black iron stove. Leon looked at Louise and then at Teresa.

"We found him under a cottonwood tree in the big arroyo near sheep camp. I guess he sat down to rest in the shade and never got up again." Leon walked toward the old man's bed.

The red plaid shawl had been shaken and spread carefully over the bed, and a new brown flannel shirt and pair of stiff new Levis were arranged neatly beside the pillow. Louise held the screen door open while Leon and Ken carried in the red blanket. He looked small and shriveled, and after they dressed him in the new shirt and pants he seemed more shrunken.

It was noontime now because the church bells rang the Angelus. They ate the beans with hot bread, and nobody said anything until after Teresa poured the coffee. Ken stood up and put on his jacket.

"I'll see about the gravediggers. Only the top layer of soil is frozen. I think it can be ready before dark."

Leon nodded his head and finished his coffee. After Ken had been gone for a while, the neighbors and clans people came quietly to embrace Teofilo's family and to leave food on the table because the gravediggers would come to eat when they were finished.

THREE

The sky in the west was full of pale-yellow light. Louise stood outside with her hands in the pockets of Leon's green army jacket that was too big for her. The funeral was over, and the old men had taken their candles and medicine bags and were gone. She waited until the body was laid into the pickup before she said anything to Leon. She touched his arm, and he noticed that her hands were still dusty from the corn meal that she had sprinkled around the old man. When she spoke, Leon could not hear her. "What did you say? I didn't hear you."

"I said that I had been thinking about something."

"About what?"

"About the priest sprinkling holy water for Grandpa. So he won't be thirsty." Leon stared at the new moccasins that Teofilo had made for the ceremonial dances in the summer. They were nearly hidden by the red blanket. It was getting colder, and the wind pushed gray dust down the narrow pueblo road. The sun was approaching the long mesa where it disappeared during the winter. Louise stood there shivering and watching his face. Then he zipped up his jacket and opened the truck door. "I'll see if he's there."

FOUR

Ken stopped the pickup at the church, and Leon got out; and then Ken drove down the hill to the graveyard where people were waiting. Leon knocked at the old carved door with its symbols of the Lamb. While he waited he looked up at the twin bells from the king of Spain with the last sunlight pouring around them in their tower.

The priest opened the door and smiled when he saw who it was. "Come in! What brings you here this evening?"

The priest walked toward the kitchen, and Leon stood with his cap in his hand, playing with the earflaps and examining the living room, the brown sofa, the green armchair, and the brass lamp that hung down from the ceiling by links of chain. The priest dragged a chair out of the kitchen and offered it to Leon.

"No thank you, Father. I only came to ask you if you would bring your holy water to the graveyard."

The priest turned away from Leon and looked out the window at the patio full of shadows and the dining-room windows of the nuns' cloister across the patio. The curtains were heavy, and the light from within faintly penetrated; it was impossible to see the nuns inside eating supper.

"Why didn't you tell me he was dead? I could have brought the Last Rites anyway."

Leon smiled. "It wasn't necessary, Father."

The priest stared down at his scuffed brown loafers and the worn hem of his cassock. "For a Christian burial it was necessary."

His voice was distant, and Leon thought that his blue eyes looked tired.

"It's O.K. Father, we just want him to have plenty of water."

The priest sank down into the green chair and picked up a glossy missionary magazine. He turned the colored pages full of lepers and pagans without looking at them.

"You know I can't do that, Leon. There should have been the Last Rites and a funeral Mass at the very least."

Leon put on his green cap and pulled the flaps down over his ears. "It's getting late, Father. I've got to go."

When Leon opened the door Father Paul stood up and said, "Wait." He left the room and came back wearing a long brown overcoat. He followed Leon out the door and across the dim churchyard to the adobe steps in front of the church. They both stooped to fit through the low adobe entrance. And when they started down the hill to the graveyard only half of the sun was visible above the mesa.

The priest approached the grave slowly, wondering how they had managed to dig into the frozen ground; and then he remembered that this was New Mexico, and saw the pile of cold loose sand beside the hole. The people stood close to each other with little clouds of steam puffing from their faces. The priest looked at them and saw a pile of jackets, gloves, and scarves in the yellow, dry tumbleweeds that grew in the graveyard. He looked at the red blanket, not sure that Teofilo was so small, wondering if it wasn't some perverse Indian trick or something they did in March to ensure a good harvest, wondering if maybe old Teofilo was actually at sheep camp corralling the sheep for the night. But there he was, facing into a cold dry wind and squinting at the last sunlight, ready to bury a red wool blanket while the faces of his parishioners were in shadow with the last warmth of the sun on their backs.

His fingers were stiff, and it took him a long time to twist the lid off the holy water. Drops of water fell on the red blanket and soaked into dark icy spots. He sprinkled the grave and the water disappeared almost before it touched the dim, cold sand; it reminded him of something, and he tried to remember what it was because he thought if he could remember he might understand this. He sprinkled more water; he shook the container until it was empty, and the water fell through the light from sundown like August rain that fell while the sun was still shining, almost evaporating before it touched the wilted squash flowers.

The wind pulled at the priest's brown Franciscan robe and swirled away the corn meal and pollen that had been sprinkled on the blanket. They lowered the bundle into the ground, and they didn't bother to untie the stiff pieces of new rope that were tied around the ends of the blanket. The sun was gone, and over on the highway the eastbound lane was full of headlights. The priest walked away slowly. Leon watched him climb the hill, and when he had disappeared within the tall, thick walls, Leon turned to look up at the high blue mountains in the deep snow that reflected a faint red light from the west. He felt good because it was finished, and he was happy about the sprinkling of the holy water; now the old man could send them big thunderclouds for sure.

I. L. Peretz

IF NOT HIGHER

Early every Friday morning, at the time of the Penitential Prayers, the rabbi of Nemirov would vanish.

He was nowhere to be seen—neither in the synagogue nor in the two study houses nor at a *minyan*. And he was certainly not at home. His door stood open: whoever wished could go in and out; no one would steal from the rabbi. But not a living creature was within.

Where could the rabbi be? Where should he be? In heaven, no doubt. A rabbi has plenty of business to take care of just before the Days of Awe. Jews, God bless them, need livelihood, peace, health, and good matches. They want to be pious and good, but our sins are so great, and Satan of the thousand eyes watches the whole earth from one end to the other. What he sees, he reports; he denounces, informs. Who can help us if not the rabbi!

Isaac Loeb Peretz, also known as Yitskhok Leybush Peretz, was born in an Orthodox Jewish home in Poland in 1851. An author and playwright, he is regarded as one of the great classical Yiddish writers and an influential figure in modern Jewish culture. His first poem, "Hashahar," was published in 1877, and his first book, a collection of stories titled *Familiar Pictures,* was published in 1890. Along with others, Peretz edited *The Jewish Library,* a series of publications on literature and social problems that became a focus of emerging Yiddish literature and literary talent. Because of his interest in the poor and his support of the labor movement, Peretz was arrested as a Socialist in 1899 and spent two months in prison. Peretz died in 1915. This short story is Marie Syrkin's 1953 translation.

That's what the people thought.

But once a Litvak came, and he laughed. You know the Litvaks. They think little of the holy books but stuff themselves with Talmud and law. So this Litvak points to a passage in the *Gemarah*—it sticks in your eyes—where it is written that even Moses our Teacher did not ascend to heaven during his lifetime but remained suspended two and a half feet below. Go argue with a Litvak!

So where can the rabbi be?

"That's not my business," said the Litvak, shrugging. Yet all the while—what a Litvak can do!—he is scheming to find out.

That same night, right after the evening prayers, the Litvak steals into the rabbi's room, slides under the rabbi's bed, and waits. He'll watch all night and discover where the rabbi vanishes and what he does during the Penitential Prayers.

Someone else might have gotten drowsy and fallen asleep, but a Litvak is never at a loss; he recites a whole tractate of the Talmud by heart.

At dawn he hears the call to prayers.

The rabbi has already been awake for a long time. The Litvak has heard him groaning for a whole hour.

Whoever has heard the rabbi of Nemirov groan knows how much sorrow for all Israel, how much suffering, lies in each groan. A man's heart might break, hearing it. But a Litvak is made of iron; he listens and remains where he is. The rabbi—long life to him!—lies on the bed, and the Litvak under the bed.

Then the Litvak hears the beds in the house begin to creak; he hears people jumping out of their beds; mumbling a few Jewish words, pouring water on their fingernails, banging doors. Everyone has left. It is again quiet and dark; a bit of light from the moon shines through the shutters.

(Afterward, the Litvak admitted that when he found himself alone with the rabbi a great fear took hold of him. Goose pimples spread across his skin, and the roots of his sidelocks pricked him like needles. A trifle: to be alone with the rabbi at the time of the Penitential Prayers! But a Litvak is stubborn. So he quivered like a fish in water and remained where he was.)

Finally the rabbi—long life to him!—arises. First, he does what befits a Jew. Then he goes to the clothes closet and takes out a bundle of peasant clothes: linen trousers, high boots, a coat, a big felt hat, and a long, wide leather belt studded with brass nails. The rabbi gets dressed. From his coat pocket dangles the end of a heavy peasant rope.

The rabbi goes out, and the Litvak follows him.

On the way the rabbi stops in the kitchen, bends down, takes an ax from the bed, puts it into his belt, and leaves the house. The Litvak trembles but continues to follow.

The hushed dread of the Days of Awe hangs over the dark streets. Every once in a while a cry rises from some minyan reciting the Penitential Prayers, or from a sickbed. The rabbi hugs the sides of the streets, keeping to the shade of the houses. He glides from house to house, and the Litvak after him. The Litvak hears the sound of his heartbeats mingling with the sound of the rabbi's heavy steps. But he keeps on going and follows the rabbi to the outskirts of town.

A small wood stands just outside the town.

The rabbi—long life to him!—enters the wood. He takes thirty or forty steps and stops by a small tree. The Litvak, overcome with amazement, watches the rabbi take the ax out of his belt and strike the tree. He hears the tree creak and fall. The rabbi chops the tree into logs and the logs into sticks. Then he makes a bundle of the wood and ties it with the rope in his pocket. He puts the bundle of wood on his back, shoves the ax back into his belt, and returns to the town.

He stops at a back street beside a small, broken-down shack and knocks at the window.

"Who is there?" asks a frightened voice. The Litvak recognizes it as the voice of a sick Jewish woman.

"I," answers the rabbi in the accent of a peasant.

"Who is I?"

Again the rabbi answers in Russian. "Vassil."

"Who is Vassil, and what do you want?"

"I have wood to sell, very cheap." And not waiting for the woman's reply, he goes into the house.

The Litvak steals in after him. In the gray light of early morning he sees a poor room with broken, miserable furnishings. A sick woman, wrapped in rags, lies on the bed. She complains bitterly, "Buy? How can I buy? Where will a poor widow get money?"

"I'll lend it to you," answers the supposed Vassil. "It's only six cents."

"And how will I ever pay you back?" asks the poor woman, groaning.

"Foolish one," says the rabbi reproachfully. "See, you are a poor, sick Jew, and I am ready to trust you with a little wood. I am sure you'll pay. While you, you have such a great and mighty God and you don't trust him for six cents."

"And who will kindle the fire?" asks the widow? "Have I the strength to get up? My son is at work."

"I'll kindle the fire," answers the rabbi.

As the rabbi puts the wood into the oven he recited, in a groan, the first portion of the Penitential Prayers.

As he kindled the fire and the wood burned brightly, he recited, a bit more joyously, the second portion of the Penitential Prayers. When the fire was set, he recited the third portion, and then shut the stove.

The Litvak who saw all this became a disciple of the rabbi.

And ever after, when another disciple tells how the rabbi of Nemirov ascends to heaven at the time of the Penitential Prayers, the Litvak does not laugh. He only adds quietly, "If not higher."

Anna Swir

THE SAME INSIDE

in *Talking to My Body*

Walking to your place for a love feast
I saw at a street corner
an old beggar woman.

I took her hand,
kissed her delicate cheek,
we talked, she was
the same inside as I am,
from the same kind,
I sensed this instantly
as a dog knows by scent
another dog.

Anna Swir was born Anna Swirszczynska in Warsaw, Poland, in 1909 to a family living in poverty. Swir put herself through college and published her first poem at the age of twenty-one. During the Nazi occupation of Poland, Swir joined the resistance movement and became a military nurse in the Warsaw Uprising. Throughout her life, Swir wrote several books of poetry. The following poem appeared in Csezlaw Milosz and Leonard Nathan's translation of her poetry for the 1996 collection, *Talking to My Body*. Swir died in 1984.

I gave her money,
I could not part from her.
After all, one needs
someone who is close.

And then I no longer knew
why I was walking to your place.

John Oskison

THE PROBLEM OF OLD HARJO

~~~

The Spirit of the Lord had descended upon old Harjo. From the new missionary, just out from New York, he had learned that he was a sinner. The fire in the new missionary's eyes and her gracious appeal had convinced old Harjo that this was the time to repent and be saved. He was very much in earnest, and he assured Miss Evans that he wanted to be baptized and received into the church at once. Miss Evans was enthusiastic and went to Mrs. Rowell with the news. It was Mrs. Rowell who had said that it was no use to try to convert the older Indians, and she, after fifteen years of work in Indian Territory missions, should have known. Miss Evans was pardonably proud of her conquest.

"Old Harjo converted!" exclaimed Mrs. Rowell. "Dear Miss Evans, do you know that old Harjo has two wives?" To the older

John Milton Oskison was born in Vinita, Oklahoma, in Indian Territory in 1874 to a Cherokee mother and a white father. After graduating from Willie Halsell College in 1894, he received a BA from Stanford University and studied literature at Harvard. A lifelong writer, Oskison first achieved success as a short story writer, then turned to journalism and later yet to novels and biography—focusing often, although not exclusively, on life in the Cherokee Nation and the intense intercultural conflicts of that place and people. He also served with the American Expeditionary Force in Europe during World War I. "The Problem of Old Harjo" was first published in 1907 in *The Southern Workman,* a journal dedicated in part to promoting interracial understanding and respect.

woman it was as if someone had said to her "Madame, the Sultan of Turkey wishes to teach one of your mission Sabbath school classes."

"But," protested the younger woman, "he is really sincere, and——"

"Then ask him," Mrs. Rowell interrupted a bit sternly, "if he will put away one of his wives. Ask him, before he comes into the presence of the Lord, if he is willing to conform to the laws of the country in which he lives, the country that guarantees his idle existence. Miss Evans, your work is not even begun." No one who knew Mrs. Rowell would say that she lacked sincerity and patriotism. Her own cousin was an earnest crusader against Mormonism, and had gathered a goodly share of that wagonload of protests that the Senate had been asked to read when it was considering whether a certain statesman of Utah should be allowed to represent his state at Washington.

In her practical, tactful way, Mrs. Rowell had kept clear of such embarrassments. At first, she had written letters of indignant protest to the Indian Office against the toleration of bigamy amongst the tribes. A wise inspector had been sent to the mission, and this man had pointed out that it was better to ignore certain things, "deplorable, to be sure," than to attempt to make over the habits of the old men. Of course, the young Indians would not be permitted to take more than one wife each.

So Mrs. Rowell had discreetly limited her missionary efforts to the young, and had exercised toward the old and bigamous only that strict charity which even a hopeless sinner might claim.

Miss Evans, it was to be regretted, had only the vaguest notions about "expediency;" so weak on matters of doctrine was she that the news that Harjo was living with two wives didn't startle her. She was young and possessed of but one enthusiasm—that for saving souls.

"I suppose," she ventured, "that old Harjo must put away one wife before he can join the church?"

"There can be no question about it, Miss Evans."

"Then I shall have to ask him to do it." Miss Evans regretted the necessity for forcing this sacrifice, but had no doubt that the Indian would make it in order to accept the gift of salvation which she was commissioned to bear to him.

Harjo lived in a "double" log cabin three miles from the mission. His ten acres of corn had been gathered into its fence-rail crib; four hogs that were to furnish his winter's bacon had been brought in from the woods and penned conveniently near to the crib; out in a corner of the garden, a fat mound of dirt rose where the crop of turnips and potatoes had been buried against the corrupting frost; and in the hayloft of his log stable were stored many pumpkins, dried corn, onions (suspended in bunches from the rafters) and the varied forage that Mrs. Harjo number one and Mrs. Harjo number two had thriftily provided. Three cows, three young heifers, two colts, and two patient, capable mares bore the Harjo brand, a fantastic "-H-" that the old man had designed. Materially, Harjo was solvent; and if the Government had ever come to his aid he could not recall the date.

This attempt to rehabilitate old Harjo morally, Miss Evans felt, was not one to be made at the mission; it should be undertaken in the Creek's own home where the evidences of his sin should confront him as she explained.

When Miss Evans rode up to the block in front of Harjo's cabin, the old Indian came out, slowly and with a broadening smile of welcome on his face. A clean gray flannel shirt had taken the place of the white collarless garment, with crackling stiff bosom, that he had worn to the mission meetings. Comfortable, well-patched moccasins had been substituted for creaking boots, and brown corduroys, belted in at the waist, for tight black trousers. His abundant gray hair fell down on his shoulders. In his eyes, clear and large and black, glowed the light of true hospitality. Miss Evans thought of the patriarchs as she saw him lead her horse out to the stable; thus Abraham might have looked and lived.

"Harjo," began Miss Evans before following the old man to the covered passageway between the disconnected cabins, "is it true that you have two wives?" Her tone was neither stern nor accusatory. The Creek had heard that question before, from scandalized missionaries and perplexed registry clerks when he went to Muscogee to enroll himself and his family in one of the many "final" records ordered to be made by the government preparatory to dividing the Creek lands among the individual citizens.

139

For answer, Harjo called, first into the cabin that was used as a kitchen and then, in a loud, clear voice, toward the small field, where Miss Evans saw a flock of half-grown turkeys running about in the corn stubble. From the kitchen emerged a tall, thin Indian woman of fifty-five, with a red handkerchief bound severely over her head. She spoke to Miss Evans and sat down in the passageway. Presently, a clear, sweet voice was heard in the field; a stout, handsome woman, about the same age as the other, climbed the rail fence and came up to the house. She, also, greeted Miss Evans briefly. Then she carried a tin basin to the well nearby, where she filled it to the brim. Setting it down on the horse block, she rolled back her sleeves, tucked in the collar of her gray blouse, and plunged her face in the water. In a minute she came out of the kitchen freshened and smiling. 'Liza Harjo had been pulling dried bean stalks at one end of the field, and it was dirty work. At last old Harjo turned to Miss Evans and said, "These two my wife—this one 'Liza, this one Jennie."

It was done with simple dignity. Miss Evans bowed and stammered.

Three pairs of eyes were turned upon her in patient, courteous inquiry.

It was hard to state the case. The old man was so evidently proud of his women, and so flattered by Miss Evans' interest in them, that he would find it hard to understand. Still, it had to be done, and Miss Evans took the plunge.

"Harjo, you want to come into our church?" The old man's face lighted.

"Oh, yes, I would come to Jesus, please, my friend."

"Do you know, Harjo, that the Lord commanded that one man should mate with but one woman?" The question was stated again in simpler terms, and the Indian replied, "Me know that now, my friend. Long time ago"—Harjo plainly meant the whole period previous to his conversion—"me did not know. The Lord Jesus did not speak to me in that time and so I was blind. I do what blind man do."

"Harjo, you must have only one wife when you come into our church. Can't you give up one of these women?" Miss Evans glanced at the two, sitting by with smiles of polite interest on their faces, understanding nothing. They had not shared Harjo's enthusiasm either for the white man's God or his language.

"Give up my wife?" A sly smile stole over his face. He leaned closer to Miss Evans. "You tell me, my friend, which one I give up." He glanced from 'Liza to Jennie as if to weigh their attractions, and the two rewarded him with their pleasantest smiles. "You tell me which one," he urged.

"Why, Harjo, how can I tell you!" Miss Evans had little sense of humor; she had taken the old man seriously.

"Then," Harjo sighed, continuing the comedy, for surely the missionary was jesting with him, "'Liza and Jennie must say." He talked to the Indian women for a time, and they laughed heartily. 'Liza, pointing to the other, shook her head. At length Harjo explained, "My friend, they cannot say. Jennie, she would run a race to see which one stay, but 'Liza, she say no, she is fat and cannot run."

Miss Evans comprehended at last. She flushed angrily, and protested, "Harjo, you are making a mock of a sacred subject; I cannot allow you to talk like this."

"But did you not speak in fun, my friend?" Harjo queried, sobering. "Surely you have just said what your friend, the white woman at the mission (he meant Mrs. Rowell) would say, and you do not mean what you say."

"Yes, Harjo, I mean it. It is true that Mrs. Rowell raised the point first, but I agree with her. The church cannot be defiled by receiving a bigamist into its membership." Harjo saw that the young woman was serious, distressingly serious. He was silent for a long time, but at last he raised his head and spoke quietly, "It is not good to talk like that if it is not in fun."

He rose and went to the stable. As he led Miss Evans' horse up to the block it was champing a mouthful of corn, the last of a generous portion that Harjo had put before it. The Indian held the bridle and waited for Miss Evans to mount. She was embarrassed, humiliated, angry. It was absurd to be dismissed in this way by—"by an ignorant old bigamist!" Then the humor of it burst upon her, and its human aspect. In her anxiety concerning the spiritual welfare of the sinner Harjo, she had insulted the man Harjo. She began to understand why Mrs. Rowell had said that the old Indians were hopeless.

"Harjo," she begged, coming out of the passageway, "please forgive me. I do not want you to give up one of your wives. Just tell me why you took them."

"I will tell you that, my friend." The old Creek looped the reins over his arm and sat down on the block. "For thirty years Jennie has lived with me as my wife. She is of the Bear people, and she came to me when I was thirty-five and she was twenty-five. She could not come before, for her mother was old, very old, and Jennie, she stay with her and feed her.

"So, when I was thirty years old I took 'Liza for my woman. She is of the Crow people. She help me make this little farm here when there was no farm for many miles around.

"Well, five years 'Liza and me, we live here and work hard. But there was no child. Then the old mother of Jennie she died, and Jennie got no family left in this part of the country. So 'Liza say to me, 'Why don't you take Jennie in here?' I say, 'You don't care?' and she say, 'No, maybe we have children here then.' But we have no children—never have children. We do not like that, but God He would not let it be. So, we have lived here thirty years very happy. Only just now you make me sad."

"Harjo," cried Miss Evans, "forget what I said. Forget that you wanted to join the church." For a young mission worker with a single purpose always before her, Miss Evans was saying a strange thing. Yet she couldn't help saying it; all of her zeal seemed to have been dissipated by a simple statement of the old man.

"I cannot forget to love Jesus, and I want to be saved." Old Harjo spoke with solemn earnestness. The situation was distracting. On one side stood a convert eager for the protection of the church, asking only that he be allowed to fulfill the obligations of humanity and on the other stood the church, represented by Mrs. Rowell, that set an impossible condition on receiving old Harjo to itself. Miss Evans wanted to cry; prayer, she felt, would be entirely inadequate as a means of expression.

"Oh! Harjo," she cried out, "I don't know what to do. I must think it over and talk with Mrs. Rowell again."

But Mrs. Rowell could suggest no way out; Miss Evans' talk with her only gave the older woman another opportunity to preach the folly of wasting time on the old and "unreasonable" Indians. Certainly the church could not listen even to a hint of a compromise in this case. If Harjo wanted to be saved there was one way and only one—unless—

"Is either of the two women old? I mean, so old that she is—an—"

"Not at all," answered Miss Evans. "They're both strong and—yes, happy. I think they will outlive Harjo."

"Can't you appeal to one of the women to go away? I dare say we could provide for her." Miss Evans, incongruously, remembered Jennie's jesting proposal to race for the right to stay with Harjo. What could the mission provide as a substitute for the little home that 'Liza had helped to create there in the edge of the woods? What other home would satisfy Jennie?

"Mrs. Rowell, are you sure that we ought to try to take one of Harjo's women from him? I'm not sure that it would in the least advance morality amongst the tribe, but I'm certain that it would make three gentle people unhappy for the rest of their lives."

"You may be right, Miss Evans." Mrs. Rowell was not seeking to create unhappiness, for enough of it inevitably came to be pictured in the little mission building. "You may be right," she repeated, "but it is a grievous misfortune that old Harjo should wish to unite with the church."

No one was more regular in his attendance at the mission meetings than old Harjo. Sitting well forward, he was always in plain view of Miss Evans at the organ. Before the service began, and after it was over, the old man greeted the young woman. There was never a spoken question, but in the Creek's eyes was always a mute inquiry.

Once Miss Evans ventured to write to her old pastor in New York, and explain her trouble. This was what he wrote in reply: "I am surprised that you are troubled, for I should have expected you to rejoice, as I do, over this new and wonderful evidence of the Lord's reforming power. Though the church cannot receive the old man so long as he is confessedly a bigamist and violator of his country's just laws, you should be greatly strengthened in your work through bringing him to desire salvation."

"Oh! it's easy to talk when you're free from responsibility!" cried out Miss Evans. "But I woke him up to a desire for this water of salvation that he cannot take. I have seen Harjo's home, and I know how cruel and useless it would be to urge him to give up what he loves—for he does love those two women who have spent half their lives and more with him. What, what can be done!"

Month after month, as old Harjo continued to occupy his seat in the mission meetings, with that mute appeal in his eyes and a persistent light of hope on his face, Miss Evans repeated the question, "What can be done?" If she was sometimes tempted to say to the old man, "Stop worrying about your soul; you'll get to heaven as surely as any of us," there was always Mrs. Rowell to remind her that she was not a Mormon missionary. She could not run away from her perplexity. If she should secure a transfer to another station, she felt that Harjo would give up coming to the meetings, and in his despair become a positive influence for evil amongst his people. Mrs. Rowell would not waste her energy on an obstinate old man. No, Harjo was her creation, her impossible convert, and throughout the years, until death—the great solvent which is not always a solvent—came to one of them, would continue to haunt her.

And meanwhile, what?

Thich Nhat Hanh

MEDITATION ON COMPASSION
and NOT TWO

from *Peace Is Every Step*

~~~

"MEDITATION ON COMPASSION"

Love is a mind that brings peace, joy, and happiness to another person. Compassion is a mind that removes the suffering that is present in the other. We all have the seeds of love and compassion in our minds, and we can develop these fine and wonderful sources of energy. We can nurture the unconditional love that does not expect anything in return and therefore does not lead to anxiety and sorrow.

An exiled Vietnamese Zen Buddhist monk, Thich Nhat Hanh is a teacher, a poet, and a peace and human rights activist. Born in central Vietnam in 1926, he joined a Zen monastery at sixteen and was ordained as a monk in 1949. He founded the School of Youth for Social Services (SYSS), a relief organization in Saigon that rebuilt bombed villages, schools, and medical centers, and resettled families during the Vietnam War. He urged the U.S. government to withdraw from Vietnam, encouraged Martin Luther King Jr. to oppose the war publicly, and led the Buddhist delegation to the Paris Peace Talks. His more than one hundred books include *Vietnam: Lotus in a Sea of Fire* (in which he coined the term *engaged Buddhism*) and *Living Buddha, Living Christ*. He currently lives in the Plum Village Monastery in France, a community he founded in 1982, and continues to be active in the peace movement. The passages selected here come from his book *Peace Is Every Step*.

145

The essence of love and compassion is understanding, the ability to recognize the physical, material, and psychological suffering of others, to put ourselves "inside the skin" of the other. We "go inside" their body, feelings, and mental formations, and witness for ourselves their suffering. Shallow observation as an outsider is not enough to see their suffering. We must become one with the object of our observation. When we are in contact with another's suffering, a feeling of compassion is born in us. Compassion means, literally, "to suffer with."

We begin by choosing as the object of our meditation someone who is undergoing physical or material suffering, someone who is weak and easily ill, poor or oppressed, or has no protection. This kind of suffering is easy for us to see. After that, we can practice being in contact with more subtle forms of suffering. Sometimes the other person does not seem to be suffering at all, but we may notice that he has sorrows which have left their marks in hidden ways. People with more than enough material comforts also suffer. We look deeply at the person who is the objet of our meditation on compassion, both during sitting meditation and when we are actually in contact with him. We must allow enough time to be really in deep contact with his suffering. We continue to observe him until compassion arises and penetrates our being.

When we observe deeply in this way, the fruit of our meditation will naturally transform into some kind of action. We will not just say, "I love him very much," but instead, "I will do something so that he will suffer less." The mind of compassion is truly present when it is effective in removing another person's suffering. We have to find ways to nourish and express our compassion. When we come into contact with the other person, our thoughts and actions should express our mind of compassion, even if that person says and does things that are not easy to accept. We practice in this way until we see clearly that our love is not contingent upon the other person being lovable. Then we can know that our mind of compassion is firm and authentic. We ourselves will be more at ease, and the person who has been the object of our meditation will also benefit eventually. His suffering will slowly diminish, and his life will gradually be brighter and more joyful as a result of our compassion.

We can also meditate on the suffering of those who cause us to suffer. Anyone who has made us suffer is undoubtedly suffering too. We only need to follow our breathing and look deeply, and naturally we will see his suffering. A part of his difficulties and sorrows may have been brought about by his parents' lack of skill when he was still young. But his parents themselves may have been victims of their parents; the suffering has been transmitted from generation to generation and been reborn in him. If we see that, we will no longer blame him for making us suffer, because we know that he is also a victim. To look deeply is to understand. Once we understand the reasons he has acted badly, our bitterness towards him will vanish, and we will long for him to suffer less. We will feel cool and light, and we can smile. We do not need the other person to be present in order to bring about reconciliation. When we look deeply, we become reconciled with ourselves, and, for us, the problem no longer exists. Sooner or later, he will see our attitude and will share in the freshness of the stream of love which is flowing naturally from our heart.

"Not Two"

When we want to understand something, we cannot just stand outside and observe it. We have to enter deeply into it and be one with it in order to really understand. If we want to understand a person, we have to feel his feelings, suffer his sufferings, and enjoy his joy. The word "comprehend" is made up of the Latin roots *cum*, which means "with," and *prehendere*, which means "to grasp it or pick it up." To comprehend something means to pick it up and be one with it. There is no other way to understand something. In Buddhism, we call this kind of understanding "non-duality." Not two.

Fifteen years ago, I helped a committee for orphans who were victims of the war in Vietnam. From Vietnam, the social workers sent out applications, one sheet of paper with a small picture of a child in the corner, telling the name, age, and conditions of the orphan. My job was to translate the application from Vietnamese into French in order to seek a sponsor, so that the child would have food to eat and books for school, and be put into the family of an aunt, an uncle, or a grandparent. Then the committee in France could send the money to the family member to help take care of the child.

Each day I helped translate about thirty applications. The way I did it was to look at the picture of the child. I did not read the application, I just took time to look at the picture of the child. Usually after only thirty or forty seconds, I became one with the child. Then I would pick up the pen and translate the words from the application onto another sheet. Afterwards I realized that it was not me who had translated the application; it was the child and me, who had become one. Looking at his or her face, I felt inspired, and I became the child and he or she became me, and together we did the translation. It is very natural. You don't have to practice a lot of meditation to be able to do that. You just look, allowing yourself to be, and you lose yourself in the child, and the child in you.

THE LEGEND OF THE LOWLY DEVOTEE

in *The Tiruvaçagam*

In the town of the Tiru-cenkattan-kudi, in the Chora land (the Tamil country round about Tanjore), there lived a man called Paranjotiyar, who was skilled as a physician, and adept in the management of horses and elephants, and also a mighty warrior. But he was a saint also. Day and night this noble and highly gifted man meditated on the perfections of Shiva the Supreme, and so humbly devoted himself and his wealth to the service of the poor mendicant devotees of Shiva that he always bore the name of the "Lowly Devotee."

On a certain occasion he had gained a great victory for his Rāja, and as he returned laden with rich spoil the courtiers sneeringly told the king that it was the singular devotion of the brave hero to his God that had gained for him the victory, which was therefore due solely to the favor of Shiva.

"What," cried the Rāja, who before this knew nothing of the saintliness of his Commander-in-Chief, "have I exposed so great a saint to peril of death in battle for my petty affairs? He shall fight no more!"

The Tiruvaçagam ("sacred utterance") is a volume of hymns composed by the ninth-century Shaivite bhakti poet Manikkavāçakar. It is composed of fifty-one *pathigams* (a form of poem), together making up the eighth volume of the *Tirumurai,* the sacred anthology of Tamil Shaiva Siddhanta, a school of Shaivite Hinduism. The main message of *The Tiruvaçagam* is that the body is temporary and we should not spend much time and money in worldly comforts, the root cause of pain and sorrow. Shaivism, which considers Shiva to be the Supreme Being, is one of the four sects of Hinduism and is prevalent in India, Nepal, Sri Lanka, Malaysia, Singapore, and Indonesia. This translation was done by G. U. Pope in 1900.

The "lowly devotee" replied: "Nay, I have merely performed the ancestral duties of my caste. No evil there, though I slew your foes!"

But the king, giving up to him the spoils of the campaign, released him at once from all further service, and bade him occupy himself henceforth wholly in the service of God, and of his devotees. So the *Nayanar* (devotee) went home, and thenceforth devoted himself exclusively to the worship and service of Shiva in the temple of his native town. And, as domestic virtue is the highest of all virtue (a Tamil proverb) ... he married a lady called Nangaiyar of Tiruvenkadu, by whom he had one son, Cirala-devar. At five years of age the boy was sent to school to learn Shiva's sacred books.

Now Shiva the Supreme was graciously pleased to make proof of the love of this devotee, and to test especially his obedience: and, therefore from among the various forms the God assumes, and under which he is worshipped by the six Shaiva sects, he chose that of Bhairava—"the terrible, the destroyer" and descended from Kailasa, his own peculiar heaven, in that dread shape, loaded with matted hair, his body smeared with ashes—weird and terrible. Yet he seemed a holy man, though of the most repellent type of fanatical mendicants. The "lowly devotee" found him thus seated under a banyan tree, and immediately discerning the sign of the sacred ashes, went to offer him hospitality.

The disguised one inquires: "Art thou the renowned 'lowly devotee'?"

The Nayanar meekly replies: "The servants of my God deign in love to style me so. I have sought in vain today for guests among the pilgrim-servants of our God. I have now found thee. Graciously take thy holy meal in my house."

"Thou cannot find me the food I need."

"If Shiva's servants need anything, the difficult becomes easy, because of Him whom they serve: I can and will provide whatever thou can require."

"Once in six months I eat the flesh of a slain victim: this is the day."

"I have flocks and herds; I can supply and offer the victim, and my wife shall prepare the food."

The Bhairava replies: "What I eat must be a HUMAN victim. It must be five years of age, its limbs without a blemish; the only child in the household; a sacrifice willingly offered. Such a little one the mother must herself hold with joyous mind while the father slays. Such food alone I eat this day."

"Such food, if THOU require, is not difficult to supply," replies the "lowly devotee," and hastens homeward with cheerful countenance. His wife meets him with wifely obeisance at the door, and asks: "What does the holy one command?"

He repeats to her the awful words.

She asks: "Where shall such an offering be obtained?"

"My life, my wife," says he, "for much wealth might even such a one be bought, but where are the mother and father able with glad and pious mind so to sacrifice? It must be our own little son and it is we who must so offer him to the servant of God."

She, with a like unflinching devotion, consents and adds: "Go, bring from the school our little one, born to be the guardian of our lives."

The devotee, with pious mind, eagerly hastens to the school.... Soon the food is ready, the fearful guest is brought in, and the father with courteous deference begs him to eat of the sacrifice.

"I cannot eat alone. None so worthy to share with me as thyself."

Another plate is set in all lowly loving obedience. But the Bhairava interposes yet another objection.

"Thou has a son, let him eat too."

"My son cannot help us in this!"

"Till he come I eat not; go, seek, call, and bring him here."

The father rises, calls the mother and they, simply obedient, but bewildered, stand without the door and cry, "Come, O son."

Then lo, even as he was wont, his bright eyes beaming with joy, his long black silken curls glistening in the sunlight, his silver anklets tinkling as he runs, their son is seen hastening on, and rushes into his mother's arms.... When they would bring him into the presence of the disguised God, the dread guest had vanished, and the dish was empty, bright and clean. It had all been delusion, the sport of the Deity!

No death, no offering—but in pious will.

Then, because what the God caused them to seem to do in a loving ecstasy was right in its motive, though forbidden in itself, all the gods appeared to them in the sky and applauded them; and while they worshipped in speechless rapture, the father, mother, son, and nurse were carried away to Kailāsa, there to adore the God and Pārvatī, his wife, and Subramanya, his son, in bliss unending.

Ruth 1–4:22

Elimelech's Family Goes to Moab

In the days when the judges ruled, there was a famine in the land, and a certain man of Bethlehem in Judah went to live in the country of Moab, he and his wife and two sons. The name of the man was Elimelech and the name of his wife Naomi, and the names of his two sons were Mahlon and Chilion; they were Ephrathites from Bethlehem in Judah. They went into the country of Moab and remained there. But Elimelech, the husband of Naomi, died, and she was left with her two sons. These took Moabite wives; the name of the one was Orpah and the name of the other Ruth. When they had lived there about ten years, both Mahlon and Chilion also died, so that the woman was left without her two sons and her husband.

Naomi and Her Daughters-in-Law

Then she started to return with her daughters-in-law from the country of Moab, for she had heard in the country of Moab that the LORD had considered his people and given them food. So she set out from the place where she had been living, she and her two daughters-in-law, and they went on their way to go back to the land of Judah. But Naomi said

The Book of Ruth is a short book of the Hebrew Bible and the Christian Old Testament that appears between Judges and I Samuel. Its chief significance to Jews is in many instances related to its treatment of compassion and conversion. For Christians, the Book of Ruth has additional significance on account of the lineage laid out in its fourth chapter. This translation comes from the New Revised Standard Version.

to her two daughters-in-law, "Go back each of you to your mother's house. May the LORD deal kindly with you, as you have dealt with the dead and with me. The LORD grant that you may find security, each of you in the house of your husband." Then she kissed them, and they wept aloud. They said to her, "No, we will return with you to your people." But Naomi said, "Turn back, my daughters, why will you go with me? Do I still have sons in my womb that they may become your husbands? Turn back, my daughters, go your way, for I am too old to have a husband. Even if I thought there was hope for me, even if I should have a husband tonight and bear sons, would you then wait until they were grown? Would you then refrain from marrying? No, my daughters, it has been far more bitter for me than for you, because the hand of the LORD has turned against me." Then they wept aloud again. Orpah kissed her mother-in-law, but Ruth clung to her.

So she said, "See, your sister-in-law has gone back to her people and to her gods; return after your sister-in-law." But Ruth said,

> "Do not press me to leave you
> > or to turn back from following you!
> Where you go, I will go;
> > Where you lodge, I will lodge;
> your people shall be my people,
> > and your God my God.
> Where you die, I will die—
> > there will I be buried.
> May the Lord do thus and so to me,
> > and more as well,
> if even death parts me from you!"

When Naomi saw that she was determined to go with her, she said no more to her.

So the two of them went on until they came to Bethlehem. When they came to Bethlehem, the whole town was stirred because of them; and the women said, "Is this Naomi?" She said to them,

"Call me no longer Naomi,

    call me Mara,

    for the Almighty has dealt bitterly with me.

I went away full,

    but the Lord has brought me back empty;

why call me Naomi

    when the LORD has dealt harshly with me,

    and the Almighty has brought calamity upon me?"

So Naomi returned together with Ruth the Moabite, her daughter-in-law, who came back with her from the country of Moab. They came to Bethlehem at the beginning of the barley harvest.

RUTH MEETS BOAZ

Now Naomi had a kinsman on her husband's side, a prominent rich man, of the family of Elimelech, whose name was Boaz. And Ruth the Moabite said to Naomi, "Let me go to the field and glean among the ears of grain, behind someone in whose sight I may find favor." She said to her, "Go, my daughter." So she went. She came and gleaned in the field behind the reapers. As it happened, she came to the part of the field belonging to Boaz, who was of the family of Elimelech. Just then Boaz came from Bethlehem. He said to the reapers, "The LORD be with you." They answered, "The LORD bless you." Then Boaz said to his servant who was in charge of the reapers, "To whom does this young woman belong?" The servant who was in charge of the reapers answered, "She is the Moabite who came back with Naomi from the country of Moab. She said, 'Please, let me glean and gather among the sheaves behind the reapers.' So she came, and she has been on her feet from early this morning until now, without resting even for a moment."

Then Boaz said to Ruth, "Now listen, my daughter, do not go to glean in another field or leave this one, but keep close to my young women. Keep your eyes on the field that is being reaped, and follow behind them. I have ordered the young men not to bother you. If you get thirsty, go to the vessels and drink from what the young men have drawn." Then she fell prostrate, with her face to the ground, and said to him, "Why have I found favor in your sight, that you should take notice of me, when I am a foreigner?" But Boaz answered her, "All that you have done for your mother-in-law since the death of your husband has been fully told me, and how you left your father and mother and your native land and came to a people that you did not know before. May the LORD reward you for your deeds, and may you have a full reward from the LORD, the God of Israel, under whose wings you have come for refuge!" Then she said, "May I continue to find favor in your sight, my LORD, for you have comforted me and spoken kindly to your servant, even though I am not one of your servants."

At mealtime Boaz said to her, "Come here, and eat some of this bread, and dip your morsel in the sour wine." So she sat beside the reapers, and he heaped up for her some parched grain. She ate until she was satisfied, and she had some left over. When she got up to glean, Boaz instructed his young men, "Let her glean even among the standing sheaves, and do not reproach her. You must also pull out some handfuls for her from the bundles, and leave them for her to glean, and do not rebuke her."

So she gleaned in the field until evening. Then she beat out what she had gleaned, and it was about an ephah of barley. She picked it up and came into the town, and her mother-in-law saw how much she had gleaned. Then she took out and gave her what was left over after she herself had been satisfied. Her mother-in-law said to her, "Where did you glean today? And where have you worked? Blessed be the man who took notice of you." So she told her mother-in-law with whom she had worked and said, "The name of the man with whom I worked today is Boaz." Then Naomi said to her daughter-in-law, "Blessed be he by the LORD, whose kindness has not forsaken the living or the dead!" Naomi also said to her, "The man is a relative of ours, one of our nearest kin." Then Ruth the Moabite said, "He even said to me, 'Stay close by my servants, until they have finished all my harvest.'" Naomi said to Ruth, her daughter-in-law, "It is better, my daughter, that you go out with his young women, otherwise you might be bothered in another field." So she stayed close to the young women of Boaz, gleaning until the end of the barley and wheat harvests; and she lived with her mother-in-law.

RUTH AND BOAZ AT THE THRESHING FLOOR

Naomi, her mother-in-law, said to her, "My daughter, I need to seek some security for you, so that it may be well with you. Now here is our kinsman Boaz, with whose young women you have been working. See, he is winnowing barley tonight at the threshing floor. Now wash and anoint yourself, and put on your best clothes and go down to the threshing floor; but do not make yourself known to the man until he has finished eating and drinking. When he lies down, observe the place where he lies; then, go and uncover his feet and lie down; and he will tell you what to do." She said to her, "All that you tell me I will do."

So she went down to the threshing floor and did just as her mother-in-law had instructed her. When Boaz had eaten and drunk, and he was in a contented mood, he went to lie down at the end of the heap of grain. Then she came stealthily and uncovered his feet and lay down. At midnight the man was startled and turned over, and there, lying at his feet, was a woman! He said, "Who are you?" And she answered, "I am Ruth, your servant; spread your cloak over your servant, for you are next-of-kin." He said, "May you be blessed by the LORD, my daughter; this last instance of your loyalty is better than the first; you have not gone after young men, whether poor or rich. And now, my daughter, do not be afraid, I will do for you all that you ask, for all the assembly of my people know that you are a worthy woman. But now, though it is true that I am a near kinsman, there is another kinsman more closely related than I. Remain this night, and in the morning, if he will act as next-of-kin for you, good; let him do it. If he is not willing to act as next-of-kin for you, then, as the LORD lives, I will act as next-of kin for you. Lie down until the morning."

So she lay at his feet until morning but got up before one person could recognize another; for he said, "It must not be known that the woman came to the threshing floor." Then he said, "Bring the

cloak you are wearing and hold it out." So she held it, and he measured out six measures of barley and put it on her back; then he went
into the city. She came to her mother-in-law, who said, "How did
things go with you, my daughter?" Then she told her all that the man
had done for her, saying, "He gave me these six measures of barley,
for he said, 'Do not go back to your mother-in-law empty-handed.'"
She replied, "Wait, my daughter, until you learn how the matter turns
out, for the man will not rest, but will settle the matter today."

THE MARRIAGE OF BOAZ AND RUTH

No sooner had Boaz gone up to the gate and sat down there than
the next-of-kin, of whom Boaz had spoken, came passing by. So
Boaz said, "Come over, friend; sit down here." And he went over and
sat down. Then Boaz took ten men of the elders of the city and said,
"Sit down here"; so they sat down. He then said to the next-of-kin,
"Naomi, who has come back from the country of Moab, is selling the
parcel of land that belonged to our kinsman Elimelech. So I thought
I would tell you of it and say: Buy it in the presence of those sitting
here, and in the presence of the elders of my people. If you will
redeem it, redeem it; but if you will not, tell me, so that I may know;
for there is no one prior to you to redeem it, and I come after you."
So he said, "I will redeem it." Then Boaz said, "The day you acquire
the field from the hand of Naomi, you are also acquiring Ruth the
Moabite, the widow of the dead man, to maintain the dead man's
name on his inheritance." At this, the next-of-kin said, "I cannot
redeem it for myself without damaging my own inheritance. Take my
right of redemption yourself, for I cannot redeem it."

Now this was the custom in former times in Israel concerning
redeeming and exchanging: to confirm a transaction, the one took
off a sandal and gave it to the other; this was the manner of attesting
in Israel. So when the next-of-kin said to Boaz, "Acquire it for yourself," he took off his sandal. Then Boaz said to the elders and all the
people, "Today you are witnesses that I have acquired from the hand
of Naomi all that belonged to Elimelech and all that belonged to
Chilion and Mahlon. I have also acquired Ruth the Moabite, the

wife of Mahlon, to be my wife, to maintain the dead man's name on his inheritance, in order that the name of the dead may not be cut off from his kindred and from the gate of his native place; today you are witnesses." Then all the people who were at the gate, along with the elders, said, "We are witnesses. May the LORD make the woman who is coming into your house like Rachel and Leah, who together built up the house of Israel. May you produce children in Ephrathah and bestow a name in Bethlehem; and, through the children that the LORD will give you by this young woman, may your house be like the house of Perez, whom Tamar bore to Judah."

THE GENEALOGY OF DAVID

So Boaz took Ruth and she became his wife. When they came together, the LORD made her conceive, and she bore a son. Then the women said to Naomi, "Blessed be the LORD, who has not left you this day without next-of-kin; and may his name be renowned in Israel! He shall be to you a restorer of life and a nourisher of your old age; for your daughter-in-law who loves you, who is more to you than seven sons, has borne him." Then Naomi took the child and laid him in her bosom and became his nurse. The women of the neighborhood gave him a name, saying, "A son has been born to Naomi." They named him Obed; he became the father of Jesse, the father of David.

Now these are the descendants of Perez: Perez became the father of Hezron, Hezron of Ram, Ram of Amminadab, Amminadab of Nahshon, Nahshon of Salmon, Salmon of Boaz, Boaz of Obed, Obed of Jesse, and Jesse of David.

حلّ

THE MEXICAN-AMERICAN
AND THE CHURCH

⁀‿⁀

The place to begin is with our own experience with the Church in the strike that has gone on for thirty-one months in Delano. For in Delano the Church has been involved with the poor in a unique way that should stand as a symbol to other communities. Of course, when we refer to the Church we should define the word a little. We mean the whole Church, the Church as an ecumenical body spread around the world, and not just its particular form in a parish in a local community.

The Church we are talking about is a tremendously powerful institution in our society, and in the world. That Church is one form of the Presence of God on Earth, and so naturally it is powerful. It is powerful by definition. It is a powerful moral and spiritual force which cannot be ignored by any movement. Furthermore, it is an

---

Cesar Chavez was born in 1927 in Yuma, Arizona, to a family of poor migrant farm workers. After serving in the U.S. Navy, Chavez became an organizer for the Community Service Organization, working to register voters, fight racial and economic discrimination, and help create new CSO chapters. In 1962, Chavez left his position with CSO to found the National Farm Workers Association, and he gradually built a nationwide coalition of unions, church groups, students, and consumers, eventually rallying millions of supporters to the United Farm Workers. Chavez died in 1993 and received the Presidential Medal of Freedom in 1994. Chavez prepared the speech below during a twenty-five-day spiritual fast and presented it at a conference of Mexican Americans in 1968 in Sacramento, California.

organization with tremendous wealth. Since the Church is to be servant to the poor, it is our fault if that wealth is not channeled to help the poor in our world. In a small way we have been able, in the Delano strike, to work together with the Church in such a way as to bring some of its moral and economic power to bear on those who want to maintain the status quo, keeping farm workers in virtual enslavement. In brief, here is what happened in Delano.

Some years ago, when some of us were working with the Community Service Organization, we began to realize the powerful effect which the Church can have on the conscience of the opposition. In scattered instances, in San Jose, Sacramento, Oakland, Los Angeles and other places, priests would speak out loudly and clearly against specific instances of oppression, and in some cases, stand with the people who were being hurt. Furthermore, a small group of priests, Frs. McDonald, McCollough, Duggan and others, began to pinpoint attention on the terrible situation of the farm workers in our state.

At about that same time, we began to run into the California Migrant Ministry in the camps and field. They were about the only ones there, and a lot of us were very suspicious, since we were Catholics and they were Protestants. However, they had developed a very clear conception of the Church. It was called to serve, to be at the mercy of the poor, and not to try to use them. After a while this made a lot of sense to us, and we began to find ourselves working side by side with them. In fact, it forced us to raise the question why our Church was not doing the same.

We would ask, why do the Protestants come out here and help the people, demand nothing, and give all their time to serving farm workers, while our own parish priests stay in their churches, where only a few people come, and usually feel uncomfortable? It was not until some of us moved to Delano and began working to build the National Farm Workers Association that we really saw how far removed from the people the parish Church was. In fact, we could not get any help at all from the priests of Delano. When the strike began, they told us we could not even use the Church's auditorium for the meetings. The farm workers' money helped build that auditorium! But the Protestants were there again, in the form of the

California Migrant Ministry, and they began to help in little ways, here and there.

When the strike started in 1965, most of our friends forsook us for a while. They ran—or were just too busy to help. But the California Migrant Ministry held a meeting with its staff and decided that the strike was a matter of life or death for farm workers everywhere, and that even if it meant the end of the Migrant Ministry they would turn over their resources to the strikers. The political pressure on the Protestant Churches was tremendous and the Migrant Ministry lost a lot of money. But they stuck it out, and they began to point the way to the rest of the Church. In fact, when 30 of the strikers were arrested for shouting Huelga, 11 ministers went to jail with them. They were in Delano that day at the request of Chris Hartmire, director of the California Migrant Ministry.

Then the workers began to raise the question: why ministers? Why not priests? What does the Bishop say? But the Bishop said nothing. But slowly the pressure of the people grew and grew, until finally we have in Delano a priest sent by the new Bishop, Timothy Manning, who is there to help minister to the needs of farm workers. His name is Father Mark Day and he is the Union's chaplain. Finally, our own Catholic Church has decided to recognize that we have our own peculiar needs, just as the growers have theirs.

But outside of the local diocese, the pressure built up on growers to negotiate was tremendous. Though we were not allowed to have our own priest, the power of the ecumenical body of the Church was tremendous. The work of the Church, for example, in the Schenley, Di Giorgio, Perelly-Minetti strikes was fantastic. They applied pressure—and they mediated. When poor people get involved in a long conflict, such as a strike, or a civil rights drive, and the pressure increases each day, there is a deep need for spiritual advice. Without it we see families crumble, leadership weaken, and hard workers grow tired. And in such a situation the spiritual advice must be given by a friend, not by the opposition. What sense does it make to go to Mass on Sunday and reach out for spiritual help, and instead get sermons about the wickedness of your cause? That only drives one to question and to despair.

The growers in Delano have their spiritual problems ... we do not deny that. They have every right to have priests and ministers who serve their needs. But we have different needs, and so we needed a friendly spiritual guide. And this is true in every community in this state where the poor face tremendous problems. But the opposition raises a tremendous howl about this. They don't want us to have our spiritual advisors, friendly to our needs. Why is this? Why indeed except that THERE IS TREMENDOUS SPIRITUAL AND ECONOMIC POWER IN THE CHURCH. The rich know it, and for that reason they choose to keep it from the people.

The leadership of the Mexican-American Community must admit that we have fallen far short in our task of helping provide spiritual guidance for our people. We may say, I don't feel any such need. I can get along. But that is a poor excuse for not helping provide such help for others. For we can also say, I don't need any welfare help. I can take care of my own problems. But we are all willing to fight like hell for welfare aid for those who truly need it, who would starve without it. Likewise we may have gotten an education and not care about scholarship money for ourselves, or our children. But we would, we should, fight like hell to see to it that our state provides aid for any child needing it so that he can get the education he desires.

Likewise we can say we don't need the Church. That is our business. But there are hundreds of thousands of our people who desperately need some help from that powerful institution, the Church, and we are foolish not to help them get it. For example, the Catholic Charities agency of the Catholic Church has millions of dollars earmarked for the poor. But often the money is spent for food baskets for the needy instead of for effective action to eradicate the causes of poverty. The men and women who administer this money sincerely want to help their brothers. It should be our duty to help direct the attention to the basic needs of the Mexican-Americans in our society ... needs which cannot be satisfied with baskets of food, but rather with effective organizing at the grass roots level.

Therefore, I am calling for Mexican-American groups to stop ignoring this source of power. It is not just our right to appeal to the Church to use its power effectively for the poor, it is our duty to do so. It should be as natural as appealing to government ... and we do that often enough.

Furthermore, we should be prepared to come to the defense of that priest, rabbi, minister, or layman of the Church, who out of commitment to truth and justice gets into a tight place with his pastor or bishop. It behooves us to stand with that man and help him see his trial through. It is our duty to see to it that his rights of conscience are respected and that no bishop, pastor or other higher body takes that God-given, human right away.

Finally, in a nutshell, what do we want the Church to do? We don't ask for more cathedrals. We don't ask for bigger churches or fine gifts. We ask for its presence with us, beside us, as Christ among us. We ask the Church to sacrifice with the people for social change, for justice, and for love or brother. We don't ask for words. We ask for deeds. We don't ask for paternalism. We ask for servanthood.

Chitra Banerjee Divakaruni

THE WALK

from *Leaving Yuba City*

~~~

Each Sunday evening the nuns took us
for a walk. We climbed carefully
in our patent-leather shoes up hillsides looped
with trails the color of earthworms. Below,
the school fell away, the sad green roofs
of the dormitories, the angled classrooms,
the refectory where we learned to cut
buttered bread into polite squares,
to eat bland stews and puddings. The sharp
metallic thrust of the church spire, small, then smaller,
and around it the town: bazaar, post office, the scab

Chitra Banerjee Divakaruni was born in 1956 in Kolkatta (Calcutta), India, and moved to the United States in 1976 to continue her education at Wright State University and the University of California, Berkeley. Divakaruni is a prize-winning poet, novelist, and short story writer and a professor of creative writing at the University of Houston in Texas. She is also actively involved with organizations that assist South Asian and South Asian–American women in abusive domestic situations, and with an organization providing educational support to children in poverty. The following selection first appeared in *Leaving Yuba City* in 1997.

coated donkeys. Straggle of huts
with hesitant woodfires in the yards. All
at a respectful distance, like the local children we passed,
tattered pants and swollen chilblained fingers
color of the torn sky, color of the Sacred Heart
in the painting of Jesus that hung above our beds
with his chest open.

We were trained not to talk to them,
runny-nosed kids with who-knew-what diseases, not even
to wave back, and of course it was improper
to stare. The nuns walked so fast,
already we were passing the plantation, the shrubs
lined up neatly, the thick glossy green
giving out a faint wild odor like our bodies
in bed after lights-out. Passing the pickers,
hill women with branch-scarred arms, bent
under huge baskets strapped to shoulder and head,
the cords in their thin necks
pulling like wires. Back at school
though Sister Dolores cracked the refectory ruler
down on our knuckles, we could not drink
our tea. It tasted salty as the bitten inside
of the mouth, its brown like the women's necks,
that same tense color.

But now we walk quicker because
it is drizzling. Drops fall on us from *pipul* leaves
shaped like eyes. We pull on
our grey rainhoods and step in time,
soldiers of Christ squelching through vales of mud.
We are singing, as always on walks,
the nuns leading us with choir-boy voices.

O Kindly Light, and then a song
about the Emerald Isle. Ireland, where they grew up,
these two Sisters not much older
than us. Mountain fog thickens like a cataract
over the sun's pale eye, it is stumbling-dark,
we must take a shortcut through the upper town. The nuns
motion us, *faster, faster,* an oval blur of hands
in long black sleeves.

Honeysuckle over a gate, lanterns
in front windows. In one, a woman in a blue sari
holds a baby, his fuzzy backlit head
against the curve of her shoulder. Smell of food
in the air, *real* food, onion pakoras, like our mothers
once made. Rain in our eyes, our mouths. Salt, salt.
A sudden streetlamp lights the nuns' faces, damp,
splotched with red like frostbitten
camellias. It prickles the backs of our throats.
The woman watches, wonder-eyed, as we pass
in our wet, determined shoes, singing
Beautiful Killarney, a long line of girls, all of us
so far from home.

Linda Gregg

THE SHOPPING-BAG LADY

in *Alma*

You told people I would know easily what the murdered
lady had in her sack which could prove she was happy
more or less. As if they were a game, the old women
who carry all they own in bags, maybe proudly,
without homes we think except the streets.
But if I could guess (nothing in sets for example),
I would not. They are like those men who lay their
few things on the ground in a park at the end of Hester.
For sale perhaps, but who can tell? Like her way
of getting money. Never asking. Sideways and disconcerting.
With no thanks, only judgment. "You are a nice girl,"
one said as she moved away and then stopped in front
of a bum sitting on the bench who yelled that he would
kill her if she did not get away from him. She walked

A poet and teacher, Linda Gregg was born in 1942 in Suffern, New York,
and grew up in Marin County, California. *Too Bright to See,* her first collection of poems, was published in 1981. Her other books include *Things and
Flesh, Sacraments of Desire*, and *Alma*, in which the selection included here
first appeared. Gregg is the recipient of multiple Pushcart Prizes, a
Guggenheim Fellowship, and the PEN/Voelcker Award for Poetry.

at an angle not exactly away but until she was the same
distance from each of us. Stood still, looking down.
Standing in our attention as if it were a palpable thing.
Like the city itself or the cold winter. Holding her hands.
And if there was disgrace, it was God's. The failure
was ours as she remained quiet near the concrete wall
with cars coming and the sound of the subway filling
and fading in the most important place we have yet
   devised.

THE CAMEL DRIVER AND THE ADDER

A Camel Driver, crossing the plains, stopped to rest where a caravan had halted and built a fire the night before; in the morning they had moved on before it had died out. As the night wind arose, it fanned the sparks and soon set all the brush-wood around on fire. In the midst of the brush-wood lay coiled an Adder, fast asleep. The flames, however, soon awoke him, but not until he was completely encircled by the fire. He was about to despair of his life, when he saw the Camel Driver and called upon him for aid. At first the Camel Driver hesitated, for he remembered the poisonous sting of the Adder. Still, he could not bear to see any living creature suffer, so he promised to help the Adder. He had a bag beneath his saddle. This he now drew forth and tied to the end of his spear. He then reached it over into the midst of the burning brush; the Adder crawled inside, and the Camel Driver drew him safely out of the fire.

Bidpai (or Pilpay) is the name attributed to the supposed author of the *Panchatantra* (also called *The Fables of Bidpai* or *Pilpay's Fables*). The *Panchatantra* (*Five Principles*) was originally a canonical collection of Hindu and Buddhist animal fables in poem and verse. Scholars believe it was composed in the third century BCE, but that it is based on older oral traditions that go back to the origins of language on the subcontinent. In the original Sanskrit version, a king asks a wise man, Vishnu Sharman, to teach his sons the ways of the world. Vishnu Sharman passes on his wisdom in the form of stories where animals speak like humans. This version of "The Camel Driver and the Adder" was adapted and translated by Maude Burrows Dunton in 1910.

"Now go your way," said the Camel Driver, loosening the neck of the bag so that the Adder could glide out. "Only remember the kindness which I have shown to you, and do you hereafter be kind to men in your turn."

"I confess," replied the Adder, slipping out on the ground, "that you have been kind to me, and yet I shall not go away until I have stung both you and your camel. I only leave it to you to decide whether I shall sting you first or the camel."

"What a monster of ingratitude you are!" cried the Camel Driver. "Is it right to return evil for good?"

"Such is the custom of men," said the Adder.

"You are not only ungrateful, but untruthful as well," the Camel Driver made reply. "It would be hard indeed for you to prove these words of yours. There is no other creature in the world, I venture to say, who will agree with you. If you can find out one other, I will allow you to sting me."

"Very well," responded the Adder, "let us put the question to yonder Cow."

The Cow stopped chewing her cud. "If you mean what is man's custom," she began, in answer to their question, "I must answer to my sorrow that he is wont to repay evil for good. For many years I have been the faithful servant of a farmer. Every day I have supplied him with milk to drink and rich cream for his butter. Now I am old and no longer able to serve him. So he has put me out in this pasture that I may grow fat, and only yesterday he brought the butcher to see me. To-morrow I am to be sold for beef. Surely this is repaying my kindness with evil."

"You see," said the Adder to the Camel Driver, "that what I said is true. Get ready for me to sting you. Shall it be you or the camel first?"

"Hold," replied the Camel Driver. "In court a decree is not passed without the testimony of two witnesses. Bring another witness, and if he agrees with the Cow, you may do with me as you please."

The Adder looked about him and saw that they were standing beneath a huge palm-tree. "Let us put the question to the tree," he said.

When the Palm had heard their question, he shook his great branches sadly. "Experience has taught me," he moaned, "that for every favor you do to men, you must expect some injury in return. I stand here in the desert, doing harm to none and good to many. Every traveler who comes by can rest beneath my shade. I bear dates for his refreshment, and gladly give my sap to quench his thirst. Yet when the traveler has eaten and slept beneath my shade, he looks up into my branches and says to himself: 'That branch would make me a good cane, or handle for my axe,' or 'What splendid wood there is in this tree! I must cut off a limb to make some new doors for my house.' And I must consent to this without a murmur. Thus is my kindness returned by men."

"The two witnesses have now testified," spoke the Adder, "and agree. Which shall I bite first, you or the camel?"

But just at that moment a Fox ran by, and the Camel Driver pleaded that they might hear one more testimony. The Adder was so pleased with what the Cow and the Tree had said, that he readily agreed to listen to the Fox.

When the Camel Driver had finished telling the whole tale to the Fox, the Fox laughed out loud. "You seem to be a clever fellow," he replied to the Camel Driver. "Why do you tell me such a falsehood?"

"Indeed, he is telling you nothing but the truth," the Adder hastened to assure the Fox.

Again the Fox laughed outright. "Do you mean to tell me," he asked scornfully, "that such a large Adder as you could possibly get into such a small bag?"

"If you do not believe it, I will crawl in again and show you," answered the Adder.

"Well," responded the Fox, thoughtfully, "if I see you in there with my own eyes, then I will consent to give my answer to your question."

The Camel Driver straightway held the bag open, and the Adder crept in and coiled up in the bottom.

"Be quick now," cried the Fox, "and draw the string. Any creature so lacking in gratitude as this Adder deserves nothing but death."

Valerie Martin

A RICH YOUNG MAN ON THE ROAD

from *Salvation: Scenes from the Life of St. Francis*

In the morning, when he leaves Foligno, his horse knows they are on the last leg of their journey and plods along at a steady pace, requiring neither guidance nor urging. Francesco is in no hurry, for his home has none of the charms of the adventure he brings to a close with his return. Everyone will want to hear about what he has seen; even his father will listen to his descriptions of Roma, the city of wonders, of the towers and bridges, the palace of the Laterano, and all the shrines and sacred relics he visited. But he will not mention the event that most fired his imagination, because anyone who hears of it will say it was a shameful, foolish exploit, the folly of a wealthy and useless young man who hasn't the sense to appreciate his position. Suppose, his father would exclaim, just suppose some neighbor from Assisi had recognized him. How could he hold his head up in the town?

For some time, something has been coming to Francesco. He cannot be sure what it is or when it began, but he can feel it moving

---

Valerie Martin was born in Missouri in 1948 and went on to graduate from the MFA Program for Poets and Writers at the University of Massachusetts, Amherst. She has published numerous short story collections and novels, including the Orange Prize–winning *Property* and *Mary Reilly,* which was adapted into a feature film. The selection below is drawn from Martin's 2001 nonfiction work, *Salvation: Scenes from the Life of St. Francis*, which explores the life of Saint Francis of Assisi.

toward him, gathering momentum. His dreams are full of triumph; voices counsel him, showing him scenes of great glory with a promise: All this will be yours. But when he is awake there are no triumphs, though he is free to indulge himself in whatever pursuits and amusements his father's money can buy. He might decide to arrange a feast or organize a singing group or, on a feast day when his father has no use for him in the stalls, he might walk into the countryside and explore the woods and streams, the various caverns in which, as a boy, he searched for hidden treasure. Nothing obstructs him, no one contradicts him. If he says he wants to be a knight, he is encouraged at every turning and provided with armor; arrangements are made for him to join a noble party, though his parents must know, he knows, that he has neither the health nor skill at arms for such a venture. When he made up his mind to visit the holy places in Roma, he received no objections. His mother provided him with a pouch full of bread and sweets, his father offered the better of their horses, and both parents made sure that his clothes were the finest and that he carried enough silver to make proper offerings at the shrines.

His horse shakes his head as if to remind him that he has at least some small obligations as a rider, and he comes to himself with a start. It is a spring day of stunning perfection; the air is cool and fresh, the sky overhead as blue as the mantle of the Holy Virgin, and on either side of the road, the fields stretch away pleasantly, olive trees on one side, grain on the other, bordered by ranks of cypress and pine. There are contingents of chaffinches chirping in the smoky leaves of the olive trees and swallows whirling overhead in undulating formations, like fallen leaves in a stream. He passes two peasants digging mud from the side of the road and another leading a reluctant goat by a bit of dirty rope. They glance at him as he goes by, a rich young man, carefree, and they give terse responses to his friendly salutations, for they have work to do and cannot ride about the countryside dressed like a fop on a fine horse. The goat makes a strangled cry, struggling at the end of his rope while his owner curses and threatens him, swearing he will not live another day. Francesco looks away, wounded as he always is by displays of pointless ferocity. He has seen too many in the last few days, especially in the city, where men and beasts are crowded together and tempers flare at the most innocent remark. At the Basilica of San Pietro he saw two men fighting on the very steps, and later, when he came out, there was such a quantity of blood—though no sign of the combatants—that he thought one had surely killed the other. And it was there, as he stood looking about nervously, that a voice called to him from the shadows of the vestibule and the peculiar and wonderful adventure began.

"Have you given it all to the thieving priests?" the voice inquired. "Or isn't there a coin to spare for those that may truly have need of it?"

Francesco stepped away from the blood soaking into the paving stones and approached the man, if he was a man, for all he could see was one bare foot, so swollen and bruised it looked more like a rotten vegetable than human flesh. "I have not given it all," he said, stepping in under the arch. He could see nothing, for the daylight had dazzled his eyes and now the shadows confounded them, but he heard the harsh laughter of several men. One of them said, "Here is the last honest man in the world," and another responded, "It proves what I have been telling you, that the judgment day is near, for here is the new Christ among us to prove it."

"And the pope is the Antichrist," the first speaker declared. Francesco gazed down as his eyes became accustomed to the dark. There were three of them; two were old fellows, the third, the one who had announced the imminence of the judgment day, was a youth of perhaps Francesco's age with thick blond hair, scarcely any beard, and an open, ingenuous expression. He looked Francesco up and down with a bold, rapacious eye. "Now that's a fine cloak such as only a nobleman could afford," he observed.

"I am not a nobleman," Francesco replied. "But my father is a cloth merchant."

The young man got to his feet awkwardly, pressing his hands behind him against the wall. When he was halfway up, he lurched forward onto his one good leg. The other was stunted and shriveled, the muscles in the calf atrophied, the skin tight against the bone. He could put his weight on this leg long enough to make a hopping step. He crossed the space to Francesco with a rolling, out-of-kilter gait,

175

then propped himself against the other wall. "Wouldn't I look a prince in such a cloak as that?" he said, smiling up into Francesco's face. He was missing the lower teeth on the right side of his face, and when he smiled his lower lip fell in over the gap.

"For the love of God," said one of the old men, "give us a coin if you won't give us the cloak."

Francesco turned, narrowing his eyes to make out the speaker, crouched beside his friend, who rubbed his face with his palms and echoed, "Yes, give us a coin, for the love of God."

"For the love of God," Francesco said.

In the church he had seen the faithful crowded around the tomb of the apostle Pietro. As the pilgrims arrived at the rail, each one placed a coin on the tomb ledge and said a brief prayer. Francesco was shocked by the paltriness of these contributions. Many of these people were dressed in the best silks, woolens, and furs, their fingers and throats covered in jewels, even the clasps on their girdles made of beaten gold, but when it came time to make an offering in the name of the apostle who was chosen by Christ to protect his church, who had been his closest companion, the witness of his crucifixion and triumph over death, who was himself crucified in this very place and gave up his life willingly in the cause of his faith, then these wealthy men and women dug into their purses and came up with a single coin. What could account for such stinginess? Did they think the Son of God was a beggar who would be grateful for their narrow charity? Did his sublime sacrifice require no more repayment than this? When Francesco's turn came, he opened his purse, took out a handful of coins, and scattered them across the stones, where they rolled and spun and slipped through the rail, clattering on the tomb. The other pilgrims turned to stare at him, and he glared back proudly, though he did not speak his reproving thoughts. Then he strode out through the crowd without looking back.

Outside, he had found the bloody steps, and then these beggars called to him, claiming whatever he had left "for the love of God."

Francesco gazed into the eager eyes of the young man who seemed to imagine no greater glory than to have such a cloak. "Will you trade your clothes for mine?" he said. For reply the youth gave a hoot of delight. The old men cackled together; here was an odd business. "Will you let me sit here with you?" Francesco continued as he pulled off his cloak, his doublet, his leather girdle. The young man began stripping off his rags, which took no time at all, as he had only a short sackcloth tunic and a pair of filthy breeches embroidered with holes. "I will have to take my other clothes back when I go," Francesco explained, examining the contents of his purse, "but I will leave you my cloak and all but two of these coins; I will need that much for my journey home."

"Giuseppe is right," one of the old men remarked. "This proves God's judgment is nigh on this world."

Francesco laughed. He was half naked, bent over to pull off his leggings. Giuseppe had already donned his shirt. "And will you share your food with me?" he added. This set them all into laughter. "Oh yes," they agreed. Giuseppe slid down the wall to the stones, clutching his new cloak, which he had bundled in his arms like a baby. "You are welcome to everything we have," he announced, with the casual grace and courtesy of a lord offering hospitality to some bedraggled traveler who has arrived at his door after days of wandering.

So Francesco stayed with them all day, and everyone who saw him assumed he was a beggar. He experienced the most thrilling and exotic sensations, he who had always been admired and envied in his own town. Even when he was taken prisoner and shoved into a black cell in Perugia, he had been treated respectfully and lodged with the nobility, because the Perugians knew his father was rich and would pay a heavy ransom for his release. Now he was an object of derision, the butt of cruel jokes. The passing crowd never stopped mocking the company in the vestibule, calling them thieves and felons and complaining that their presence fouled the pure air of the holy shrine. "For the love of God," Francesco pleaded with his hand out, and he saw contempt in the faces of all who heard him, even in those who vouchsafed to toss him a coin. It was a mystery, impenetrable and tantalizing. By changing his clothes and taking these low fellows as his companions, he was himself entirely altered. He would not, he knew, even admit to his own name, for to do so would be to shame his father, who was proud, who held his head high and believed his son to be one of the many excellent products of his own industry and business acumen.

What was this sensation, so delicious and unexpected, when a lady paused to look down at him with a haughty yet pitying eye? As he stretched out his hand to her, she turned away, drawing her skirt in close, lest he should touch it. Did she thank heaven no son of hers would ever be found in such disgraceful circumstances? And what would she say if she knew this importuning beggar was a sham, deserving neither charity nor pity, for he had a horse, a purse, fine clothes, and would return in a day or two to his father's comfortable house, where a servant would greet him at the door?

When evening came, two more men joined the group, and they all sat down in the street to share the food they had begged. It was poor stuff, black bread and a little grain which they made into a porridge, for one of them possessed an iron pot and another had begged some sticks of firewood. Francesco listened to their lively conversation, full of profanity and derision for the vanity of the world. Though he was wealthy, they included him, as if he, too, did not know when he would find a meal again. After they had eaten, he changed back into his own clothes and laughed with them over the miracle of his transformation. Yet he felt an aching premonitory sadness as the linen settled across his shoulders: it was as though he was putting on a costume that would deceive only a fool, for a wise man would see at once that it did not suit him, that it must belong to some other man, an elegant, stylish young man, and that Francesco, in his own clothes, was an impostor. He folded the cloak and laid it in Giuseppe's lap, accepting his enthusiastic blessing and the boisterous farewells of the others who promised him their hospitality whenever he should return. Then, bowing and waving as they repeatedly called out his name, he wandered into the dark streets alone.

Now he is himself again, but not himself; something has changed, and the world looks different because of it. He has acquired, among other novelties, a memory he will not share. His horse carries him back over the same road he traveled. His senses are open; he is prey to sudden and conflicting emotions; he sees himself from the outside, and he is not entirely gratified by what he sees.

His back is stiff and sore from days of riding and from the long rounds of the shrines. He shrugs, attempting to shake out the soreness, and rolls his head in a slow circle, easing the knotted muscles in his neck. As he does this, his horse starts, making a panicked sidestep that nearly unseats him. He catches up the reins as he lifts himself out of the saddle, then, when he drops back into his seat, he loosens his knees, gripping the horse's flanks with his calves. He knows as he goes through these automatic calming responses that there is something in the road just ahead, something that was not there a moment ago. The horse comes to a standstill in a cloud of dust that rises to his knees, and he stands working his head back and forth against the bit. Francesco rests a hand upon his mane and says his name softly, reassuring him as he looks down past the foaming lips to see what has so terrified this normally reliable creature.

The leper stands in the middle of the road, perfectly still. One hand rests on the bell cord around his neck, the other hangs limply at his side. He is dressed in a filthy garment, patched together from bits of sacking and undyed wool, which hangs loosely upon his emaciated body. He regards Francesco and the horse steadily, his head slightly turned and his chin lifted, the better to see them, for his disease has eaten away half of his face and he has only one eye.

Francesco does not speak, he cannot move. They face each other on the road, and the sun pours down over them, so that there are no shadows anywhere, nothing to soften or dim the reality of this encounter and nowhere to hide from the necessity of playing it out. The leper's eye drills into Francesco; he can feel it penetrating into his brain. From childhood he has had a horror of lepers, and he has always avoided the *lazaretto* at the foot of Mount Subasio, where they sometimes congregate in the road, ringing their bells and calling out for alms. The stench rising from their rotting flesh, their grotesque faces, their phlegmy, guttural voices, pursue him in dreams, from which he wakes sweating and shouting for help.

But this is no dream, and there is no point in shouting now, for no one will hear. He glances back down the road and into the neat ranks of the olive trees. The world is uncommonly still. Even the birds have been silenced, frightened, no doubt, by the brief commotion of the horse.

He could ride on. There is no reason to stop. As he passes, he can throw down his last coin to the leper. His horse lifts one hoof and paws the dirt. It is time to go on, to go home. As Francesco drops his hand to the reins, his eyes fall upon his own expensive, well-fitting glove, and it dawns on him that this leper is not wearing gloves, which is odd; he and his kind are required to wear them when they leave their hospitals, just as they are required to wear and ring their bells to warn the unwary traveler of their approach.

Again Francesco looks down upon the solitary figure of the leper, who has not moved a muscle. His hand is still wrapped about the cord of the bell, his head arrested at an angle. He is like a weatherbeaten statue, and Francesco has the sense that he has been standing there, in this path, forever.

Something has been coming toward him, or he has been coming to something; he has known this for some time, and he has bent his energy in the direction of finding out what it might be. This was the reason for his pilgrimage to Roma. At the shrines he recited the requisite prayers, gazed upon the relics, bones, bits of hair and cloth, vials of blood and tears, proffered the proper offerings, but he did not feel the burden of his sins lifted, and this spiritual restlessness drove him on. Only when he was with the beggars beneath the portico at the basilica did he feel some respite from this condition of urgent expectancy.

He is in the grip of it again as he swings one leg over the saddle and drops to the ground beside his horse. The stillness of the world makes every sound acute: the clinking of the bridle chain as he leads the animal to a green patch nearby, the sound of grass tearing, and then the big jaws grinding as the horse chews the first clump. Francesco runs his hands through his hair, bats the dust from the front of this doublet, and turns to face the man, who is there, waiting for him.

The leper watches him with interest. His blasted face is bathed in sunlight; the black hole that was his eye has a steely sheen, and a few moist drops on his lips glitter like precious stones. He moves at last, releasing his bell cord and extending his hand slowly, palm up before him.

This supplicating gesture releases Francesco, for it dictates the countergesture, which he realizes he longs to make. Without hesitation, he strides across the distance separating him from his obligation, smiling all the while as if stepping out to greet an old and dear friend. He opens his purse, extracts the thin piece of silver inside it, and closes it up again. He is closer now than he has ever been to one of these unfortunate beings, and the old familiar reaction of disgust and nausea rises up, nearly choking him, but he battles it down. He can hear the rasp of the leper's diseased, difficult breath, rattling and wet. The war between Francesco's will and his reluctance overmasters him; he misses a step, recovers, then drops to one knee before the outstretched hand, which is hardly recognizable as a hand but is rather a lumpish, misshapen thing, the fingers so swollen and callused that they are hardly differentiated, the flesh as hard as an animal's rough paw. Carefully, Francesco places his coin in the open palm, where it glitters, hot and white. For a moment he tries to form some simple speech, some pleasantry that will restore him to the ordinary world, but even as he struggles, he understands that this world is gone from him now, that there is no turning back; it was only so much smoke, blinding and confusing him, but he has come through it somehow, he has found the source of it, and now, at last, he is standing in the fire. Tenderly he takes the leper's hand, tenderly he brings it to his lips. At once his mouth is flooded with an unearthly sweetness, which pours over his tongue, sweet and hot, burning his throat and bringing sudden tears to his eyes. These tears moisten the corrupted hand he presses to his mouth. His ears are filled with the sound of wind, and he can feel the wind chilling his face, a cold, harsh wind blowing toward him from the future, blowing away everything that has come before this moment, which he has longed for and dreaded, as if he thought he might not live through it. He reaches up, clinging to the leper's tunic, for the wind is so strong, so cold, he fears he cannot stand against it. Behind him, the horse lifts his head from his grazing and lets out a long, impatient whinny, but Francesco does not hear him. He is there in the road, rising to his feet, and the leper assists him, holding him by the shoulders. Then the two men clutch each other, their faces pressed close together, their arms entwined. The sun beats down, the air is hot and still, yet they appear to be caught in a whirlwind. Their clothes whip about; their hair stands on end; they hold on to each other for dear life.

Rumi

SAY YES QUICKLY

Forget your life. Say *God is Great.* Get up.
You think you know what time it is. It's time to pray.
You've carved so many little figurines, too many.
Don't knock on any random door like a beggar.
Reach your long hand out to another door, beyond where
you go on the street, the street
where everyone says, "How are you?"
and no one says *How aren't you?*

Tomorrow you'll see what you've broken and torn tonight,
thrashing in the dark. Inside you
there's an artist you don't know about.
He's not interested in how things look different in the
    moonlight.

Mowlana Jalaluddin Rumi, best known to English-speaking audiences as Rumi, is considered to be one of the greatest of Sufi poets. Born in 1207 in Balkh (now Afghanistan), Rumi was a teacher, theologian, and philosopher, as well as a mystic poet, whose influence spread throughout Afghanistan and central Asia, Turkey, and India. His most significant work is the *Mathnawi,* a multivolume work of stories and lyric poetry on teaching and Sufi lore. He also brought us the Mawlawiya (Mevlevi), a Sufi order that engages dance in its spiritual practices and that is better known in the West as the Whirling Dervishes. This translation was done by John Moyne and Coleman Barks.

If you are here unfaithfully with us,
you're causing terrible damage.
If you've opened your loving to God's love,
you're helping people you don't know
      and have never seen.

Is what I say true? Say *yes* quickly,
if you know, if you've known it
from before the beginning of the universe.

Mikhail Naimy

HIS GRACE

~~~

I was having supper at a Syrian restaurant in New York with a friend of mine. It was after nine and the place had emptied of customers; the owner came over and sat with us, adding his own interesting anecdotes to help us consume and digest his fare. He was a convivial fellow, who took a liking to us and went out of his way to please us because we were regulars. Indicating his watch, my friend said to him: "We're late tonight, Abu 'Assaf; I imagine you're ready to shut up shop and go home, so don't delay on account of us."

Abu 'Assaf shook his head and swore he counted it an honor to sit with us and would stay open on our account until midnight; and that both he and his restaurant were at our disposal. He added that he seldom locked his door before ten o'clock, because "the Bey" never came before half-past nine.

We both asked him the same question at once: "Who's 'the Bey,' Abu 'Assaf?"

Mikhail Naimy (or Mikha'il Na'ima) was born in 1889 in Mount Sannine in what is now Lebanon. Naimy studied at the Baskinta school, the Russian Teachers' Institute in Nazareth, the Theological Seminary in Poltava, Ukraine, and the University of Washington. After graduating and beginning his writing career in Walla Walla, Washington, Naimy moved to New York, where he, along with Khalil Gibran and several other writers, founded the New York Pen League, a movement dedicated to the rebirth of Arabic literature. Naimy wrote ninety-nine books before his death in Baskinta in 1988. "His Grace" was written around 1925; the translation here is by J. A. Perry.

You would have thought we had blasphemed against the prophets and saints, whom Abu 'Assaf worshipped more than his Lord, or had denied the existence of the Almighty, or at least found a beetle in our soup. Abu 'Assaf's eyes widened and he said, as if he could not believe his ears, "Are you joking, or do you really not know the Bey? How can you not know him?"

And before Abu 'Assaf could get over his amazement at our utter ignorance, the door opened, and in came a man tall and erect, narrow-shouldered and pot-bellied, with long hands and fingers. In his right hand he carried a stick, crooked as a dog's hind leg, and in his left an Arabic newspaper. He wore a suit consisting of gray trousers and a brown jacket, all worn and frayed at the edges, from which dangled threads of varying lengths. All I could see of his face at first was a pair of bushy whiskers that reached right up to his ears, a bulbous nose and leathery brown skin.

The newcomer strode slowly to the back of the restaurant, laid his stick and his hat on one side of the table, sat down and began to read his paper. Intrigued by his curious costume and demeanor, I studied his features more closely. What struck me as most odd about him was the shape of his head, like a pinecone, the size of his ears, flat and stuck to the side of his head like two pieces of dough, and his short hair, which began little more than an inch above his eyebrows.

"Abu 'Assaf, bring me a zucchini with stuffed vineleaves, tripe with *hummus, hummus* and sesame oil, and a bit of watermelon," said our visitor, without raising his eyes from his newspaper, and in a voice accustomed to giving orders since early youth without risk of refusal. The moment he saw him come in, Abu 'Assaf had scurried to the kitchen; he prepared his order in a trice and brought it to him with every sign of awe and reverence, and without uttering a word, as if his client were some redoubtable potentate. Abu 'Assaf bustled back and forth with plates and dishes until the visitor finished his meal, put on his hat, picked up his stick in one hand and his newspaper in the other, and left as he had arrived—with a slow, steady pace, looking neither left nor right, and without paying Abu 'Assaf a solitary cent.

A moment later, Abu 'Assaf came back to us, apologizing for having neglected us while this third customer was in the restaurant, but in strangely subdued tones, as if tongue-tied. Before we could reply at all, he told us: "That was the Bey. Did you see him?"

We asked him "The Bey's" name and what he did, and he told us.

"His name is As'ad al-Da'waq, and he is from my own village in Lebanon—the last of the sheikhs of the house of Da'waq, who have ruled our village for a long time. Their power was absolute: the local people were like their slaves, they did not own so much as a clod of the land they tilled. Then after a while, fortune turned against them, as it has against so many other emirs and sheikhs. One of their former tenants emigrated to America, came back rich and bought a large part of the land that had belonged to the Da'waq estate. And so the house of Da'waq steadily declined generation after generation, until the only one left was Sheikh As'ad, and all *he* had left was the title and astronomical debts.

"Then it so happened that one of the villagers, and a former servant of Sheikh As'ad's at that, amassed a great deal of money in America, then returned home, built a splendid mansion and bought himself the title of 'Bey.' You know how such titles are bought and sold in our part of the world.

"Up to that time Sheikh As'ad had been happy enough, content with his lot, satisfied still to be the local sheikh, the accepted and unrivaled celebrity. But once there was a Bey in the community, there was no longer any place for a mere sheikh. And how could a Da'waq possibly accept that there should be someone in the community of higher status than himself?

"Worse than anything was the fact that this Bey was a former servant of the Sheikh. This was a disgrace not to be endured! And all of a sudden the Sheikh changed completely, as if an unseen hand had whisked him away and substituted someone else. He no longer went to church, though he never used to miss a single Sunday or holiday; he forbade his wife to set foot outside the house; he took his sons away from school; he locked his doors to all comers and never received a single visitor.

"When he walked through the streets he would not look to left or right. When passers-by greeted him, he never returned the greeting. And if he happened to run across the Bey, he would turn up his nose, twirl his moustache, swing his stick, clear his throat loudly and spit on the ground with full force.

"The villagers were baffled by the Sheikh's behavior, and many and varied were the interpretations put on it. Some said that all the sins and crimes of the house of Da'waq had been hung like a millstone round his neck, and as a result the Sheikh had lost his wits. Some said he had simply become chronically unsociable ever since the glory of his ancestors had dwindled and disappeared. Others thought the Sheikh was too embarrassed to face people because of his many debts, and that he would not receive visitors because he had nothing to offer them in the way of hospitality.

"So the talk went on in the village, till the news went around that the Sheikh had been snatched away by a jinni—for nobody had seen hide nor hair of him for nearly a week. The community was most alarmed, and the elders assembled, headed by the priest, to look into this serious matter and see how they might save the Sheikh from the clutches of the jinni, or else get rid of the rest of the Sheikh's family in order to ward off from the village the danger of evil spirits. And while they were gabbling prayers and charms in utter consternation, and the priest was explaining how they would have to break into the Sheikh's house to sprinkle it with holy water, and send his wife and children away from the village for fear that by means of them the jinn might extend their power over the whole community—lo and behold, the Sheikh suddenly reappeared. For a moment they all sat rooted to the spot; then they rose to their feet as one man. They remained standing like statues for several minutes, without a one opening his mouth, totally numbed by fear. Finally the priest plucked up courage and, first crossing himself, quavered: 'Welcome back, Sheikh As'ad!'

"With a twirl of his moustache, the Sheikh broke in, 'His Grace As'ad Bey Da'waq, Father, His Grace As'ad Bey, if you please. Sheikh As'ad is dead, and as from now is succeeded by His Grace As'ad Bey!'

"That night the church bell pealed for almost an hour, announcing to the populace the glad tidings that their Sheikh had become a Bey. The news spread through the village like wildfire that the reason Sheikh As'ad had been absent so long was that the Ottoman governor had summoned him to tell him of his elevation to the beylik. The villagers used up all their dry straw and petroleum for bonfires, danced the *dabka*, cheered 'their Bey' to the echo; and for the last time in the history of the Da'waq family their house was once more packed with throngs of people, once again the lights shone from its balconies, again it was surrounded by young men and girls cheering and singing and ululating, and all convinced that the glory of the house of Da'waq was on the way to being fully restored and might well surpass that of the previous generations.

"The first thing Sheikh As'ad did on becoming 'His Grace' was to set his wife at liberty and send his children back to school (admonishing the teacher to seat them at the head of the class since they were sons of '*the* Bey,' and not to take it into his head ever to place the sons of the other bey above them), and to call a truce with God and resume his visits to church.

"So proud was he of his new title that he refused to accept a letter that came addressed merely to 'His Excellency As'ad Bey Da'waq,' and notified the village postmaster that henceforth he would not accept any mail unless correctly addressed to 'His Grace As'ad Bey.' He no longer referred to his wife by her name, or even her maiden name, in front of other people, but by the title of 'Begum.' 'The Begum is at home,' he would say, or, 'The Begum is not at home to visitors today,' and resented anyone's mentioning her in his presence without using her title.

"And here I must take you back to the first bey, the one who was a servant of Sheikh As'ad's and emigrated, came back wealthy and bought himself the title before the Sheikh obtained his. This man, whose name was Roukus Nusour, harbored a grudge against the Sheikh: he had asked the hand of the Sheikh's daughter in marriage, at which the Sheikh had flown into a rage and driven him from the house with the injunction never again to set foot on his threshold and not to forget he was a servant, and how dare a servant ask the hand of a gentleman's daughter? Roukus Nusour left the Sheikh's house with a burning resentment. He resolved to deal him a crushing blow in his most sensitive spot—his pride in his ancestry, and in still being the foremost in the whole community in rank and station. So he went and bought himself the title of Bey, and thought he had floored his adversary for good. All too soon, however, word spread of the Sheikh's journey to the provincial capital and his return with the beylik. What was to be done now?

"Roukus Nusour racked his brains for a way to revenge himself on his rival, till one day a novel thought occurred to him. Where had the Sheikh got the money to buy himself a beylik, when Roukus Nusour knew that he was up to his ears in debt and had long since pawned all but what he stood up in?

"This thought led him to the provincial capital, where he made extensive inquiries only to find no one who knew the Sheikh or had even heard of him; and it became abundantly clear that the Sheikh had not visited the governor's seat and had not obtained any beylik, but had fabricated the whole thing in order to fight his rival with his own weapon. And the trick had taken in the villagers because they were simple folk, to whom the name of Da'waq meant power and glory.

"No sooner had Roukus Nusour returned with his discovery than the news spread from house to house in record time that 'His Grace As'ad Bey Da'waq' was not His Grace at all, but was still plain Sheikh As'ad. That same day the Sheikh left the village, and no more was heard of him.

"Time went by, and I emigrated to America and opened a restaurant in New York. One night I happened to overhear three of my customers talking about 'His Grace the Bey': one of them said he had seen him in a park a long way from the Syrian neighborhood, polishing shoes. Another mentioned that he sold newspapers in the street. The third said he had found him one night sleeping on a bench in a subway station. I asked them who this 'Bey' was they were talking about, and was told he was a Syrian who called himself As'ad Bey Da'waq, and defied anyone to call him by name without using his title. Now I was certain that Sheikh As'ad was in New York, and became keen to meet him. And only a few days later, I saw him come in of his own accord.

"It was on a night when I had no other customers, about half-past nine. I recognized him at once, and knew that he recognized me, and I rushed up to shake his hand and welcome him. He didn't give me his hand or ask how I was keeping or anything. And when I made the inevitable slip of tongue and greeted him as 'Sheikh As'ad,' he glared at me enough to wither me on the spot and said: 'As'ad *Bey*, Bu 'Assaf! As'ad Bey!' Then he went straight to a table, sat down, and ordered a meal. I brought him all he ordered and more, and tried several times to talk to him, but he wouldn't speak to me. When he had eaten his fill he stood up, said: 'Put it on my bill, Abu 'Assaf,' and left.

"Almost seven years have passed since that happened, and ever since, every night without fail, he visits me at the same time and in the very same way as he first did. He comes as you saw him tonight: with a walking-stick, and a newspaper he pretends to read, though I know he can't read or write much. Then he eats, and leaves without paying a cent, and I wish him goodnight and thank him for coming.

"I just can't bring myself to disillusion him. It wouldn't be right. He's nothing if not a Da'waq. I've offered him money more than once, but he won't accept a penny. Poor fellow!'"

And our host heaved a deep sigh that came from the very depths of his heart.

عام

PART III

How Do I Serve?

In the actual human situation, "to be" is inseparable from "how to be."

Rabbi Abraham Joshua Heschel

Let's imagine for a moment that we know with great certainty why we are engaging in service and whom our service will benefit. Still there is this question: what should we actually do? How should we serve?

The question of how to serve can be answered in all sorts of ways. We could give a man a fish, teach a man to fish, pray for fish, transcend fish, act like a fish, advocate for a policy that increases the number of fish, and so on. Beneath any one answer or any combination of answers lies the hope, presumably, that the service we provide will be good for those we serve and good for us, too. This is, of course, a hope, and with the hope comes this accompanying concern: what is best for those we serve might interfere with what is best for us, or what is best for us might not leave room for others. So what should we think about, what criteria—if any—should we adhere to, when we decide how to serve?

In a 1930 letter included in this section, Mahatma Gandhi, internationally know for his resistance to tyranny through nonviolence, declares that voluntary service "must take precedence over service of self." In this view, the "how" of service is primarily an internal matter: how do we understand ourselves as we serve? How do we feel about the service we provide? Political writer George

Orwell, in a passage from his larger essay on Gandhi, writes that Gandhi would have us become saints rather than human beings—a way of serving and living that Orwell deems neither possible nor desirable. But Orwell, like Gandhi, emphasizes especially the internal character of our service.

The Hindu monk Swami Vivekananda speaks to the internal character of service as well, but he also makes the clear assertion that, in his view, physical help is "the last" and "the least" kind of help we can give. British poet and priest Gerard Manley Hopkins's poem "God's Grandeur" seems to go at least one step further than Vivekananda and to imply that our physical activity, our work, has never been anything but harmful. Yet Hopkins nonetheless holds out hope for "renewal," a hope that cannot be separated from his faith in God.

Chilean poet Gabriela Mistral and sixteenth president of the United States Abraham Lincoln, in different ways, connect Gandhi and Hopkins in an active form of inaction: the fast. In both cases, the fast seems to serve as a corrective to future action and as a kind of penance for what has come before. Yiddish writer Sholom Aleichem's short story "Reb Yozifl and the Contractor" sheds a softer light on the ways in which guilt can be used to motivate service. Japanese poet Ryokan's poem shares Aleichem's playful tone but ends up in a very different place: play, rather than work, seems to be the highest form of service. Rumi's poem "Come Out and Give Something" is playful in tone but serious about the internal alchemy it describes.

For Maimonides, a renowned twelfth-century Jewish philosopher, the highest form of service, or of giving, consists at the start in taking the hand of another. Irish writer William Trevor's short story "Sitting with the Dead" also illustrates the importance of being with, almost irrespective of what action is actually performed. Novelist Mark Helprin's short story describes a different kind of fellowship in service in which few of the feelings seem to be positive.

American writer Anne Lamott's essay "Why I Make Sam Go to Church" makes a moving case for the relationship between being with fellow churchgoers and acting in certain ways: if we are around certain kinds of people, Lamott implies, we are more likely to become people that give to those in need. Islamic scholar Umar Faruq Abd-Allah's essay on Islam as a religion of mercy establishes a similar link between living within a religious community and generosity to those around us.

Kabir, a fifteenth-century revered Indian mystic, in his poem "The Yogi Dyes His Garments," returns us to the question of whether religious or spiritual practice is primarily external or internal. But if Kabir's yogi dyes his garments and not his heart, the minister at the center of American writer Peggy Payne's novel *Revelation* has a different problem: he is concerned that he will reveal too much of himself to his congregation and wonders whether he ought to serve by withholding or by sharing even what is bound to unsettle. Prize-winning American poet Mary Oliver, in "The Buddha's Last Instruction," depicts an unsettled crowd surrounding the Buddha as he approaches his death, perhaps because the kind of service the Buddha espouses is at once confounding and enlightening.

Service, for the Buddha and for all of us, can be both confounding and enlightening. It can be internally and externally transformative, and it may be both spiritually and materially needful. The significance of service, in every case, deepens as we reflect on why we serve, whom we serve, and how we serve.

علم

Gerard Manley Hopkins

GOD'S GRANDEUR

The world is charged with the grandeur of God.
　　It will flame out, like shining from shook foil;
　　It gathers to a greatness, like the ooze of oil
Crushed. Why do men then now not reck his rod?
Generations have trod, have trod, have trod;
　　And all is seared with trade; bleared, smeared with toil;
　　And wears man's smudge and shares man's smell: the soil
Is bare now, nor foot can feel, being shod.

And for all this, nature is never spent;
　　There lives the dearest freshness deep down things;
And though the last lights off the black West went
　　Oh, morning, at the brown brink eastward, springs—
Because the Holy Ghost over the bent
　　World broods with warm breast and with ah! bright wings.

Born in England in 1844, Gerard Manley Hopkins began writing poetry at an early age. In his early twenties, Hopkins converted from Anglicanism to Roman Catholicism and in 1868 joined the Society of Jesuits. Hopkins continued to write poems thereafter, while serving as a priest and university teacher, but he burned most of his early poems out of a deep sense of conflict between his art and his faith, and he published very little in his lifetime. "God's Grandeur" appeared in the first collection of his poems, edited by his friend Robert Bridges and published in 1918, long after the poet's death in 1889.

THE SECRET OF WORK

in *The Complete Works, I:3*

~~~~~

Helping others physically, by removing their physical needs, is indeed great, but the help is great according as the need is greater and according as the help is far reaching. If a man's wants can be removed for an hour, it is helping him indeed; if his wants can be removed for a year, it will be more help to him; but if his wants can be removed for ever, it is surely the greatest help that can be given him. Spiritual knowledge is the only thing that can destroy our miseries for ever; any other knowledge satisfies wants only for a time. It is only with the knowledge of the spirit that the faculty of want is annihilated for ever; so helping man spiritually is the highest help that can be given to him. He who gives man spiritual knowledge is the greatest benefactor of mankind and as such we always find that those were the most powerful of men who helped man in his spiritual

---

Swami Vivekananda was born to an aristocratic family in Kolkatta (Calcutta), India, in 1863. As a young man, Swami Vivekananda embraced agnosticism and science, but after studying with Sri Ramakrishna, Vivekananda became a Hindu monk and traveled around India. In 1893, Vivekananda represented Hinduism at Chicago's Parliament of the World's Religions. He went on to raise awareness of Vedanta, Yoga, and Hinduism throughout the United States and England before returning to India to found the Ramakrishna Math and Mission. One of India's leading nation-builders, Swami Vivekananda died in 1902. This selection is the third chapter in his volume on karma yoga.

needs, because spirituality is the true basis of all our activities in life. A spiritually strong and sound man will be strong in every other respect, if he so wishes. Until there is spiritual strength in man even physical needs cannot be well satisfied. Next to spiritual comes intellectual help. The gift of knowledge is a far higher gift than that of food and clothes; it is even higher than giving life to a man, because the real life of man consists of knowledge. Ignorance is death, knowledge is life. Life is of very little value, if it is a life in the dark, groping through ignorance and misery. Next in order comes, of course, helping a man physically. Therefore, in considering the question of helping others, we must always strive not to commit the mistake of thinking that physical help is the only help that can be given. It is not only the last but the least, because it cannot bring about permanent satisfaction. The misery that I feel when I am hungry is satisfied by eating, but hunger returns; my misery can cease only when I am satisfied beyond all want. Then hunger will not make me miserable; no distress, no sorrow will be able to move me. So, that help which tends to make us strong spiritually is the highest, next to it comes intellectual help, and after that physical help.

The miseries of the world cannot be cured by physical help only. Until man's nature changes, these physical needs will always arise, and miseries will always be felt, and no amount of physical help will cure them completely. The only solution of this problem is to make mankind pure. Ignorance is the mother of all the evil and all the misery we see. Let men have light, let them be pure and spiritually strong and educated, then alone will misery cease in the world, not before. We may convert every house in the country into a charity asylum, we may fill the land with hospitals, but the misery of man will still continue to exist until man's character changes.

We read in the Bhagavad-Gita again and again that we must all work incessantly. All work is by nature composed of good and evil. We cannot do any work which will not do some good somewhere; there cannot be any work which will not cause some harm somewhere. Every work must necessarily be a mixture of good and evil; yet we are commanded to work incessantly. Good and evil will both have their results, will produce their Karma. Good action will entail upon us good effect; bad action, bad. But good and bad are both bondages of the soul. The solution reached in the Gita in regard to this bondage-producing nature of work is that, if we do not attach ourselves to the work we do, it will not have any binding effect on our soul. We shall try to understand what is meant by this "non-attachment to" to work.

This is the one central idea in the Gita: work incessantly, but be not attached to it. Samskâra can be translated very nearly by "inherent tendency." Using the simile of a lake for the mind, every ripple, every wave that rises in the mind, when it subsides, does not die out entirely, but leaves a mark and a future possibility of that wave coming out again. This mark, with the possibility of the wave reappearing, is what is called Samskâra. Every work that we do, every movement of the body, every thought that we think, leaves such an impression on the mind-stuff, and even when such impressions are not obvious on the surface, they are sufficiently strong to work beneath the surface, subconsciously. What we are every moment is determined by the sum total of these impressions on the mind. What I am just at this moment is the effect of the sum total of all the impressions of my past life. This is really what is meant by character; each man's character is determined by the sum total of these impressions. If good impressions prevail, the character becomes good; if bad, it becomes bad. If a man continuously hears bad words, thinks bad thoughts, does bad actions, his mind will be full of bad impressions; and they will influence his thought and work without his being conscious of the fact. In fact, these bad impressions are always working, and their resultant must be evil, and that man will be a bad man; he cannot help it. The sum total of these impressions in him will create the strong motive power for doing bad actions. He will be like a machine in the hands of his impressions, and they will force him to do evil. Similarly, if a man thinks good thoughts and does good works, the sum total of these impressions will be good; and they, in a similar manner, will force him to do good even in spite of himself. When a man has done so much good work and thought so many good thoughts that there is an irresistible tendency in him to do good in spite of himself and even if he wishes to do evil, his mind, as the sum total of his tendencies, will not allow him to do so; the tendencies will turn him back; he is completely under the influence of the good tendencies. When such is the case, a man's good character is said to be established.

As the tortoise tucks its feet and head inside the shell, and you may kill it and break it in pieces, and yet it will not come out, even so the character of that man who has control over his motives and organs is unchangeably established. He controls his own inner forces, and nothing can draw them out against his will. By this continuous reflex of good thoughts, good impressions moving over the surface of the mind, the tendency for doing good becomes strong, and as the result we feel able to control the Indriyas (the sense-organs, the nerve-centres). Thus alone will character be established, then alone a man gets to truth. Such a man is safe for ever; he cannot do any evil. You may place him in any company, there will be no danger for him. There is a still higher state than having this good tendency, and that is the desire for liberation. You must remember that freedom of the soul is the goal of all Yogas, and each one equally leads to the same result. By work alone men may get to where Buddha got largely by meditation or Christ by prayer. Buddha was a working Jnâni, Christ was a Bhakta, but the same goal was reached by both of them. The difficulty is here. Liberation means entire freedom—freedom from the bondage of good, as well as from the bondage of evil. A golden chain is as much a chain as an iron one. There is a thorn in my finger, and I use another to take the first one out; and when I have taken it out, I throw both of them aside; I have no necessity for keeping the second thorn, because both are thorns after all. So the bad tendencies are to be counteracted by the good ones, and the bad impressions on the mind should be removed by the fresh waves of good ones, until all that is evil almost disappears, or is subdued and held in control in a corner of the mind; but after that, the good tendencies have also to be conquered. Thus the "attached" becomes the "unattached." Work, but let not the action or the thought produce a deep impression on the mind. Let the ripples come and go, let huge actions proceed from the muscles and the brain, but let them not make any deep impression on the soul.

How can this be done? We see that the impression of any action, to which we attach ourselves, remains. I may meet hundreds of persons during the day, and among them meet also one whom I love; and when I retire at night, I may try to think of all the faces I saw, but only that face comes before the mind—the face which I met perhaps only for one minute, and which I loved; all the others have vanished. My attachment to this particular person caused a deeper impression on my mind than all the other faces. Physiologically the impressions have all been the same; every one of the faces that I saw pictured itself on the retina, and the brain took the pictures in, and yet there was no similarity of effect upon the mind. Most of the faces, perhaps, were entirely new faces, about which I had never thought before, but that one face of which I got only a glimpse found associations inside. Perhaps I had pictured him in my mind for years, knew hundreds of things about him, and this one new vision of him awakened hundreds of sleeping memories in my mind; and this one impression having been repeated perhaps a hundred times more than those of the different faces together, will produce a great effect on the mind.

Therefore, be "unattached"; let things work; let brain centres work; work incessantly, but let not a ripple conquer the mind. Work as if you were a stranger in this land, a sojourner; work incessantly, but do not bind yourselves; bondage is terrible. This world is not our habitation, it is only one of the many stages through which we are passing. Remember that great saying of the Sânkhya, "The whole of nature is for the soul, not the soul for nature." The very reason of nature's existence is for the education of the soul; it has no other meaning; it is there because the soul must have knowledge, and through knowledge free itself. If we remember this always, we shall never be attached to nature; we shall know that nature is a book in which we are to read, and that when we have gained the required knowledge, the book is of no more value to us. Instead of that, however, we are identifying ourselves with nature; we are thinking that the soul is for nature, that the spirit is for the flesh, and, as the common saying has it, we think that man "lives to eat" and not "eats to live." We are continually making this mistake; we are regarding nature as ourselves and are becoming attached to it; and as soon as this attachment comes, there is the deep impression on the soul, which binds us down and makes us work not from freedom but like slaves.

The whole gist of this teaching is that you should work like a *master* and not as a *slave*; work incessantly, but do not do slave's work. Do you not see how everybody works? Nobody can be altogether at rest; ninety-nine per cent of mankind work like slaves, and the result is misery; it is all selfish work. Work through freedom! Work through love! The word "love" is very difficult to understand; love never comes until there is freedom. There is no true love possible in the slave. If you buy a slave and tie him down in chains and make him work for you, he will work like a drudge, but there will be no love in him. So when we ourselves work for the things of the world as slaves, there can be no love in us, and our work is not true work. This is true of work done for relatives and friends, and is true of work done for our own selves. Selfish work is slave's work; and here is a test. Every act of love brings happiness; there is no act of love which does not bring peace and blessedness as its reaction. Real existence, real knowledge, and real love are eternally connected with one another, the three in one: where one of them is, the others also must be; they are the three aspects of the One without a second—the Existence—Knowledge—Bliss. When that existence becomes relative, we see it as the world; that knowledge becomes in its turn modified into the knowledge of the things of the world; and that bliss forms the foundation of all true love known to the heart of man. Therefore true love can never react so as to cause pain either to the lover or to the beloved. Suppose a man loves a woman; he wishes to have her all to himself and feels extremely jealous about her every movement; he wants her to sit near him, to stand near him, and to eat and move at his bidding. He is a slave to her and wishes to have her as his slave. That is not love; it is a kind of morbid affection of the slave, insinuating itself as love. It cannot be love, because it is painful; if she does not do what he wants, it brings him pain. With love there is no painful reaction; love only brings a reaction of bliss; if it does not, it is not love; it is mistaking something else for love. When you have succeeded in loving your husband, your wife, your children, the whole world, the universe, in such a manner that there is no reaction of pain or jealousy, no selfish feeling, then you are in a fit state to be unattached.

Krishna says, "Look at Me, Arjuna! If I stop from work for one moment, the whole universe will die. I have nothing to gain from work; I am the one Lord, but why do I work? Because I love the world." God is unattached because He loves; that real love makes us unattached. Wherever there is attachment, the clinging to the things of the world, you must know that it is all physical attraction between sets of particles of matter—something that attracts two bodies nearer and nearer all the time and, if they cannot get near enough, produces pain; but where there is *real* love, it does not rest on physical attachment at all. Such lovers may be a thousand miles away from one another, but their love will be all the same; it does not die, and will never produce any painful reaction.

To attain this unattachment is almost a life-work, but as soon as we have reached this point, we have attained the goal of love and become free; the bondage of nature falls from us, and we see nature as she is; she forges no more chains for us; we stand entirely free and take not the results of work into consideration; who then cares for what the results may be?

Do you ask anything from your children in return for what you have given them? It is your duty to work for them, and there the matter ends. In whatever you do for a particular person, a city, or a state, assume the same attitude towards it as you have towards your children—expect nothing in return. If you can invariably take the position of a giver, in which everything given by you is a free offering to the world, without any thought of return, then will your work bring you no attachment. Attachment comes only where we expect a return.

If working like slaves results in selfishness and attachment, working as master of our own mind gives rise to the bliss of non-attachment. We often talk of right and justice, but we find that in the world right and justice are mere baby's talk. There are two things which guide the conduct of men: might and mercy. The exercise of might is invariably the exercise of selfishness. All men and women try to make the most of whatever power or advantage they have. Mercy is heaven itself; to be good, we have all to be merciful. Even justice and right should stand on mercy. All thought of obtaining return for the work we do hinders our spiritual progress; nay, in the end it brings misery.

There is another way in which this idea of mercy and selfless charity can be put into practice; that is, by looking upon work as "worship" in case we believe in a Personal God. Here we give up all the fruits of our work unto the Lord, and worshipping Him thus, we have no right to expect anything from mankind for the work we do. The Lord Himself works incessantly and is ever without attachment. Just as water cannot wet the lotus leaf, so work cannot bind the unselfish man by giving rise to attachment to results. The selfless and unattached man may live in the very heart of a crowded and sinful city; he will not be touched by sin.

This idea of complete self-sacrifice is illustrated in the following story: After the battle of Kurukshetra the five Pândava brothers performed a great sacrifice and made very large gifts to the poor. All people expressed amazement at the greatness and richness of the sacrifice, and said that such a sacrifice the world had never seen before. But, after the ceremony, there came a little mongoose, half of whose body was golden, and the other half brown; and he began to roll on the floor of the sacrificial hall. He said to those around, "You are all liars; this is no sacrifice." "What!" they exclaimed, "you say this is no sacrifice; do you not know how money and jewels were poured out to the poor and everyone became rich and happy? This was the most wonderful sacrifice any man ever performed." But the mongoose said, "There was once a little village, and in it there dwelt a poor Brahmin with his wife, his son, and his son's wife. They were very poor and lived on small gifts made to them for preaching and teaching. There came in that land a three years' famine, and the poor Brahmin suffered more than ever. At last when the family had starved for days, the father brought home one morning a little barley flour, which he had been fortunate enough to obtain, and he divided it into four parts, one for each member of the family. They prepared it for their meal, and just as they were about to eat, there was a knock at the door. The father opened it, and there stood a guest. Now in India a guest is a sacred person; he is as a god for the time being, and must be treated as such. So the poor Brahmin said, 'Come in, sir; you are welcome.' He set before the guest his own portion of the food, which the guest quickly ate and said, 'Oh, sir, you have killed me; I have been starving for ten days, and this little bit has but increased my hunger.' Then the wife said to her husband, 'Give him my share,' but the husband said, 'Not so.' The wife however insisted, saying, 'Here is a poor man, and it is our duty as householders to see that he is fed, and it is my duty as a wife to give him my portion, seeing that you have no more to offer him.' Then she gave her share to the guest, which he ate, and said he was still burning with hunger. So the son said, 'Take my portion also; it is the duty of a son to help his father to fulfill his obligations.' The guest ate that, but remained still unsatisfied; so the son's wife gave him her portion also. That was sufficient, and the guest departed, blessing them. That night those four people died of starvation. A few granules of that flour had fallen on the floor; and when I rolled my body on them, half of it became golden, as you see. Since then I have been traveling all over the world, hoping to find another sacrifice like that, but nowhere have I found one; nowhere else has the other half of my body been turned into gold. That is why I say this is no sacrifice."

This idea of charity is going out of India; great men are becoming fewer and fewer. When I was first learning English, I read an English storybook in which there was a story about a dutiful boy who had gone out to work and had given some of his money to his old mother, and this was praised in three or four pages. What was that? No Hindu boy can ever understand the moral of that story. Now I understand it when I hear the Western idea—every man for himself. And some men take everything for themselves, and fathers and mothers and wives and children go to the wall. That should never and nowhere be the ideal of the householder.

Now you see what Karma-Yoga means; even at the point of death to help anyone, without asking questions. Be cheated millions of times and never ask a question, and never think of what you are doing. Never vaunt of your gifts to the poor or expect their gratitude, but rather be grateful to them for giving you the occasion of practicing charity to them. Thus it is plain that to be an ideal householder is a much more difficult task than to be an ideal Sannyasin; the true life of work is indeed as hard as, if not harder than, the equally true life of renunciation.

Sholom Aleichem

REB YOZIFL AND THE CONTRACTOR

in *Inside Kasrilevke*

~~~

Everything in the world is progressing and marching onward. So is our town of Kasrilevke. Kasrilevke has taken a great stride ahead latterly. So much so, that you will be positively surprised if you go there now.

There is one sight in Kasrilevke especially that you will never tire of gazing at. You will see in the heart of the town, where the mud is at its deepest, a massive, yellow brick building—tall and wide—ornamented with iron, with a host of windows, a beautiful, high, carved door, and above it a marble slab bearing the following Hebrew inscription in golden letters:

MOSHAV Z'KENIM

As you look at the building you can't help thinking of a gorgeous velvet patch atop a threadbare lustrine gaberdine, green with age. How comes this luxurious Home for the Aged in the midst of poverty-stricken Kasrilevke? you ask. Was it put up to spite anybody? Or just as

Sholom Aleichem was born in 1859 in a small village in what is now Ukraine, and went on to re-create this village, or *shtetl*, in much of his work. Aleichem worked as a tutor, a rabbi, and a trader, and he and his family lived in Russia, Switzerland, Italy, Denmark, and the United States. His fame, if not his fortune, increased throughout his life, and he is still considered the fore-most writer of Yiddish literature. Aleichem died in New York in 1916. This story from *Inside Kasrilevke* is Isadore Goldstick's 1948 translation.

a practical joke? Or did somebody make a mistake? Here is the story as it was told to me the last time I was there to visit my parents' grave.

It happened at the time when the railway was being put through Kasrilevke. All kinds of curious creatures came down from Moscow: engineers, surveyors, excavators and such like, and at the head of them all a contractor—a personage of importance and a Jew into the bargain. His name is unknown to this day. Maybe he was one of Poliakov's men, or maybe he was the great financier Poliakov himself, for all anybody knows. But even a child could see that he was worth a fortune—a veritable millionaire. For how else could he afford the luxury of occupying two rooms by himself, gorge himself with chicken, swill wine on weekdays, and dally with the hotel proprietor's young daughter-in-law, the hussy? (She wears no wig even in public and despises her husband, as everybody knows.)

In those days our old friend the rabbi, Reb Yozifl, conceived a plan to erect a *moshav z'kenim* in Kasrilevke—a home for the poor and sick old folk. But why a home for the aged? you might ask. Why not a hospital? There you are again with your questions! Supposing he had set his mind on a hospital; then you'd ask: Why not a home for the aged? I can assure you of one thing, however: he certainly had no personal motive; nothing was further from his mind than the thought of a refuge for his own old age. He simply concluded that a sick old man was to be pitied more than a sick young man. To be sure, an ailing young person was in a bad way too. But if you are ill and old into the bargain, you're simply a burden to the world. Just a loathed dead weight. People despise an infirm old man—there's no gainsaying that.

In short, he made up his mind once and for all: Kasrilevke simply must have a *moshav z'kenim*. A home for the aged must take precedence over everything else. And in order to bring home to everybody how necessary it was, Reb Yozifl delivered a sermon in the synagogue on Saturday afternoon, illustrating his talk with a parable: "Once upon a time there was a king who had an only son …" But since I am telling you a story, I'd rather not interrupt it with another one. So we'll just defer Reb Yozifl's parable for some other time. I might tell you, however, that although the parable may not have quite fitted the moral in question, nevertheless his audience was completely carried away by it, as they were by all the parables that Reb Yozifl used to tell them. One could only wish that he had been as good at earning his daily bread as he was talented in telling parables.

On hearing his parable, one of the prominent citizens spoke up—one of the most honored, it goes without saying, for who else would dare to contradict a rabbi before a congregation of Jews?

"Yes, indeed, rabbi, there's no denying that you are right. That was a beautiful parable. The only trouble is: where do we get the cash? A home for the aged costs a lot of money, and Kasrilevke is a town of nothing but indigent, poverty-stricken, penniless, impoverished, destitute starvelings."

"Pshaw! There is a parable that applies to this case too. Once upon a time there was a king who had an only son ..."

Anyway, the fate of the king and his only son is of no importance. What is important is that on the following day, on a Sunday, our Reb Yozifl in company of two of the most prominent householders, with a kerchief in his hand, set out for the market square and started making the rounds, going from shop to shop and from house to house—the old Kasrilevke method of "raising funds." It goes without saying that no vast fortune can be amassed in this way. Reb Yozifl, however, had plenty of time. He could well afford to wait another week. Rome wasn't built in a day either. It just couldn't be helped: a townful of poor Jews! The only hope were the outsiders—merchants that come down to Kasrilevke, or other transients putting up at the local hotels.

In Kasrilevke, if ever they lay their hands on a bird of passage, they pluck it so bare that it'll warn all and sundry to shun the town: "If ever you have to pass through Kasrilevke, go miles out of your way to stay clear of it. The town beggars there are simply intolerable!"

On hearing that a Jewish contractor had come down from Moscow, one of Poliakov's men, or maybe Poliakov himself, a multimillionaire—Reb Yozifl donned his Sabbath best, threw his cloak over it and put his fur hat on his head. Somehow the ceremonial hat didn't go well with the big weekday stick; and he had everybody puzzled. The people argued: it's either one thing or another. If it's the

Sabbath, then why a stick; if it's a weekday, why a fur hat? The problem was not solved until Reb Yozifl was seen taking along with him the two most prominent citizens and making straight for the wealthy contractor in the hotel.

I don't know what other Moscow contractors are like. But this contractor who had come to Kasrilevke to put the railway through was a curious sort. Of low stature, limber, with chubby cheeks, fleshy lips, and short arms, he was a frisky little man, running more often than walking, shouting rather than talking and bursting now and then into an explosive little laugh: He-he-he! His little eyes were always moist with tears. All his movements were brisk, hurried, precipitate, and he was dangerously nervous! Not to satisfy his every whim or to irritate him with as much as a single remark was to invite disastrous consequences. His eyes immediately caught fire and he was ready to trample you underfoot or tear you to pieces. He was a very unusual contractor indeed.

He had given instructions at the hotel that no matter who came to see him, no matter who he might be, even if it should be the Governor himself (these were his very words), he was not to be admitted without the proprietor first rapping at his door and being told by the contractor to enter. Only then the proprietor was to report to him who the caller was. Then he would either see him at once or ask him to come the next day.

Needless to say, Kasrilevke had a good laugh at this odd person and his curious ways. Surely only a Moscow contractor could conceive such outlandish notions.

Isn't it enough when a man goes to all the trouble of calling on you—so they argued—must he also stand outside your door and wait till he gets your permission to enter, or else be told to come tomorrow? No, only a Moscow contractor could do a thing like that. There can be little doubt that there isn't a greater man than Reb Yozifl the rabbi, a man of learning and a God-fearing man. Nevertheless his door is open at all times for anybody who may need him. Surely this is an established Jewish custom.

On seeing Reb Yozifl in person and, what's more, wearing his Sabbath best, the hotel proprietor, a man with a good-sized paunch, unbuttoned coat and waistcoat, and a pipe in his mouth, became all flustered:

"I bid you welcome! Welcome indeed! Such a visitor! Just imagine, the rabbi in person in my house! Such a privilege! Do be seated, rabbi! What's that? Oh, you wish to see our guest? With the greatest pleasure!"

The proprietor in his confusion forgot all about the injunction "no matter who he might be" and "even if it should be the Governor," put away his pipe, buttoned his coat, showed the rabbi and the two most prominent citizens to the guest's door, and himself disappeared.

It is hard to say what the guest was busy doing at the moment. Perhaps he was in the very act of planning the railway, figuring where to lay the tracks and where to put up the station. Or maybe he was lying down in the adjoining room and dozing. Or maybe, for all one can tell, he was just sitting there and having a chat with the proprietor's young daughter-in-law, the hussy, who wears no wig and despises her husband, as everybody knows. Who is to say what a Jewish contractor from Moscow, a personage of importance and a Jew into the bargain, might be doing—a lone man occupying two rooms? In any event, when the deputation stepped into the first room, he wasn't there. The door to the adjoining room was open and there wasn't a sound. They didn't want to step any farther. That would be bad manners; he might be sleeping. So they had a brilliant idea: the three of them gave a cough (that's a Kasrilevke custom). Hearing the noise, the contractor bolted out of his room more dead than alive. When he saw the strangers, he flared up and burst out in the true Moscow manner:

"Who are you? What do you want, you so-and-so and so-and-so? Who let you in? Haven't I told them time and again to admit no one unannounced?"

Some say that he used the word *zhidy*, kikes, although it's hard to believe that a Jew would do that. All the same, when a man's wrath is kindled, and especially a millionaire's, there's no telling what he might do.

Our readers who are acquainted with the rabbi of Kasrilevke know full well what a humble man Reb Yozifl was. Why, he'd never dream of being forward. He always preferred to be last. For it was his idea that mortal man must not be in too great a hurry; he has nothing to lose and will never miss anything. But this time he had to step forward, because those "most prominent citizens" were plainly frightened by the millionaire, who was wildly waving his hands at them and emphasizing his fury by stamping his feet. Who could say who he was? Maybe he was one of Poliakov's men, and maybe even Poliakov himself. Such being the case, they naturally had to recede a bit, get a little closer to the door. For there was no telling what might happen. Only Reb Yozifl didn't get frightened this time. He argued this way. It's one of two things: he is either a *big* man or a *little* man. If he is a big man, I don't need to be afraid of him; if he is a little man, there surely can be no occasion for fear. So he spoke right up to him in these words:

"Pardon me, you are shouting at us. Maybe you are right. Forgive us for disturbing you. But we are engaged in the performance of a good deed, and the messengers of a good deed—so our sages tell us—can suffer no injury. You see, we are collecting contributions for a great cause, a home for the aged."

The Moscow contractor stood speechless. The intrusion of the three men into his room, unannounced, like a bolt from the blue, and the conduct of this old man (the fellow with the fur hat) which struck him as both foolish and impudent, so enraged our Muscovite, so infuriated him, that he felt a tickling sensation in his nose, a sense of pressure against his brain, and all his blood rushed to his face. He was simply frantic and so completely lost control of himself that he just didn't know what he was doing. His hand was raised, as if against his own will, he swung it with all his might and dealt the old man a resounding, flaming slap.

"Take this! This is for your old folks' home!"

The slap sent the old man's fur hat and skullcap flying off his head together, and for a moment the rabbi of Kasrilevke stood with uncovered head—perhaps for the first time in his life. But this lasted no more than a second. Reb Yozifl quickly bent down, snatched up the fur hat and covered his bared head. Then he cautiously felt his cheek and looked at his hand to see if there was any blood. At the

211

same time he said to the guest, speaking softly, sweetly, and with a curious smile on his deathly pale face:

"That's that. I take it that this was meant for me. Now, my dear man, what are you going to give for the sick old folk—I mean the home for the aged?"

What happened next can't be told. No one knows, for "the most prominent citizens," on hearing the language of Moscow from the lips of the contractor, had beaten a hasty retreat. And Reb Yozifl just wouldn't talk about the affair. This is known, however: on leaving the hotel, the old rabbi's face beamed strangely. One of his cheeks—the left—beamed even more than the other. He said with a sweet smile:

"*Mazeltov,* congratulations, fellow Jews, I have good news for you: we are going to have now, with the aid of the Almighty, a home for the aged—a home that will be a delight to God and man."

The "little folk" might have had some doubts about the rabbi's statement, if they hadn't heard with their own ears the contractor himself say, while tapping his shirt-front with his pudgy fingers:

"Men, I'm putting up a home for the aged in your town. I, I ..."

Not only did they hear this with their own ears, but they soon saw with their own eyes the contractor walking about the town with the rabbi, then stopping to measure a plot with his stick and saying:

"This is where the building is going to stand; it'll have this frontage and this depth ..."

Before they knew it, loads of brick, lumber, and other building materials arrived. The structure was under way.

To be sure, there were the curious who tried to question the rabbi, sound him out, get him to talk:

"Rabbi, just what did happen? Just how did this man make it up to you for his harsh words? ... What did *you* say to *him* and what did he answer *you?* ..."

Reb Yozifl, however, took no notice of what was said and avoided the subject, merely saying with his ever sweet smile:

"All the same, we are going to have a home for the aged, God willing. I'm telling you, it will be a delight to God and man."

Too bad—the home for the aged is unoccupied to this day. Reb Yozifl departed from this world long ago—there is no money to run the institution with.

This has ever been the fate of the little folk of Kasrilevke: when they dream of good things to eat—they haven't a spoon; when they have a spoon—they don't dream of good things to eat.

Ryokan

FIRST DAYS OF SPRING

First days of Spring—the sky
is bright blue, the sun huge and warm.
Everything's turning green.
Carrying my monk's bowl, I walk to the village
to beg for my daily meal.
The children spot me at the temple gate
and happily crowd around,
dragging at my arms till I stop.
I put my bowl on a white rock,
hang my bag on a branch.
First we braid grasses and play tug-of-war,
then we take turns singing and keeping a kick-ball in the air:
I kick the ball and they sing, they kick and I sing.
Time is forgotten, the hours fly.
People passing by point at me and laugh:

Ryokan, whose name means "broad-hearted and generous," was born in 1758 in Niigata, Japan. At the age of eighteen, Ryokan became a priest and took to a life of wandering until he met his teacher in Zen Buddhist practice, Kokusun Roshi. Ryokan inherited Roshi's temple but left that post to continue wandering, begging, and living as a hermit. Toward the end of his life, Ryokan fell in love with a young nun, Teishin, who collected and published his poetry after his death in 1831. This poem was translated by Stephen Mitchell.

"Why are you acting like such a fool?"
I nod my head and don't answer.
I could say something, but why?
Do you want to know what's in my heart?
From the beginning of time: just this! just this!

William Trevor

SITTING WITH THE DEAD

in *A Bit on the Side*

~ ~ ~

His eyes had been closed and he opened them, saying he wanted to see the stable-yard.

Emily's expression was empty of response. Her face, younger than his and yet not seeming so, was empty of everything except the tiredness she felt. "From the window?" she said.

No, he'd go down, he said. "Will you get me the coat? And have the boots by the door."

She turned away from the bed. He would manage on his own if she didn't help him: she'd known him for twenty-eight years, been married to him for twenty-three. Whether or not she brought the coat up to him would make no difference, any more than it would if she protested.

"It could kill you," she said.

"The fresh air'd strengthen a man."

Downstairs, she placed the boots ready for him at the back door. She brought his cap and muffler to him with his overcoat. A stitch

---

William Trevor was born in County Cork, Ireland, in 1928 to a middle-class Protestant family. After earning a degree in history from University College Dublin, Trevor worked as a sculptor and teacher. In 1954, he and his wife moved to England, where Trevor became a copywriter and a fiction writer. He has published many books and won many prizes, and he currently lives in Devon, England. This story comes from his 2004 collection, *A Bit on the Side*.

was needed where the left sleeve met the shoulder, she noticed. She hadn't before and knew he wouldn't wait while she repaired it now.

"What're you going to do there?" she asked, and he said nothing much. Tidy up a bit, he said.

He died eight days later, and Dr. Ann explained that tidying the stable-yard with only a coat over his pyjamas wouldn't have hastened anything. An hour after she left, the Geraghtys came to the house, not knowing that he was dead.

It was half past seven in the evening then. At the same time the next morning, Keane the undertaker was due. She said that to the Geraghtys, making sure they understood, not wanting them to think she was turning them away for some other reason. Although she knew that if her husband had been alive he wouldn't have agreed to have the Geraghtys at his bedside. It was a relief that they had come too late.

The Geraghtys were two middle-aged women, sisters, the Misses Geraghty, who sat with the dying. Emily had heard of them, but did not know them, not even to see: they'd had to give their name when she opened the door to them. It had never occurred to her that the Geraghtys would attempt to bring their good works to the sick-room she had lived with herself for the last seven months. They were Legion of Mary women, famed for their charity, tireless in their support of the Society of St. Vincent de Paul and their promulgation of the writings of Father Xavier O'Shea, a local priest who, at a young age in the 1880s, had contracted malaria in the mission fields of the East.

"We only heard of your trouble Tuesday," the thinner and smaller of the two apologized. "It does happen the occasional time we wouldn't hear."

The other woman, more robust and older, allowed herself jewellery and make-up and took more care with her clothes. But it was her quiet, sharp-featured sister who took the lead.

"We heard in MacClincy's," she said.

"I'm sorry you've had a wasted journey."

"It's never wasted." There was a pause, as if a pause was necessary here. "You have our sympathy," was added to that, the explanation of why the journey had not been in vain.

The conversation took place entirely at the hall door. Dusk was becoming dark, but over the white-washed wall of the small front garden Emily still could see a car drawn up in the road. It was cold, the wind gone round to the east. They meant well, these women, even if they'd got everything wrong, driving out from Carra to visit a man who wouldn't have welcomed them and then arriving too late, a man whose death had spared them an embarrassment.

"Would you like a cup of tea?" Emily offered.

She imagined they'd refuse and then begin to go, saying they couldn't disturb her at a time like this. But the big, wide-shouldered one glanced at her sister, hesitating.

"If you're alone," the smaller one said, "you'd be welcome to our company. If it would be of help to you."

The dead man had been without religion. Anyone could have told them that, Emily reflected, making tea. He would have said that there was more to their sitting at the bedsides of the ill than met the eye, and she wondered if that could possibly be so. Did they in their compassionate travels hope for the first signs of the belief that often came out of nowhere when death declared its intention? Did they drive away from the houses they visited, straight to a presbytery, their duty done? She had never heard that said about the Geraghtys and she didn't want to believe it. They meant well, she said to herself again.

When they left, she wouldn't go back upstairs to look at the dead features. She'd leave him now to Keane in the morning. In the brief time that had elapsed a day had been settled for the funeral, Thursday of next week; in the morning she would let a few people know; she'd put a notice in the *Advertiser*. No children had been born: when Thursday had passed everything would be over except for the unpaid debts. She buttered slices of brack and stirred the tea in the pot. She carried in the tray.

They hadn't taken their coats off, but sat as still as statues, a little apart from one another.

"It's cold," she said, "I'll light the fire."

"Ah no. Ah no, don't bother." They both protested, but she did anyway, and the kindling that had been in the grate all summer flared up at once. She poured their tea, asking if they took sugar, and then offering the brack. They began to call her Emily, as if they knew her well. They gave their own names: Kathleen the older sister, and Norah.

"I didn't think," Kathleen began to say, and Norah interrupted her.

"Oh, we know all right," she said. "You're Protestant here, but that never made a difference yet."

They had sat with the Methodist minister, the Reverend Wolfe, Kathleen said. They'd read to him, they'd brought in whatever he wanted. They were there when he went.

"Never a difference," Norah repeated, and in turn they took a slice of brack. They commented on it, saying it was excellent.

"It isn't easy," Kathleen said when the conversation lapsed. "The first few hours. We often stay."

"It was good of you to think of him."

"It's cheerful with that fire, Emily," Kathleen said.

They asked her about the horses because the horses were what they'd heard about, and she explained that they'd become a thing of the past. She'd sell the place now, she said.

"You'd find it remote, Emily." Kathleen said. Her lipstick had left a trace on the rim of the teacup and Norah drew her attention to it with a gesture. Kathleen wiped it off. "We're town people our-selves," she said.

Emily didn't consider the house she'd lived in for nearly thirty years remote. Five minutes in the car and you were in the middle of Carra. Mangan's Bridge, in the other direction, was no more than a minute.

"You get used to a place," Emily said.

They identified for her the house where they lived themselves, on the outskirts of Carra, on the Athy road. Emily knew it, a pleasant creeper-covered house with silver railings in front of it, not big but prosperous-looking. She's thought it was Corrigan's, the surveyor's.

"I don't know why I thought that."

"We bought it from Mr. Corrigan," Norah said, "when we came to Carra three years ago." And her sister said they'd been living in Athy before that.

"Carra was what we were looking for," Norah said.

They were endeavouring to lift her spirits, Emily realized, by keeping things light. Carra had improved in their time, they said, and it would again. You could tell with a town; some of them wouldn't rise out of the doldrums while a century'd go by.

"You'd maybe come in to Carra now?" Kathleen said.

"I don't know what I'll do."

She poured more tea. She handed round the brack again. Dr. Ann had given her pills to take, but she didn't intend to take them. Exhausted as she was, she didn't want to sleep.

"He went out a week ago," she said. "He got up and went out to the yard with only a coat over his pyjamas. I thought it was that that hurried it on, but seemingly it wasn't."

They didn't say anything, just nodded, both of them. She said he had been seven months dying. He hadn't read a newspaper all that time, she said. In the end all the food he could manage was cornflour.

"We never knew your husband," Norah said, "any more than yourself. Although I think we maybe met him on the road one day."

A feeling of apprehension began in Emily, a familiar dread that compulsively caused one hand to clench the other, fingers tightly locking. People often met him, exercising one of the horses. A car would slow down for him but he never acknowledged it, never so much as raised the crop. For a moment she forgot that he was dead.

"He was often out," she said.

"Oh, this was long ago."

"He sold the last of the horses twelve months ago. He didn't want them left."

"He raced his horses, we're to understand?" Kathleen said.

"Point-to-points. Punchestown the odd time."

"Well, that's great."

"There wasn't much success."

"It's an up and down business, of course."

Disappointment had filled the house when yet again a horse trailed in, when months of preparation went for nothing. There had never been much reason for optimism, but even so expectation had been high, as if anything less would have brought bad luck. When Emily married, her husband had been training a string of yearlings on the Curragh. Doing well, he'd said himself, although in fact he wasn't.

"You never had children, Emily?" Kathleen asked.

"No, we never did."

"I think we heard that said."

The house had been left to her by an aunt on her mother's side. Forty-three acres, sheep kept; and the furniture had been left to her too. "I used come here as a child. A Miss Edgill my aunt was. Did you hear of her?"

They shook their heads. Way before their time, Kathleen said, looking around her. A good house, she said.

"She'd no one else to leave it to." And Emily didn't add that neither the property nor the land would ever have become hers if her aunt had suspected she'd marry the man she had.

"You'll let it go though?" Kathleen pursued her enquires, doing her best to knit together a conversation. "The way things are now, you were saying you'd let it go?"

"I don't know."

"Anyone would require a bit of time."

"We see a lot of widowing," Norah murmured.

"Nearly to the day, we were married twenty-three years."

"God took him because He wanted him, Emily."

The Geraghtys continued to offer sympathy, one following the other in what was said, the difference in tone and manner continuing also. And again—and more often as more solace was pressed upon her—Emily reflected how fortunate it was that they had escaped the awkwardness of attempting to keep company with her husband. He would have called her back as soon as she'd left them with him. He would have asked her who they were, although he knew; he would have told her to take them away. He'd never minded what he said— the flow of coarse language when someone crossed one of the fields, every word shouted out, frighteningly sometimes. It was always that: raising his voice, the expressions he used; not once, not ever, had there been violence. Yet often she had wished that there had been, believing that violence would have been easier to bear than the power of this articulated anger. It was power she had always felt coming from him, festering and then released, his denial of his failure.

"The horses. Punchestown. The world of the racecourse," Kathleen said. "You've had an interesting life, Emily."

It seemed to Emily that Norah was about to shake her head, that for the first time the sisters were on the verge of disagreement. It didn't surprise her: the observation that had been made astonished her.

"Unusual is what my sister means," Norah nodded her correction into place, her tone softening the contradiction.

"There's many a woman doesn't get out and about," Kathleen said.

Emily poured more tea and added turf to the fire. She had forgotten to draw the curtains over and she did so now. The light in the room was dim; he'd been particular about low-wattage electric bulbs. But the dimness made the room cosy and it seemed wrong that anywhere should be so while he lay only a few hours dead. She wondered what she'd do when another bulb went, either here or somewhere else, if she would replace it with a stronger one or if low-wattage light was part of her now. She wondered if her nervousness was part of her too. It didn't seem that it had always been, but she knew she could be wrong about that.

"I didn't go out and about much," she said because a silence in the conversation had come. Both visitors were stirring sugar into their tea. When their teaspoons were laid down, Norah said:

"There's some wouldn't bother with that."

"He was a difficult man. People would have told you."

They did not contradict that. They did not say anything. She said:

"He put his trust in the horses. Since childhood what he wanted was to win races, to be known for it. But he never managed much."

"Poor man," Kathleen murmured. "Poor man."

"Yes."

She shouldn't have complained, she hadn't meant to: Emily tried to say that, but the words wouldn't come. She looked away from the women who had visited her, gazing about her at the furniture of a room she knew too well. He had been angry when she'd taken the curtains down to wash them; everyone staring in, he'd said, and she hadn't known what he'd meant. Hardly anyone passed by on the road.

"He married me for the house," she said, unable to prevent herself from saying that too. The women were strangers, she was speaking ill of the dead. She shook her head in an effort to deny what she'd said, but that seemed to be a dishonesty, worse than speaking ill.

The women sipped their tea, both lifting the cups to their lips in the same moment.

"He married me for the forty acres," Emily said, compelled again to say what she didn't want to. "I was a Protestant girl that got passed by until he made a bid for me and I thought it was romantic, like he did himself—the race cards, the race ribbons, the jockeys' colours, the big crowd there'd be. That's how it happened."

"Ah now, now," Kathleen said. "Ah now, dear."

"I was a fool and you pay for foolishness. I was greedy for what marriage might be, and you pay for greed. We'd a half acre left after what was paid back a year ago. There's a mortgage he took out on the house. I could have said to him all the time he was dying, 'What'll I do?' But I didn't, and he didn't say anything either. God knows what his last thoughts were."

They told her she was upset. One after the other they told her any widow would be, that it was what you had to expect. Norah said it twice. Kathleen said she could call on them in her grief.

"There's no grief in the house you've come to."

"Ah now, now," Kathleen said, her big face puckered in distress. "Ah, now."

"He never minded how the truth came out, whether he'd say it or not. He didn't say I was a worthless woman, but you'd see it in his eyes. Another time, I'd sweep the stable-yard and he'd say what use was that. He'd push a plate of food away untouched. We had two collies once and they were company. When they died he said he'd never have another dog. The vet wouldn't come near us. The man who came to read the meter turned surly under the abuse he got for driving his van into the yard."

"There's good and bad in everyone, Emily." Norah whispered that opinion and, still whispering, repeated it.

"Stay where you are, Emily," Kathleen said, "and I'll make another pot of tea."

She stood up, the teapot already in her hand. She was used to making tea in other people's kitchens. She'd find her way about, she said.

Emily protested, but even while she did she didn't care. In all the years of her marriage another woman hadn't made tea in that kitchen, and she imagined him walking in from the yard and finding someone other than herself there. The time she began to paint the scullery, it frightened her when he stood in the doorway, before he even said a thing. The time she dropped the sugar bag and the sugar spilt out all over the floor he watched her sweeping it on to the dust-pan, turf dust going with it. He said what was she doing, throwing it away when it was still fit to stir into your tea? The scullery had stayed half-painted to this day.

"He lived in a strangeness of his own," Emily said to the sister who was left in the room with her. "Even when he was old, he believed a horse could still reclaim him. Even when the only one left was diseased and fit for nothing. When there was none there at all he scoured the empty stables and got fresh straw in. He had it in mind to begin all over again, to find some animal going cheap. He never said it, but it was what he had in mind."

The house wasn't clean. It hadn't been clean for years. She'd lost heart in the house, and in herself, in the radio that didn't work, her bicycle with the tyres punctured. These visitors would have noticed that the summer flies weren't swept up, that nowhere was dusted.

"Three spoons and one for the pot," Kathleen said, setting the teapot down in the hearth. "Is that about right, Emily? Will we let it draw a minute?"

She had cut more brack, finding it on the breadboard, the bread saw beside it, the butter there too. She hoped it wasn't a presumption, she hoped it wasn't interference, she said, but all that remained unanswered.

"He'd sit there looking at me," Emily said. "His eyes would follow me about the kitchen. There was a beetle got on the table once and he didn't move. It got into the flour and he didn't reach out for it."

"Isn't it a wonder," Norah said, "you wouldn't have gone off, the way things were, Emily? Not that I'm saying you should have."

Emily was aware that that question was asked. She didn't answer it; she didn't know why she hadn't gone off. Looking back on it, she didn't. But she remembered how when she had thought of going away what her arguments to herself had been, how she had wondered where she could go to, and had told herself it would be wrong to leave a house that had been left to her in good faith and with affection. And then, of course, there was the worry about how he'd manage.

"Will you take another cup, Emily?"

She shook her head. The wind had become stronger. She could hear it rattling the doors upstairs. She'd left a light burning in the room.

"I'm wrong to delay you," she said.

But the Geraghtys had settled down again, with the fresh tea to sustain them. She wasn't delaying them in any way whatsoever, Kathleen said. In the shadowy illumination of the single forty-watt bulb the alarm clock on the mantelpiece gave the time as twenty past eleven, although in fact it was half an hour later.

"It's just I'm tired," Emily said. "A time like this, I didn't mean to go on about what's done with."

Kathleen said it was the shock. The shock of death changed everything, she said; no matter how certainly death was expected, it was always a shock.

"I wouldn't want you to think I didn't love my husband."

The sisters were taken aback, Kathleen on her knees adding turf to the fire, Norah pouring milk into her tea. How could these two unmarried women understand? Emily thought. How could they understand that even if there was neither grief nor mourning there had been some love left for the man who'd died? Her fault, her foolishness from the first it had been; no one had made her do anything.

The talk went on, back and forth between the widow and the sisters, words and commiseration, solace and reassurance. The past came into it when more was said: the wedding, his polished shoes and shiny hair, the party afterwards over on the Curragh, at Jockey Hall because he knew the man there. People were spoken of, names known to the Geraghtys, or people before their time; occasions were spoken of—the year he went to Cheltenham, the shooting of the old grey when her leg went at Glanbyre point-to-point. The Geraghtys spoke of their growing up in Galway, how you wouldn't recognize the City of the Tribes these days so fashionable and lively it had become; how later they had lived near Enniscorthy; how Kathleen had felt the draw of the religious life at that time but then had felt the receding of it, how she had

225

known ever since that she'd been tested with her own mistake. In this way the Geraghtys spread themselves into the conversation. As the night went on, Emily was aware that they were doing so because it was necessary, on a bleak occasion, to influence the bleakness in other ways. She apologized for speaking ill of the dead, and blamed herself again. It was half past three before the Geraghtys left.

"Thank you," she said, holding open the hall door. The wind that had been slight and then had got up wasn't there any more. The air was fresh and clean. She said she'd be all right.

Light flickered in the car when the women opened the doors. There was the red glow of the tail-light before the engine started up, a whiff of exhaust before the car moved slowly forward and gathered speed.

In the room upstairs, the sheet drawn up over the raddled, stiffening features, Emily prayed. She knelt by the bedside and pleaded for the deliverance of the husband who had wronged her for so long. Fear had drained to a husk the love she had spoken of, but she did not deny that remnant's existence, as she had not in the company of her visitors. She could not grieve, she could not mourn; too little was left, too much destroyed. Would they know that as they drove away? Would they explain it to people when people asked?

Downstairs, she washed up the cups and saucers. She would not sleep. She would not go to bed. The hours would pass and then the undertaker's man would come.

The headlights illuminated low stone walls, ragwort thriving on the verges, gorse among the motionless sheep in gated fields. Kathleen drove, as she always did, Norah never having learnt how to. A visit had not before turned out so strangely, so different from what had been the sisters' familiar expectation. They said all that, and then were silent for a while before Kathleen made her final comment: that what they had heard had been all the more terrible to listen to with a man dead in an upstairs room.

Hunched in the dark of the car, Norah frowned over that. She did not speak immediately, but when they'd gone another mile she said:

"I'd say, myself, was the dead we were sitting with."

In the house the silence there had been before the visitors disturbed it was there again. No spectre rose from the carnal remains of the man who was at last at peace. But the woman sitting by the turf fire she kept going was aware, as dawn lightened the edges of the curtains, of a stirring in her senses. Her tiredness afflicted her less, a calm possessed her. In the neglected room she regretted nothing now of what she had said to the women who had meant well; nor did it matter if, here and there, they had not quite understood. She sat for a while longer, then pulled the curtains back and the day came in. Hers was the ghost the night had brought, in her own image as she once had been.

Umar Faruq Abd-Allah

MERCY: THE STAMP OF CREATION

The explicit link between the Arabic words *Islām,* literally "entering into peace," and *salām,* "peace" or "perfect peace," has been frequently highlighted of late. It is mainly because of this etymological connection that many Muslims and others advance the claim that Islam is a religion of peace, just as Christianity is customarily called a religion of love. Certainly, in terms of their creed and the historical record, Muslims are no less justified in equating Islam with peace than Christians are in identifying their faith with love. From a theological perspective, however, it would be more precise to describe Islam as the religion of mercy. Islamic revelation designates the Prophet Muhammad as "the prophet of mercy," and Islam's scriptural sources stress that mercy—above other divine attributions—is God's hallmark in creation and constitutes his primary relation to the world from its inception through eternity, in this world and the next. Islam enjoins its followers to be merciful to themselves, to others, and the whole of creation, teaching a karma-like law of universal

Umar Faruq Abd-Allah was born in 1948 to a Protestant family in Columbus, Nebraska. Abd-Allah was a graduate student in English literature when, in early 1970, he read *The Autobiography of Malcom X* and embraced Islam. He then transferred to the University of Chicago to pursue Arabic and Islamic studies. Abd-Allah has taught Islamic studies, comparative religion, and Arabic at various universities, and he is the chair and scholar-in-residence at the Nawawi Foundation, whose mission is to increase American Islamic cultural and religious literacy. This article was written for the Nawawi Foundation in 2004.

reciprocity by which God shows mercy to the merciful and with-holds it from those who hold it back from others.

The Prophet Muhammad said: "People who show mercy to others will be shown mercy by the All-Merciful. Be merciful to those on earth, and he who is in heaven will be merciful to you." Because these words epitomize Islam's fundamental ethos, it was called "the Tradition of Primacy" and, for generations of Classical Muslim teachers, constituted the first text that many of them handed down to their students and required them to commit to memory with a full chain of transmitters going back to the Prophet Muhammad.

GOD: THE ALL-MERCIFUL

In Arabic, God is called by many names, but his primary and most beautiful name, embracing all others, is *Allāh* (God, the true God). *Allāh* is a derivative of the same Semitic root as the Biblical *Elōhîm* (God) and *hā-Elôh* (the true God) of Moses and the Hebrew prophets or the Aramaic *Alāhā* (God, the true God) of Jesus and John the Baptist. The formula "In the name of God, the All-Merciful, the Mercy-Giving" (*bismi-Llāhi 'r-Rahmāni 'r-Rahīm*), occurs one hundred and fourteen times in the Qur'ān—Islam's holy book—at the beginning of all but one chapter and twice in another. The phrase is central to Islamic ritual. In Islam, the All-Merciful (*ar-Rahmān*) and the Mercy-Giving (*ar-Rahīm*) may be said to be the greatest names of God after Allah. Of all his names, they are most descriptive of his relation to the world and emphasize his will in salvation history and throughout eternity to benefit creation and ultimately bring about the triumph of supreme good over evil.

The Qur'ān states: "It is the All-Merciful who assumed the Throne," meaning that God designs the world and rules the universe in his aspect as the All-Merciful. Consequently, mercy is the stamp of creation and the ontological thread that runs through everything. All that transpires—even temporal deprivation, harm, and evil—will, in due course, fall under the rubric of cosmic mercy. One Islamic lumi-nary maintained: "If God had revealed instead that 'the Overpowering (*al-Jabbār*) [another of God's ninety-nine principal names] had assumed the throne,' creation would melt." Another verse reads: "God ordained mercy upon himself," again emphasizing that mercy is a universal law (*sunna*), the dominant theme of the cosmos, and the fundamental purpose of the creative act. Two prophetic Traditions reveal God as saying: "My mercy has vanquished my wrath" and, in the second: "My mercy takes precedence over my wrath." Because we live in a universe bearing mercy's imprint, harmony and beauty permeate all things: "Our Lord, you have embraced all things in mercy and knowledge." In the verse, mercy—technically an attribute of act—is given priority of reference over knowledge—an attribute of essence—again emphasizing mercy's predominance in the universal plan.

THE PROPHET OF MERCY

According to Islamic revelation, Muhammad was the last and greatest of God's messengers, fulfilling the legacy of the Biblical and extra-Biblical prophets and confirming the teachings of Abraham, Moses, and Jesus. As the All-Merciful's chief emissary, he was fittingly called the "prophet of mercy" (*nabīy ar-rahma*). The Qur'ān says of him: "We did not send you but as a special mercy to all the worlds." The Prophet stated: "In certainty, I was not sent to bring down curses; I was only sent as a special mercy."

As in English, "mercy" in Arabic is tied to compassion and closely linked with the act of forgiveness and pardon. Theologically, Islamic tradition defines mercy as the intent to bring good to others and cause them benefit. As such, being merciful implies the desire to avert evil and harm. When associated with acts of pardon and forgiveness, mercy is retroactive and after the fact. But as it relates to the intent to bring about good or avert evil, mercy assumes an elemental and proactive dimension and is often before the fact, evincing a forward-looking quality that seeks to set things right, make a break with the past, and foster new beginnings where goodness and benefit can thrive.

The thread of proactive mercy ran throughout the fabric of the Prophet's life and was the key to his phenomenal, hard-earned, and lasting success. The loyalty and love of his followers and the awe and respect he evoked among his enemies were the fruits of such magnanimity. He said: "The closest of you to me on the Day of Judgment will be the best of you in character."

Muḥammad jested with children, showed a kindly humor toward adults, and even gave his followers friendly nicknames. He visited the sick, inquired after the welfare of neighbors, friends, followers, and even those who disbelieved in him. He was a warm egalitarian and shared everything with those around him, including their poverty. He was always willing to forgive, rarely chastising those who disobeyed him. He did not restrict his mercy to his followers. One day in Medina, he was sitting with his Companions, who later related: "A funeral procession passed us by, and the Prophet, may God bless and keep him, stood up so we all stood up because he had. Then we said: 'O Messenger of God, it is only the funeral procession of a Jew.' He replied: 'Was he not a human being?'"

Like Moses and other Biblical prophets, Muḥammad took part in battle. He was victorious but not a "world-conqueror." Although he engaged in war, he waged peace, and his inclination toward amnesty and diplomatic solutions is unmistakable. Above all it was the attitude of perpetual mercy that enabled him ultimately to forge for the first time in history a *pax islamica* in the Arabian Peninsula. That same attitude combined with masterly statesmanship enabled him not only to rescue the city of Medina—which had invited him for that purpose—from generations of civil war between its feuding clans but to create an island of stability in a sea of chaos and then extend that island gradually until it claimed the sea.

Those who died in the Prophet's battles were relatively few, and, according to some estimates, numbered around two hundred on both sides. He laid down rules of engagement and parameters of war that became a central part of Islamic law, forbidding the predation of civilian populations, the wanton destruction of lands and livestock, and the use of fire, flooding, and poisons that kill indiscriminately. The Prophet accepted people at their word and forgave them easily. He harbored no desire for vengeance and rejected the pagan custom of blood feuds and revenge. There was nothing mindless or fanatic about his piety. He was never intransigent or bent on war. Men who had been numbered among his most relentless and unforgiving enemies—like Abū Sufyān ibn Ḥarb, 'Ikrima ibn Abī Jahl, and Ṣafwān ibn Umayya—ultimately came not only to accept and follow the Prophet but, during the last years of their lives, devoted themselves heroically to his mission with a passion surpassing the enmity that had driven them before.

Even in the midst of bitter war, the Prophet inclined toward peaceful solutions. The Armistice of Ḥudaybiyya exemplified this spirit and his desire for the ultimate welfare of his enemies, in this case the pagans of Mecca. It was reached at a time when Muslim strength was reaching a high point and the power of the Prophet's pagan opponents—now in irreversible decline—was vulnerable and could have been ruthlessly crushed. Yet Muḥammad accepted without hesitation conciliatory concessions which initially appeared so humiliating that they bewildered his followers. The Qur'ānic revelation proclaimed the armistice a "manifest victory," and within weeks it was clear that it had set the stage for winning the hearts of the Prophet's harshest enemies and opening doors of reconciliation, which for years had been stubbornly shut.

In due course, the Prophet "conquered" Mecca peacefully. As he approached the city with the largest army ever assembled on the Arabian Peninsula till that time, he noticed a wild dog on the roadside nursing her litter and posted one of his Companions, Ju'ayl aḍ-Ḍamarī, to stand guard near her so that the entire contingent could pass without disturbing her or the pups.

After years of bitter conflict, some of the Prophet's Companions—in keeping with the ancient Arabian code of revenge—were sure that the day they took Mecca would be the hour of vengeance. One of Medina's tribal chieftains, Sa'd ibn 'Ubāda, noticed Abū Sufyān ibn Ḥarb, former leader of pagan Mecca, standing near the Prophet and told Abū Sufyān ominously: "This will be a day of slaughter." Sa'd was proudly bearing his tribal banner. The Prophet took it from him, handed it to Sa'd's son, and declared: "What Sa'd has said is wrong. No, this will be the day that God glorifies his House (the temple of Abraham in Mecca) and decorates it with a new covering."

By any measure, it was a day of mercy. In Mecca, the Prophet gathered his former enemies at the House of Abraham and asked them: "What do you think I am about to do with you?" They replied: "You are a magnanimous brother, the son of a magnanimous brother." He answered: "Go to your houses. You have been set free." It was this merciful and forgiving nature that finally established the Prophet's authority in Mecca after its peaceful conquest, fostered mutual understanding, and forged new bonds. In the end, it was above all this proactive mercy that spelled the death of idolatry and paganism in Mecca and throughout Arabia and prepared the way for Islam's unparalleled triumph in the world beyond.

THE COMMAND TO BE MERCIFUL

In imitation of the Prophet, Muslims are expected to be merciful, to bring good, and to seek the benefit of others—all others—not wish them harm or rejoice in the evil that befalls them. Indeed, the Tradition of Primacy promotes a doctrine of universal, all-embracing mercy. Commentators emphasize this point, clarifying that the mercy Muslims are commanded to show is not exclusively for themselves or the righteous amongst them. It extends to all human beings: Jews, Christians, the believing and unbelieving, the upright and the immoral, and it goes beyond the human family to include both the animate and inanimate: birds and animals, even plants and trees. In English, "be merciful to those on earth" tends to imply human beings. Translated here as "those," the Arabic word *man* is broad and inclusive. Its primary reference is to rational beings, but it includes, by secondary reference, non-rational ones also: animals, plants, and, by extension, what today would be termed the environment.

The Prophet told an anecdote of a sinful man suffering from thirst one oppressively hot day who came across a well. He went down into it—(Middle Eastern wells are often open and with deep, winding staircases)—drew water, and drank. When he came back up, he noticed a dog, panting from thirst and eating the clay around the well for moisture. The man said to himself: "This dog is suffering from thirst like I was." He went down into the well a second time, filled his shoe with water, and let the dog drink. God loved the man's humane act, showed him mercy, and forgave all his sins. When Muhammad's Companions heard the story, they asked: "O Messenger of God, will we be rewarded for being good to animals?" He answered: "Yes, there is reward in showing good to every living creature." In another Tradition, the Prophet emphasized the atrociousness of merciless behavior in God's eyes and told of a woman condemned to hell for intentionally starving a cat to death.

Mercy begins with the individual by taking care of the self physically, emotionally, and spiritually and includes exercise and diet, pursuing education, and keeping good company. It also means having a good opinion of oneself—without being arrogant or blind to one's faults—living in constant anticipation of God's help and mercy along with other Islamic corollaries of behavior like the categorical prohibition of suicide and despair. From the individual, concentric rings of mercy extend outward, taking in parents, spouse, children, family, neighbors, community, and the world. Part of being merciful toward others is having a good opinion of them, defending their good name, and doing whatever makes their lives better and averts harm.

The Qur'ān looks upon marital life as a primary locus of mercy and, consequently, exalts the institution of marriage as one of creation's marvels and chief proofs of God, next to the creation of the heavens and the earth and of humankind itself. Marriage is not just the basic mode of human generation, manifesting the biological continuity of divine creation, but forms the primary social nucleus of love: "Among God's signs is his creating for you partners in marriage from yourselves so that you find happiness in them and his putting between you bonds of affection and mercy. Certainly in that there are signs for people who think."

The Arabic words for "affection" and "mercy" in the verse are *mawadda* and *rahma*. Matrimonial "mercy" means that both husband and wife seek to make each other happy, desiring what is good, prosperous, and beneficial for each. It implies that each spouse treat the other honorably and that neither be content with evil or harm as the other's lot.

Mawadda—translated above as "affection" but more frequently as "love"—precedes *rahma* in the verse, implying that love is mercy's spiritual bedrock. While Arabic has many words for love, *mawadda* represents a special type. One of the ninety-nine principal names of God in Arabic—*al-Wadūd*, "the Loving"—is derived from the same linguistic root. *Mawadda* does not refer to physical love but to an active, emotive love that is direct and personal, involving affectionate care and abiding attention to others' needs. With regard to God, *al-Wadūd* ("the Loving"), *mawadda* refers to his providential care for creation and the personal bounty and protection that he grants those he loves. With regard to human interaction, both in a general and marital context—as in the above-quoted verse—mawadda refers to loving involvement in the life of another, not simply through care or concern for that person's well-being but also by personal faithfulness, emotional support, good counsel, and a general regard for that person's interests.

THE LAW OF UNIVERSAL RECIPROCITY

As discussed at the beginning of this essay and as the Traditions above concerning kindness to animals indicate, mercy—God's signature in creation—is linked to a law of universal reciprocity: Mercy will be shown to the merciful, and it will be withdrawn from the merciless. The positive side of this universal law is reflected in the words of the Tradition of Primacy: "Be merciful to those on earth, and he who is in heaven will be merciful to you," a lesson often repeated in the Islamic scriptures. The Prophet taught: "Truly, God only shows mercy to those of his servants who are themselves merciful." Here the complementary side of the law of mercy is clarified. The Prophet said elsewhere: "Whoever shows no mercy will be shown no mercy." In the same authoritative collections, we find: "God will show no mercy to those who show no mercy to humankind." The Prophet warned his community: "Being merciful is only stripped away from the damned," implying that mercy is the natural condition of the human soul and is only stripped away and exchanged for mercilessness in people with callous, unnatural hearts that can no longer receive it. A heart that no longer has the capacity to feel mercy cannot be a receptacle of salvation either or a container of true faith; to become ruthless and void of compassion is to carry the mark of divine wrath and bear the brand of damnation and is the sure sign of an evil end.

Thus, the reciprocity inherent in the universal law of mercy embodies another dimension: the fact that mercy is linked with faith and opens the door of salvation, while mercilessness is linked with the rejection of God and invites damnation. Classical commentators explain that mercy springs from a healthy heart, one that is spiritually alive and suitable for sincere faith. Utter lack of mercy, on the other hand, reflects a heart that is spiritually dead. The implications are profound: Mercy and true belief do not cohabit hearts where hatred and the utter disregard for others reign.

CONCLUSION

The imperative to be merciful—to bring benefit to the world and avert harm—must underlie a Muslim's understanding of reality and attitude toward society. Islam was not intended to create a chosen people, fostering exclusive claims for themselves, while looking down upon the rest of humanity like a sea of untouchables or regarding the animate and inanimate worlds around them as fields readied for wanton exploitation. Wherever Muslims find themselves, they are called upon to be actively and positively engaged as vanguards of mercy, welfare, and well-being.

Islam's call to mercy should not render Muslims incapable of a wise and measured response to transgression, oppression, or injustice, which in some cases can only be checked by force. Islam is not a pacifist religion, although it commands its followers to incline toward merciful solutions and seek peace, while always remaining within dignified bounds and proper parameters consistent with Islam's overarching doctrine of mercy. In a faith like Islam, which teaches that a person may be condemned to hell for starving a cat, it goes without saying that acts of ruthless barbarity must be rejected and never given the aura of religious sanctity.

The merciless heart abides in the spirit of the damned, while the healthy heart is instinctively humane and comprehends the pricelessness of mercy. It is to people who are not "damaged goods" but humanly intact and spiritually alive that the Prophet directed his admonition: "Take an informed opinion (literally, *fatwā*) from your heart. What is good puts your self and your heart at rest. What is wrong is never fully acceptable to your self and wavers in your heart, even if people give you a different opinion (*fatwā*) and keep on giving it to you."

علم

Mahatma Gandhi

Yajna, Welfare, and Service

from a letter to Narandas Gandhi, October 28, 1930

~ ~ ~

Tuesday morning, October 28, 1930

I wrote about *yajna* last week, but feel like writing more about it. It will perhaps be worthwhile further to consider a principle which has been created along with mankind. Yajna is duty to be performed, or service to be rendered, all the twenty-four hours of the day, and hence a maxim like "The powers of the good are always exercised for a benevolent purpose" is inappropriate, if benevolence has any taste of favour about it. To serve without desire is to favour not others, but ourselves even as in discharging a debt we serve only ourselves, lighten our burden and fulfil our duty. Again, not only the good, but all of us are bound to place our resources at the disposal of humanity. And if such is the law, as evidently it is, indulgence ceases to hold

---

Mohandas Karamchand Gandhi, born in 1869, led India to independence and inspired movements for civil rights and freedom across the world. Known as Mahatma ("Great Soul") internationally and Bapu ("Father") in India, Gandhi employed and wrote prodigiously about *satyagraha* and *ahimsa*—resistance to tyranny through civil disobedience and nonviolence. Before his assassination in 1948, Gandhi also led campaigns for easing poverty, expanding women's rights, and building bridges across ethnic and religious differences. The passage below appears in a letter dated October 28, 1930, which Gandhi wrote to Narandas Gandhi, secretary of the ashram.

a place in life and gives way to renunciation. For human beings renunciation itself is enjoyment. This is what differentiates man from the beast.

Some object that life thus understood becomes dull and devoid of art, and leaves no room for the householder. But I think in saying this they misinterpret the word "renunciation." Renunciation here does not mean abandoning the world and retiring into the forest.

The spirit of renunciation should rule all the activities of life. A householder does not cease to be one if he regards life as a duty rather than as an indulgence. A cobbler, a cultivator, a tradesman or a barber may be inspired in their work or activities either by the spirit of renunciation or merely by the desire for self-indulgence.

A merchant who carries on his business in a spirit of sacrifice will have crores passing through his hands, but he will, if he follows the law, use his abilities for service. He will, therefore, not cheat or speculate, will lead a simple life, will not injure a living soul and will lose millions rather than harm anybody. Let no one run away with the idea that this type of merchant exists only in my imagination. Fortunately for the world, he does exist in the West as well as in the East. It is true such merchants may be counted on one's fingers but the type ceases to be imaginary as soon as even one living specimen can be found to answer to it.

All of us know of a philanthropic tailor in Wadhwan. I know of one such barber. Everyone of us knows of such a weaver. And if we go deeply into the matter, we shall come across men in every walk of life who lead dedicated lives. No doubt these sacrificers obtain their livelihood by their work. But livelihood is not their objective, but only a by-product of their vocation. Motilal was a tailor at first, and continued as a tailor afterwards. But his spirit was changed and his work was transmuted into worship. He began to think about the welfare of others and his life became artistic in the real sense of the term.

A life of sacrifice is the pinnacle of art and is full of true joy. Such life is the source of ever fresh springs of joy which never dry up and never satiate. Yajna is not yajna if one feels it to be burdensome or annoying. Self-indulgence leads to destruction and renunciation to immortality. Joy has no independent existence. It depends upon our attitude to life. One man will enjoy theatrical scenery, another the ever new scenes which unfold themselves in the sky. Joy, therefore, is a matter of education. We shall delight in things which we have been taught to delight in as children. And illustrations can be easily cited of different national tastes. Again, many sacrificers imagine that they are free to receive from the people everything they need and many things they do not need, because they are rendering disinterested service. Directly this idea sways a man, he ceases to be a servant and becomes a tyrant over the people.

One who would serve others will not waste a thought upon his own comforts, which he leaves to be attended to or neglected by his Master on high. He will not, therefore, encumber himself with everything that comes his way; he will take only what he strictly needs and leave the rest. He will be calm, free from anger and unruffled in mind even if he finds himself inconvenienced. His service, like virtue, is its own reward, and he will rest content with it. Again, one dare not be negligent in service or be behindhand with it. He who thinks that he must be diligent only in his personal business and unpaid public business may be done in any way and at any time he chooses, has still to learn the very rudiments of the science of sacrifice. Voluntary service of others demands the best of which one is capable, and must take precedence over service of self. In fact, the pure devotee consecrates himself to the service of humanity without any reservation whatever.

Blessings from BAPU

ॐ

George Orwell

REFLECTIONS ON GANDHI

from the *Partisan Review*

~~~

Close friendships, Gandhi says, are dangerous, because "friends react on one another" and through loyalty to a friend one can be led into wrong-doing. This is unquestionably true. Moreover, if one is to love God, or to love humanity as a whole, one cannot give one's preference to any individual person. This again is true, and it marks the point at which the humanistic and the religious attitude cease to be reconcilable. To an ordinary human being, love means nothing if it does not mean loving some people more than others. The autobiography leaves it uncertain whether Gandhi behaved in an inconsiderate way to his wife and children, but at any rate makes it clear that on three occasions he was willing to let his wife or child die rather than administer the animal food prescribed by the doctor. It is true that the threatened death never actually occurred, and also that Gandhi—with, one gathers, a good deal of moral pressure in the opposite direction—always gave the patient the choice of staying

---

George Orwell was born Eric Blair in the British colony of Bengal in 1903. After going to school at Eton and serving with the Indian Imperial Police in Burma, Orwell returned to Europe and earned his living as a writer of essays and novels, most of which are deeply political. For several years Orwell lived in poverty, though he eventually found work as a schoolteacher and then a journalist. Orwell died from tuberculosis in 1950 and is now most famous for two novels, *1984* and *Animal Farm*. The following selection first appeared as part of a larger essay in the *Partisan Review* in 1949.

alive at the price of committing a sin: still, if the decision had been solely his own, he would have forbidden the animal food, whatever the risks might be. There must, he says, be some limit to what we will do in order to remain alive, and the limit is well on this side of chicken broth. This attitude is perhaps a noble one, but, in the sense which—I think—most people would give to the word, it is inhuman. The essence of being human is that one does not seek perfection, that one *is* sometimes willing to commit sins for the sake of loyalty, that one does not push asceticism to the point where it makes friendly intercourse impossible, and that one is prepared in the end to be defeated and broken up by life, which is the inevitable price of fastening one's love upon other human individuals. No doubt alcohol, tobacco and so forth are things that a saint must avoid, but sainthood is also a thing that human beings must avoid. There is an obvious retort to this, but one should be wary about making it. In this yogi-ridden age, it is too readily assumed that "non-attachment" is not only better than a full acceptance of earthly life, but that the ordinary man only rejects it because it is too difficult: in other words, that the average human being is a failed saint. It is doubtful whether this is true. Many people genuinely do not wish to be saints, and it is probable that some who achieve or aspire to sainthood have never felt much temptation to be human beings. If one could follow it to its psychological roots, one would, I believe, find that the main motive for "non-attachment" is a desire to escape from the pain of living, and above all from love, which, sexual or non-sexual, is hard work. But it is not necessary here to argue whether the otherworldly or the humanistic ideal is "higher." The point is that they are incompatible. One must choose between God and Man, and all "radicals" and "progressives," from the mildest Liberal to the most extreme Anarchist, have in effect chosen Man.

Maimonides

LEVELS OF GIVING

in *Mishneh Torah*

~~~

There are eight degrees of almsgiving, each one superior to the other. The highest degree, than which there is none higher, is one who upholds the hand of an Israelite reduced to poverty by handing him a gift or a loan, or entering into a partnership with him, or finding work for him, in order to strengthen his hand, so that he would have no need to beg from other people. Concerning such a one Scripture says, "Thou shalt uphold him; as a stranger and a settler shall he live with thee" (Lev. 25:35), meaning uphold him, so that he would not lapse into want.

Below this is he who gives alms to the poor in such a way that he does not know to whom he has given, nor does the poor man know from whom he has received. This constitutes the fulfilling of religious duty for its own sake, and for such there was a chamber of secrets in the temple, whereunto the righteous would contribute secretly, and

Moses Maimonides was born in Spain in 1135, the son of a judge in the rabbinical court of Cordoba. Soon after his birth, Christians reconquered Spain from its Muslim rulers, and Maimonides spent his childhood moving to avoid persecution, living first in Andalusia and later in Morocco, Israel, and Egypt. In time he became a physician, rabbi, and philosopher of great influence. Among his most famous works are *The Guide for the Perplexed* and the *Mishneh Torah,* a code of Jewish law from which this selection is taken. Maimonides died in 1204. This translation was done by Philip Birnbaum.

wherefrom the poor of good families would draw their sustenance in equal secrecy. Close to such a person is he who contributes directly to the alms fund.

One should not, however, contribute directly to the alms fund unless he knows that the person in charge of it is trustworthy, is a sage, and knows how to manage it properly, as was the case of Rabbi Hananiah ben Teradion.

Below this is he who knows to whom he is giving, while the poor man does not know from whom he is receiving. He is thus like a great among the sages who were wont to set out secretly and throw the money down at the doors of the poor. This is a proper way of doing it, and a preferable one if those in charge of alms are not conducting themselves as they should.

Below this is the case where the poor man knows from whom he is receiving, but himself remains unknown to the giver. He is thus like the great among the sages who used to place the money in the fold of a linen sheet that they would throw over their shoulder, whereupon the poor would come behind them and take the money without being exposed to humiliation.

Below this is he who hands alms to the poor man before being asked for them.

Below this is he who hands alms to the poor man after the latter has asked for them.

Below this is he who gives the poor man less than what is proper but with a friendly countenance.

Below this is he who gives alms with a frowning countenance.

The Buddha's Last Instruction

in *House of Light*

~~~

"Make of yourself a light"
said the Buddha,
before he died.
I think of this every morning
as the east begins
to tear off its many clouds
of darkness, to send up the first
signal—a white fan
streaked with pink and violet,
even green.
An old man, he lay down
between two sala trees,
and he might have said anything,
knowing it was his final hour.
The light burns upward,

Mary Oliver was born in Cleveland, Ohio, in 1935. After attending Vassar College, Oliver went on to write more than a dozen books of poetry and prose. Her collection of poetry, *American Primitive,* won the Pulitzer Prize for Poetry in 1984, and *New and Selected Poems* won the National Book Award for Poetry in 1992. This poem appeared in her 1990 collection, *House of Light*.

it thickens and settles over the fields.
Around him, the villagers gathered
and stretched forward to listen.
Even before the sun itself
hangs, disattached, in the blue air,
I am touched everywhere
by its ocean of yellow waves.
No doubt he thought of everything
that had happened in his difficult life.
And then I feel the sun itself
as it blazes over the hills,
like a million flowers on fire—
clearly I'm not needed,
yet I feel myself turning
into something of inexplicable value.
Slowly, beneath the branches,
he raised his head.
He looked into the faces of that frightened crowd.

Mark Helprin

NORTH LIGHT—A RECOLLECTION IN THE PRESENT TENSE

in *Ellis Island and Other Stories*

~~~

W e are being held back. We are poised at a curve in the road on the southern ridge of a small valley. The sun shines from behind, illuminating with flawless light the moves and countermoves of several score tanks below us. For a long time, we have been absorbed in the mystery of matching the puffs of white smoke from tank cannon with the sounds that follow. The columns themselves move silently: only the great roar rising from the battle proves it not to be a dream.

A man next to me is deeply absorbed in sniffing his wrist. "What are you doing?" I ask.

"My wife," he says. "I can still smell her perfume on my wrist, and I taste the taste of her mouth. It's sweet."

Mark Helprin was born in 1947 and was raised in the United States and in the British West Indies. He went on to serve in the British Merchant Navy, the Israeli infantry, and the Israeli Air Force, and to write several short story collections, children's books, and novels, including *Refiner's Fire: The Life and Adventures of Marshall Pearl, a Foundling* and *A Soldier of the Great War*. His essays and columns have appeared in *The New Yorker*, *The Atlantic Monthly*, the *Wall Street Journal*, and the *National Review*. He also served as a policy advisor and speechwriter to presidential candidate Bob Dole in 1996. This story appeared in his collection *Ellis Island and Other Stories*.

We were called up this morning. The war is two days old. Now it is afternoon, and we are being held back—even though our forces below are greatly outnumbered. We are being held back until nightfall, when we will have a better chance on the plain; for it is packed with tanks, and we have only two old half-tracks. They are loaded with guns—it is true—but they are lightly armored, they are slow, and they present high targets. We expect to move at dusk or just before. Then we will descend on the road into the valley and fight amid the shadows. No one wants this: we all are terrified.

The young ones are frightened because, for most of them, this is the first battle. But their fear is not as strong as the blood which is rising and fills their chests with anger and strength. They have little to lose, being, as they are, only eighteen. They look no more frightened than members of a sports team before an important match: it is that kind of fear, for they are responsible only to themselves.

Married men, on the other hand, are given away by their eyes and faces. They are saying to themselves, "I must not die; I *must not die.*" They are remembering how they used to feel when they were younger; and they know that they have to fight. They may be killed, but if they don't fight they will surely be killed, because the slow self-made fear which demands constant hesitation is the most efficient of all killers. It is not the cautious who die, but the overcautious. The married men are trying to strike an exact balance between their responsibility as soldiers, their fervent desire to stay alive, and their only hope—which is to go into battle with the smooth, courageous, trancelike movements that will keep them out of trouble. Soldiers who do not know how (like dancers or mountain climbers) to let their bodies think for them are very liable to be killed. There is a flow to hard combat; it is not (as it has often been depicted) entirely chance or entirely skill. A thousand signals and signs speak to you, much as in music. And what a sad moment it is when you must, for one reason or another, ignore them. The married men fear this moment. We should have begun hours ago. Being held back is bad luck.

"What time is it?" asks one of the young soldiers. Someone answers him.

"Fourteen hundred." No one in the Israeli Army except high-ranking officers (colonels, generals—and we have here no colonels or generals) tells time in this fashion.

"What are you, a general?" asks the young soldier. Everyone laughs, as if this were funny, because we are scared. We should not be held back like this.

Another man, a man who is close to fifty and is worrying about his two sons who are in Sinai, keeps on looking at his watch. It is expensive and Japanese, with a black dial. He looks at it every minute to see what time it is, because he has actually forgotten. If he were asked what the time was, he would not be able to respond without checking the watch, even though he has done so fifty times in the last hour. He too is afraid. The sun glints off the crystal and explodes in our eyes.

As younger men who badly wanted to fight, we thought we knew what courage was. Now we know that courage is the forced step of going into battle when you want anything in the world but that, when there is every reason to stay out, when you have been through all the tests, and passed them, and think that it's all over. Then the war hits like an artillery shell and you are forced to be eighteen again, but you can't be eighteen again; not with the taste of your wife's mouth in your mouth, not with the smell of her perfume on your wrists. The world turns upside down in minutes.

How hard we struggle in trying to remember the easy courage we once had. But we can't. We must either be brave in a different way, or not at all. What is that way? How can we fight like seasoned soldiers when this morning we kissed our children? There is a way, hidden in the history or war. There must be, for we can see them fighting in the valley; and, high in the air, silver specks are dueling in a dream of blue silence.

Why are we merely watching? To be restrained this way is simply not fair. A quick entrance would get the fear over with, and that would help. But, then again, in the Six Day War, we waited for weeks while the Egyptian Army built up against us. And then, after that torture, we burst out and leapt across the desert, sprinting, full of energy and fury that kept us like dancers—nimble and absorbed—and kept us alive. That is the secret: You have to be angry. When we arrived on the ridge this morning, we were anything but angry. Now we are beginning to get angry. It is our only salvation. We are angry because we are being held back.

We swear, and kick the sides of the half-tracks. We hate the voice on our radio which keeps telling us to hold to our position. We hate that man more than we hate the enemy, for now we want engagement with the enemy. We are beginning to crave battle, and we are getting angrier, and angrier, because we know that by five o'clock we will be worn out. They should let us go now.

A young soldier who has been following the battle, through binoculars, screams. "God!" he says. "Look! Look!"

The Syrians are moving up two columns of armor that will overwhelm our men on the plain below. The sergeant gets on the radio, but from it we hear a sudden waterfall of talk. Holding the microphone in his hand, he listens with us as we discover that they know. They are demanding more air support.

"What air support?" we ask. There is no air-to-ground fighting that we can see. As we watch the Syrians approach, our hearts are full of fear for those of us below. How did our soldiers know? There must be spotters or a patrol somewhere deep in, high on a hill, like us. What air support? There are planes all over the place, but not here.

Then we feel our lungs shaking like drums. The hair on our arms and the back of our necks stands up and we shake as flights of fighters roar over the hill. They are no more than fifty feet above us. We can feel the heat from the tailpipes, and the orange flames are blinding. The noise is superb. They come three at a time; one wave, two, three, four, five, and six. These are our pilots. The mass of the machinery flying through the air is so great and graceful that we are stunned beyond the noise. We cheer in anger and in satisfaction. It seems the best thing in the world when, as they pass the ridge (How they hug the ground; what superb pilots!) they dip their wings for our sake. They are descending into a thicket of anti-aircraft missiles and radar-directed guns—and they dip their wings for us.

Now we are hot. The married men feel as if rivers are rushing through them, crossing and crashing, for they are angry and full of energy. The sergeant depresses the lever on the microphone. He identifies himself and says, "In the name of God, we want to go in *now*. Damn you if you don't let us go in."

There is hesitation and silence on the other end. "Who is this?" they ask.

"This is Shimon."

More silence, then, "Okay, Shimon. Move! Move!"

The engines start. Now we have our own thunder. It is not even three o'clock. It is the right time; they've caught us at the right time. The soldiers are not slow in mounting the half-tracks. The sound of our roaring engines has magnetized them and they *jump* in. The young drivers race the engines, as they always do.

For a magnificent half minute, we stare into the north light, smiling. The man who tasted the sweet taste of his wife kisses his wrist. The young soldiers are no longer afraid, and the married men are in a perfect sustained fury. Because they love their wives and children, they will of think of them until the battle is over. Now we are soldiers again. The engines are deafening. No longer are we held back. We are shaking; we are crying. Now we stare into the north light, and listen to the explosions below. Now we hear the levers of the gearshifts. Now our drivers exhale and begin to drive. Now we are moving.

COME OUT AND GIVE SOMETHING

Every prophet is a beggar calling, "Something for God's sake!
Please, lend something

to God." The people they ask this of are truly destitute, but
still prophets and teachers

go from door to door. Though all the doors of heaven
      are open
to them, they beg for

pieces of bread. They eat the bread they get, but they didn't
ask from appetite. In fact,

don't say they eat bread; they eat light. God has said *be
moderate* when eating and

Mowlana Jalaluddin Rumi, best known to English-speaking audiences as
Rumi, is considered to be one of the greatest of Sufi poets. Born in 1207
in Balkh (now Afghanistan), Rumi was a teacher, theologian, and philosopher, as well as a mystic poet, whose influence spread throughout
Afghanistan and central Asia, Turkey, and India. His most significant work
is the *Mathnawi,* a multivolume work of stories and lyric poetry on teaching and Sufi lore. He also brought us the Mawlawiya (Mevlevi), a Sufi
order that engages dance in its spiritual practices and that is better known
in the West as the Whirling Dervishes. This translation was done by
Coleman Barks.

drinking bread and wine, but God never said *be satisfied*
when taking in light.

God offers a teacher the treasures of the world, and the
teacher responds, "To be

in love with God and expect to be paid for it!" A servant
wants to be rewarded for what he does.

A lover wants only to be in love's presence, an ocean whose
depth will never be known.

This cannot be said! Let us return, Husam, to the story of the
teacher begging in the street.

Listen to him: "Love is reckless. Love makes the sea boil
like a kettle. Love crumbles

a stone mountain to sand. Out of love God says to
    Muhammad,
'But for you, I would not have

created the universe.' Love says, 'This world is the egg. You
are the chick.' Everything

helps us understand this." The ground is low to give some
notion of humility. Spring's

green comes to reveal an alchemy that happens *inside* us.
Every experience begs

like a dervish for us to come out and give something.

عِلم

Peggy Payne

THE PURE IN HEART

in *Revelation*

~~~

Swain hits the brakes and all the books on the car seat beside him shoot forward onto the floor. A Datsun swerves out around him, the driver yelling, but Swain can't hear a sound through his closed window. The last Swain sees as the car window flashes past is the guy's finger pointing him to look up. He does as he's told and looks: red light. When did they put a light in here? There was never a light here.

He sighs, shrugs, backs his car out of the intersection and sits motionless, his elbow on the hot window frame in the midsummer heat. Six o'clock and it's still this hot. The smell of the road tar rises up around him.

He stares for a moment at the books spilled onto the floor, then slowly piles them back on the seat. *Eschatology and Ethics. New World Metaphysics. The Science of Theology.* He shakes the cold coffee off the bottom book. Damn. He finds the mug, empty now, and puts it back on the seat. Somebody behind him honks. Okay, okay, he thinks, and pulls out.

Peggy Payne was born in 1949 in North Carolina, where she has lived all her life. After graduating from Duke University and writing for two years for the *Raleigh Times,* Payne became a freelance writer. She is now a novelist, a nonfiction writer, and an editorial consultant whose work has been supported by the National Endowment for the Humanities and others. The following selection is the first chapter of her 1988 novel, *Revelation.*

I should have demolished the one in the Datsun, kept going and plowed right through him. Him and his window closed to keep in the air-conditioning. He could have looked where he was going. I should have bashed him, or at least yelled something. One good "fuck you." Once in my life I'd like to do that. The one time I ever do, it'll turn out to be somebody from the congregation.

He presses his head back against the headrest, trying to loosen up his neck muscles. Nothing is more irritating than sitting in a seminar with a bunch of other ministers all day. All of them working so hard at being warm and sensitive. They act as if they're teaching kindergarten for a living, not working with adults. I'd rather deal with my own congregation any time, he thinks. At least they don't expect me to act like Captain Kangaroo.

He pulls to a stop for another light, putting a hand out to hold back the stack of books beside him. He glances out each of the side windows, as if maybe somebody had been listening and heard what he was thinking.

In all his life, Swain would never have said that he was "called" to the ministry. After spending a day with his colleagues, he still occasionally questions how it happened. But in his heart, he knows.

He simply grew up certain that it would be so—that he would be a preacher. Not because of any belief he could actually pin down. Instead, it was because of a powerful lifelong desire that there be "something else." He wanted there to be more to life than he himself had seen or felt so far—something to ease his chronic vague dissatisfaction, something to subdue the irritation which he had always reined in ... even in his moment alone in traffic. Some would consider that yearning a too-slim, or very selfish, reason for the choice he made, but it was enough for Swain. So, after Yale and one brief stint as an associate minister, he came home to Chapel Hill to be the pastor at Westside Presbyterian.

He and Julie live in a neighborhood a few blocks back from the fraternity and sorority houses along Franklin Street, the wide main street that divides the campus from the town. Turning now onto his own narrow shaded street, Swain feels the tension inside him let go a little. He loves it here. It's an old neighborhood. The houses all look different from each other, big white-columned ones next to more modest ones like his own. In summer, the big yards are lush and unkempt around the huge oaks and magnolias. He and Julie have left theirs wooded and no one around them seems to mind. He edges his car over to the side, and lets an old Mercedes pass.

Several other families from church live in the surrounding blocks. Westside has a liberal congregation full of academics from the university community. Lots of bright, interesting people, but as a group, they tend to be a bit stiff … like Swain, a bit overly intellectual. The church was an excellent choice for the careful, self-controlled man that Swain has grown up to be.

Now he pulls slowly up into his own gravel driveway, sits still for a moment to recover from the day, then gathers up his books and goes in.

The house is quiet. Julie is already out back on the patio, arranging skewers of pork and green peppers on the rack of the charcoal grill.

Swain gets a beer out of the fridge. He knocks on the kitchen window and waves to Julie.

Julie is a medical librarian at the hospital, though if you met her you would never think of libraries. You might think of Hayley Mills in those movies from her teenage years. She has the same full features and thick red hair. "I'll be out in a minute," Swain calls to her through the pane. He goes back into the bedroom and changes into shorts and a T-shirt. Their bedroom, shaded on two sides by a big oak tree, is cool and dim. He stands, damp still, in front of the rattling window air conditioner and feels the cold column of air wrap around his middle. He feels his mind slow down as his temperature drops. He takes a swallow of the beer and closes his eyes. A peaceful moment. Why can't it all be this way?

The backyard smell of lighter fluid and searing meat reaches him. He goes out to find Julie.

"Hey," she says, and still holding the basting brush, turns to kiss him. He holds on to her for a moment, until she pulls away to take care of the fire.

"What can I do?" he says.

"Set the table. Otherwise it's mostly done. I got home a little early."

"Lucky you. I wish I had." He unloads the tray of plates and silver she has brought out, then squints up the slight hill of their wooded backyard. There's a spot of color there he hasn't noticed before. "Isn't that a lady's slipper?" he says. "Was that out yesterday?" But Julie is busy. She doesn't look.

Swain's long white feet still bare, he carefully picks his way up the hill to examine the flower. It's then, as he stops yards away from the plant—not at all a lady's slipper—that he hears God for the first time.

The sound comes up and over the hill. He stands frozen and feels it coming. One quick cut. Like a hugely amplified PA system, blocks away, switched on for a moment by mistake. "... Know that truth is ..."

There is no mistaking the voice. At the first sound, the first rolling syllable, he's swimming up out of a sleep, shocked into wakefulness. He stands where he stood, feeling all through him the murmuring life of each of his million cells. Each of them all at once. He feels the line where his two lips touch, the fingers of his left hand pressed against his leg, the spears of wet grass against the flat soles of his feet, the burning half-circles of tears that stand in his eyes. His bone marrow hums inside him like colonies of bees. He feels the breath pouring in and out of him, through the damp red passages of his skull. Swain is dizzy, stunned ... the force of it coursing through him. The last vowel, the "i" of "is," lies quivering on the air like a note struck on a wineglass.

Then it stops. In the slow way that fireworks die, the knowledge fades. He is left again with his surfaces and the usual vague darkness within. He sinks back toward what he has always known. Then he takes a breath, blinks his eyes, runs a hand down his chest, down one leg. All the same, still there. He turns back around to see if Julie has heard.

But her back is turned, she's serving the two plates that he has set on the patio table. He put them there himself. A breeze is moving the edge of the outdoor tablecloth. She turns back around toward him, looking up the hill at him. It's as if he's watching her in a TV commercial. She's pretty; he doesn't know her; she doesn't know he's there. She's looking into a TV camera, about to hold up a product. "Soup's on," she says, smiling. "Come eat." She stands and waits for him, as he walks, almost runs, barefooted, stepping on rocks and sticks and pine cones, back down to her. He has to reach her, break through whatever is suddenly between them and get to her. He rushes straight for her—seeing her eyes widen, her smile waver—he grabs her with both arms, ignoring her surprise and the half second of her resistance, pulling her close, right against him, one hand in her hair, one arm down the length of her back. He's as close as he can get.

"Swain," she says, trying to pull back so she can see him.

He holds her tighter. He starts to speak and nothing comes out. He feels the force of his own heartbeat in her body. "Something happened," he says.

She waits for more, but he doesn't say anything. What is going on? "Swain, this is scaring me. Please say something." Still nothing. She feels him take a breath to speak and then stop. "What happened?" she says. She wants to shake him. Why won't he say? "Are you okay?" She runs her hands up and down his back, looking for something wrong. His shirt is wet. "Swain, what is it?"

He tries to say it: "Julie, I heard God." But it won't come out. Then a wave of fatigue washes through him. He lets his arms loosen. "I don't know how to tell you. You'll think I'm crazy."

She shakes her head. "I won't."

But he still can't say it.

She glances at the table. Swain looks where she looks; there is food on the plates.

"Let's sit down," she says. "Then we can talk...." Did he have a stroke? If he did, could he still be standing up? She sees the shelves at the library where she files the books on circulatory diseases. Swain doesn't act like this.

He continues to stare at the table. The fork looks so foreign, so strange. The meat, shining in the patio light. It looks terrible. He shivers. The sweat that soaked his shirt is starting to chill him.

"I'm going to get a jacket," he says. "I'm cold." She nods. He can feel her eyes on his back as he walks into the house.

There are no lights on inside, only the yellowish glow of the patio light through the window, shining on one patch of floor. He can feel the hair standing up on his arms. This is insane, he thinks— I'm not afraid of the dark. He doesn't touch the switch—he forces himself to wait—until he gets to the closet at the end of the hall. There it is. His jacket. He has his hand in the closet, reaching for it, when he hears the voice again. One syllable. "Son." The sound unfurls down the long hall toward him. The word and its thousand echoes hit him all at once. He holds on to the wooden bar where the coat hangs, while the shock washes over his back.

He stays where he is, his back and neck bent, his hand bracing him, waiting. Nothing else happens. Again, it is over. He straightens painfully, as if he had held the position for hours. He walks out onto the patio. Julie, at the table, strains to see his face against the light beside the door.

"Are you all right?" she says.

He sits, looks down at his plate. She thinks, He is not all right.

Swain holds the jacket, lays it across his lap like a napkin. He shakes his head. A sob is starting low in his chest, dry like a cough. He feels it coming. He's crying, his own voice tearing and breaking through him. He hears his father's voice saying, "Swain, I cannot have noise. Not in this house." But he can't stop. Inside him, walls are falling. Interior walls cave in like old plaster, fall away to dust. He feels it like the breaking of living bones. In the last cool retreat of his reason, he thinks, I am seeing my own destruction. Then that cool place is invaded too. He feels the violent tide of whatever is in him flooding his last safe ground. He holds himself with both arms; Julie, on her knees beside his chair, holds him. God has done this to him. This is God. Tears drip from his face and trickle down his neck.

An hour later, he lies quietly beside her in bed. He has let himself be put to bed like a sick child. She finally believed him that he didn't need a doctor and crawled in beside him. The sheets feel cool, making a little tent over him. He keeps his arms close to his sides under the covers. He says, "Out there in the yard, I heard something. A voice."

"Yes? A voice?"

"God," he says. His mouth is dry. His eyes follow the patterns of swirls in the plaster of the ceiling.

She turns her head toward him, the light is shining on his face. She looks at him carefully now, her eyes scanning his eyes. He is going to tell me. She feels her heart thumping.

"Standing up there on the hill," he says. "I heard God."

She hesitates. "So ... what did it—what did the voice sound like?"

Swain repeats the words he heard. He still cannot say what happened: that hearing the voice, he felt the living hum of his every cell. That he is as weak now as a child who has had a terrible fever.

She reaches over and touches his hair, strokes it. So this is what it's about. The voice of God. All the air goes out of her. What a relief. Her whole body lets go worrying and sinks right down into the mattress. When all this time I was thinking he was sick, or that it was something awful. She says, "I don't think you're crazy. It's all right."

If one of us was to hear God, it should have been her, he thinks. But a different God, not this ... She deserves the one he has believed in until now.

"For you it would be all right," he says. He means it as a compliment. He has envied her imaginings, felt left behind sometimes by the unfocused look of her eyes. Though she'll always tell him where she is, if he asks: that she goes back, years back, to particular days with particular weathers. That she plays in the backyard of her grandparents' house, shirtless, in seersucker shorts, breathing the heavy summer air, near the blue hydrangeas. Swain wants to be with her then. He wants to go with her: "Except ye become as little children, ye shall not enter...." He wants to, and yet he doesn't. Certainly, he doesn't want to go without her. That was never what he had in mind.

He gets up and goes to the church in the morning as usual. He says nothing about it to anyone, that day or the next or the next. Maybe silence will make the whole thing go away.

Thursday night after supper he is lying on the living room floor. Julie is in the armchair reading, her feet in old white sneakers, her ankles crossed near his head. What is she reading? He twists his head around so he can see. P. D. James. She could try staying in the real world for a while for a change, he thinks. All she ever does is read. He watches her feet move, tapping in a rhythm, as if she were listening to music in her head. Maybe she's hearing Smetana's *Moldau*— which she's played so many times he's sick of it. She could be imagining the whole thing, close enough to the orchestra to hear in a pause the creaking of musicians' chairs. She could do this and think nothing of it. She lives in a daze half the time anyway, daydreaming. It's as if she doesn't really take anything seriously. At least she could quit tapping her feet.

Finally he has had the big religious revelation he always wanted, and there's no joy in it. None at all. He has never felt so cheated. As a kid, he wanted something like this to happen. He did think though that it would bring with it some pleasure—great happiness, in fact. He had a daydream of how it would be, set in the halls and classrooms of his elementary school, where he first imagined it. A column of warm pink light would pour over him, overpowering him with a sensation so intensely sweet it was unimaginable. He tried and tried to feel how it would feel. The warmth would wrap around his heart inside his chest, like two hands cradling him there. He would be full of happiness, completely at peace. The notion stayed with him past childhood, though certainly in his teenage years, he didn't talk about it.

But he did what he could to make it happen. Divine revelation. He wanted it. He was so hungry, so eager for some sign. He lay on the floor of his room at home, and he waited. Sometimes he got his mother's car and drove out to a state park, where he'd find a bend in a creek to stare at. He stared until his mind was lulled into receptive quiet. In classes he lost himself in the deep chalky green of blackboards, as beckoning as a limestone quarry pond. But nothing happened. The quiet always passed, without interruption, at least by anything divine.

The search must have ended finally, at least the purposeful part of it. He realizes that now, lying here with the front door standing open and moths batting against the screen. When did I give it up? He doesn't recall any such preoccupation during divinity school, though there was that one thing that happened in his last year.

He was sitting out on the outdoor stair landing of his apartment that was the second floor of an old house. He and Julie, not married then, were in one of their off times. He was feeling bad. His roommate was out somewhere. The concordance and the notepad had slid off his lap. His legs were sprawled, completely motionless, in front of him, hanging off the end of the butt-sagged recliner. He had lost Julie; he was bone-tired of school; he wouldn't have cared if he died.

He was staring at the dark trunks of the trees at the back of the yard, at the mud ruts of the makeshift parking lot, at the falling-down shed. Nothing mattered at all. Then while he watched, everything—without motion or shift of light—everything he saw changed. He stared at the peeling boards of the shed, at the water standing in the tire tracks. It was all alive and sharing one life. The trees, the bare ground, his own being and the porch around him had become the varied skin, the hide of one living being. In the stillness, he waited for the huge creature to move. Nothing stirred. Yet he felt the benevolence of the animal, its power, rising off the surface before him like waves of heat.

What he felt then was a lightness, a sort of happiness. A touch of that power stayed behind with him, fading slowly until he was back to his usual pale, forgettable self. But briefly, it was at least a hint of what he had always imagined—something he could be part of.

That afternoon, he was buoyed. He finished the work he had sat with for hours. He fried himself a hamburger and ate it and was still hungry. He watched a few minutes of the news on his little portable black and white TV. He did not die nor had he thought further of dying since that day, other than for the purposes of sermons, counseling, and facing the inevitable facts.

Facts. He is lying on the floor of his living room, the warm damp air coming in through the screen. Julie is reading in the chair. God has spoken to him, in English, clearly, in an unmistakable voice. And he is miserable. He wants to grab the rocker of Julie's chair, her tapping fee, and say "Stop that noise, goddamnit." He wants to get up and break something, that pink and white vase that he hates. Instead he lies here quietly and does nothing, the way he has all his life.

"What would you do, Julie?" he says. He's looking at the ceiling, he doesn't turn his head. "Would you stand up in the pulpit and tell them, 'I have heard the voice of God'? Would you do it?" He rolls over on his side and looks at her. Her foot has stopped moving. She has put her book down.

"I've been thinking about it," she says. As if I could think about one other thing, when he's lying here in a funk every night since it happened.

"What did you decide?"

"Yes," she says. "I would."

"Oh?" There's an edge in his voice. "What else would you say? How would you explain it? Explain to me, if you understand so well."

"Say as much as you know," she says.

"What is that? One piece of a sentence? I've got nothing to say."

"It's the whole point of your job, isn't it?" she says. "To tell them. Isn't it?"

"Yes," he says, slowly and carefully, "it is. But if you'll remember, Presbyterians do not make a habit of getting up in the pulpit and talking about their personal lives. I'm supposed to be talking about Scripture—"

"Swain, you can't go over there and talk about some Bible verse when this has happened."

If she had to get up there and do it herself, he thinks, she wouldn't be such a know-it-all. "Of course," he says, forcing his voice to stay level, "when I have a little better understanding of what is going on, I will have something to say—"

"Now is when you have something to say. I can't see the point in waiting until you've written a dissertation on a bunch of other people who have been through the same thing."

"And what if I don't do it?" he says, the anger rising in his voice. "What if I never say a word and you spend the rest of your life thinking I don't have the balls to get up and say it? What happens to us then?"

She shakes her head. "That's not going to happen."

Swain gets to his feet, straightens his pants leg. Then he looks at her, making sure she sees the coldness in his eyes.

She stares back at him, just as hard as he's looking at her, then goes back to her book, or at least pretends to. She hasn't read three pages in an hour. What did he expect me to say? she wonders. It's perfectly plain what he should do. She stares at the book. Not that it mattered in the least what I said, he was going to be mad anyway. You'd think if God spoke to you, there'd be something good about it.

He leaves the room, goes into the kitchen, gets out a small tub of Haagen Dazs and a spoon. Standing near the fridge, he eats from the container. There is no sound, total silence from the other room. Pink light—what a joke ... childish sentimental crap. "Suppose ye that I am come to give peace on earth? I tell you, Nay; but rather division." The voice didn't warn him, didn't remind him. He shakes his head. This whole thing has done nothing but piss him off, that's all it has done. He digs and scrapes at the ice cream.

The following morning, he sits alone in his office. How is he supposed to tell this congregation about anything so bizarre as this? His notepad is blank. He tosses his pen away, onto his desk. What am I going to do—get up and say that I heard the voice of God and the whole things was a rip-off? "Know that truth is"—what a piece of shit.

He props his elbows on his knees and stares at the floor of his office. His eyes follow one of the cracks over to the wall, follow another one back. The afternoon is like a night when you can't get to sleep: hot, itchy, restless, it's never going to end. He has to write a sermon. There's no way to avoid it. The topic is already out front in the yard on the sign. The secretary is holding his calls—it's a rare moment of quiet. How often does he have such a luxury? He hates it, he wants out of here. He has already gotten up and opened the window behind his desk. Now he stares out into the shimmering heat and listens to the churning of a lawnmower. I'd feel better pushing a lawnmower. Maybe I can do yards for a living after this is over.

"Son." He keeps coming back to that one word in his mind. But it wasn't his dad. His father would never in any of Swain's wildest fantasies have blasted out like that. He would have simply appeared there on the hill, standing quietly, looking at Swain, distant and disappointed. He pictures the old guy standing in shirtsleeves on the side porch of their house, which, up until it was old and torn down, was only three miles from the church. His father could walk to the campus to teach his classes. At home, he would step out the door of his study onto the open porch for air. He did it a dozen times in a day, no matter what the weather. When Swain was little, it seemed to be one more proof that his father was very special, that he could stand out there in the cold and not even seem to notice it. Snow on the ground and there he was in his white shirtsleeves and his big baggy pleated pants, staring off somewhere, his breath smoking up the air.

If he closes his eyes, he can hear the clock ticking in his father's study. He's sitting on the edge of a chair, his feet dangling halfway to the floor, his father saying, "Swain, I cannot have noise. Not in this house. I have work to do. Please exercise some consideration, if you will."

Swain saying, "I was coloring in my coloring book. I was being quiet."

"You have not been a problem today. But at other times I've heard too much running in the house, bouncing balls ... I don't want any more of it. I wanted to mention this while I was thinking of it."

"Yes, sir." Swain slid off the chair. He was going out the door when his father said, "I'm sorry but I can only tolerate so much." Swain went back upstairs to his coloring book—*Roadrunner and Wile E. Coyote.* All the time he was coloring then, he was careful not to bang his foot against the leg of the chair. For a long time after that, he tried to be so quiet that nobody could even tell he was there. He wanted to be the quietest person in the world. At the table, he would put his fork down in slow motion so nobody could hear it.

Swain twists in his office chair, resettles his legs. He sees again the reddish-gold light of the late sun in the backyard. He feels the electrifying surge that he could almost see pushing the air in front of it. A tidal wave of sound rushing over him and drowning him. Then his memory stops, as if he'd ripped a cassette out of the deck, pulled out the tape and destroyed it. He doesn't want to feel it again. Ever. Do you hear that? Not ever. I've spent thirty-eight years, my whole life, waiting for something that turns out to be this.

What am I going to tell them? He imagines himself in the pulpit, staring out at the congregation. He sees the horror waking on their faces, as they understand him. He sees them glancing at each other diagonally across the pews. I'd be out. It would cost me the church. They'd gradually, delicately ease me out, help me make "other arrangements." I'd get shipped off to some church with a sign out front that tallies up the number saved on a Sunday, the kind of church that has buses and an all-white congregation. Better to mow lawns.

Why go through with it anyway? Nobody in the church is going to believe me. Unless maybe Bernie, as far back as we go. Bernie will listen at least. And Patrice. He smiles. She'll listen to me. And Julie ... But most of the rest of them—coming here and saying they believe in something. I'd like to slam a few of them against a wall. Get their attention, for once.

He turns his chair away from the window, back to his desk. I have nothing to say. Know what truth is? A half sentence? Absurd. I could get up there and tell them that God is the biggest letdown a man could ever imagine. Swain stops. Then the longing that he has felt so often sweeps over him again. He wanted there to be something … He can't think about that now. The congregation is what he has to deal with. He'll have to tell them. I have to stand up in front of them and make an ass of myself. That's what will happen. I might start to cry—like I did that night. Swain reconsiders. He despises the kind of minister who gets up and makes a display of himself.

He rubs his face in his hands. He wants to be left alone. With Julie. With God, but not with the God that is doing this. The last thing in the world he wants is to get up and talk about this. But, Swain thinks, a man couldn't remain a minister with such a secret.

Swain Hammond's picture, like that of every other member of Westside, is in the church directory. The congregation compiled this book two years ago, after a brainstorming session on a weekend retreat to the beach. This was one of the ideas for bringing people together and helping to make Westside more of a community. The picture of Swain and Julie, seated side by side on a sofa in the church parlor, is listed under "H." Swain modestly objected to the idea of putting himself at the front of the book. So there they are, the same size as everybody else, in black and white sharing the page with Mike and Sally Griffin and Mary Ellen Highstaff.

Swain is tall. You notice that even when he's sitting. His big bony knees and his long legs make sharp angles in the foreground of the picture. One arm drapes along the back of the couch, lightly encircling Julie. He's a good-looking man, but you can see from the way he's sitting and the expression on his face that he still doesn't believe it. He looks as if he might spring off the couch in a second if anyone questioned his right to be there. And there's something about his smile that's a little tentative too. His face looks as if it stopped halfway between two clear-cut expressions. There's a slight curve to his lips, but it doesn't tell you a thing.

What's obvious and unequivocal about him is dark eyes and a lot of brown hair. His hair falls forward on his forehead, a thick pile of it. Just looking at the picture, without knowing him, you could almost see him reaching to push it back, as he constantly does. Then you notice his eyes, how carefully they watch, the way people watch the needle on a scale, waiting for it to come to a stop. Though it's hard to see in this picture, one eye is slightly different from the other. There's a notch in the oval of his lower right lid, a little break in the circle. When he was a kid, about six, he climbed up on the roof of the backyard garage, using the wisteria vines to get up there. Then, somehow, he fell. One the way down, one of those same vines he used for climbing raked across his face. The only mark that stayed on him was that slight irregularity. Sometimes Swain thinks he notices people staring at it, and it's true, he's not imagining it. For most of the people who know him as an adult, it's the only thing about him that has ever been a little out of line. Swain, as even Julie would say, has until recently been a very deliberate and careful kind of man.

Julie sits on the sofa next to him, slightly inclined into the curve beneath his arm, smiling easily for the camera. Her body looks as if it has taken this position naturally, not been placed and arranged by a photographer. Her hands lie open in the folds of her loose sleeveless dress, her shoulders, arms, neck as strong as a swimmer's. She is short, large-breasted, and it's easy to imagine her sunburned from working outdoors. Looking at her calls up a certain sort of image: a white pitcher of milk in a patch of sunlight on a table, or a yellow bowl of daisies. Of course, she is not as simple as all that. And it's that very complacency and ease before the camera that's the clue. But at first blush, there she is: freckled, full-bodied, wide-eyed, disarming. A preacher's wife who has until recently seemed to treat that demanding role as something she hardly noticed. She has given her warmth and her presence, and if the church has expected anything else of her, they've never let her know.

What was portrayed in this picture of the two of them—if a picture can portray a marriage—was Swain's only real success in human relations. Then as now, and this was taken about two years ago, they were happy. Swain and Julie, married thirteen years, are very close. And though they have endured the usual difficulties, from the start this marriage seemed like a pretty sure thing.

Swain's personal ministry has been a different matter. He has always privately considered the counseling part of his work a disaster. Although he got by very respectably—no one seemed to notice his discomfort. At worst he seemed a little distant, stilted, aloof. And at Westside, a reserved, perhaps too intellectual sort of person is, at the least, easily tolerated.

Swain, pulling up into the driveway, stops to watch what's happening in the yard next door. A mob of kids running around yelling. The Gustafsons and some of their buddies out playing under the sprinkler. He slowed the car when he first saw them jumping around in the spray and running from it, pushing each other into it. Now he sits in his own driveway, watching. He always thought somehow that if he found what he was looking for—from God—he would be able to run around and have fun like that. God was supposed to unlock whatever it is that keeps Swain Hammond so tied up. Sometimes he feels as if his arms are tied to his chest with barbed wire, and all around him, everywhere he goes, people are reaching over and touching each other, as if that were an easy, ordinary thing to do. If I went around telling people that God had picked me to talk to, they would all know why: the last shall go first. So it is written. Swain Hammond, tight-ass. Who could be more last?

Water splats against the back of the oldest boy, then comes the softer sound against the grass as the spray swizzles away. His own skin feels dry and dirty. Julie isn't home yet, her car isn't here. I could go over there and try it, act like a kid for once. Wash the dust off me. Now. Fast, before I can change my mind—go over there and act like a happy kid. Run around yelling and getting wet like the rest of them and having fun.

He gets out of the car, slams the door, goes into the house, straight to the bedroom. He doesn't pause. He puts on his bathing suit, then looks at himself in the mirror. He is so long and white, just a touch of softness at the sides of his waist. But so white. He puts his undershirt back on and inspects himself again. Better. I can take it off as soon as I get over there and throw it aside on the grass.

Now, Swain, go, he tells himself. Out the front door, passing his briefcase, where he dropped it, with the new book on bereavement.

He picks his way, barefooted, across the concrete driveway and the Gustafsons' gravel path.

"Hi, Dr. Hammond," the biggest boy says. Swain can't keep up with their names. The kid has a stretchy red striped bathing suit that looks as if it was rolled down onto his skinny frame, the way you put a sweat band around your wrist to play tennis.

"Dad's not home," the kid says. The boy stands there and waits for him to say something and then go away. They all do, all five of them. The sprinkler swishes back and forth over them and they don't even notice. The littlest one puts two fingers in her mouth and continues to stare. Their scruffy dog stands with the water dripping off him, looking from one kid to the other.

"I wasn't looking for your dad. I wanted to come play under the sprinkler with you."

"Oh ... uh, okay," the kid says, shrugging, looking down the street, as if he'd sent somebody to call for help and the police ought to be on the way. "Sure," he says. They all continue to stand there. Swain has succeeded in turning the whole crew of them into a statuary garden, with all the alabaster eyes on him. They wait for him, then, to go play under the sprinkler while they stand and watch.

All right, then. The little bastards. He pulls his T-shirt off and throws it over onto the sidewalk. He walks deliberately onto the circle of dripping grass. And he stands there until the stream of water spatters and jerks its way around to him, and for three beats of its trip—he stands motionless with his eyes closed—the needles of water drill against his chest. Then it swishes away, hitting grass, circling with the same inevitable rhythm.

He opens his eyes. The kids are still staring, pretending that they didn't exchange glances and that nothing happened while he stood blind under the shower. But now they are standing farther apart. He has dispersed them a little more, like a game of billiards. They are each a little more distant from him and a little farther from each other. He has done that, and it was so easy. It is all exactly the way it has always been. Nothing is any different.

When he tells the congregation that he heard the voice of God, they're going to stare at him just like this. Like these kids and their damn dog. As if he's some kind of alien, which he is, but now they'll all know it.

He waits until Saturday night to decide that he will definitely do it this Sunday—so he won't spend the whole week dreading it. He has scrapped the sermon that he was supposed to give, that he had finally forced himself to write. He is going to tell them, and he's doing it at the first possible opportunity, the first Sunday after it happened.

He is still in the safety of his bench behind the pulpit. The last notes of the organ have died away into a vibration. They're all out there, waiting for him. This is it. He swallows and makes himself start to move, walk forward into the pulpit, stand with his hands on the wooden rail. His fingers seek out their familiar places along the tiered wood.

Sam Bagdikian settles back in his pew, rests his hands on his stomach. Time to lie back for a little snooze. Swain can say some interesting stuff. But his voice has such a rhythm to it, kind of lulls you. You're supposed to be able to learn languages if you listen to the tapes in your sleep.

"Friends," Swain says, his eyes moving back and forth across them. "I have struggled with what I must tell you today.

"I have come before you this morning to say that I have heard the voice of God."

He looks past the faces, stares just beyond the last row at the back wall, and waits for the explosion or at least a sudden freezing silence. Nothing happens. His eyes sweep forward again, from the window back across the three hundred faces. They're blank, waiting, mildly interested. No one is alarmed. They can't have understood.

He starts again. "I think you know that I believe in an immanent God. I think you know that I believe in the presence and power of God in all our lives. I have come to tell you today that something has happened to me in recent days which I do not understand.

"A voice has spoken to me. I know that it is the voice of God." He pauses. He looks at them: no reaction. He can't believe it.

Halfway back, Bill Bartholomew recrosses his legs, twists his wrists inside his cuffs. Get to the point. We've all heard God. Everybody that got out of Korea knew what God was. Operating in

270

a tent with the shelling going on night and day. He drums the tips of his fingers against the hymnbook, then rakes a hand through his stiff gray hair.

Swain continues, "My wife, Julie, and I were cooking dinner on the grill of our back patio...."

Now the rustlings of movement stop. Face after face grows taut with attention. Joe Miles slowly pulls his gaze away from the long blond hair of the girl in front of him. What's he saying? The voice of God on his patio? *Patrice picked a good day to lean on me to come.* He looks over Jakey's head at her. She's staring up at Hammond as though he's the one who's God. He watches her, just the way she sits there ... elegant. *The woman is a Rolls, a 500 Benz. And sitting there staring at Hammond, of all people. It's a hell of a line, hearing God.* He looks back at the girl in the pew in front of him. *How can anything that looks like that be Bruce Hoggard's child?*

DeWitt Chambers, seated alone in the same corner of a pew where he has sat for more than forty years, looks over at Julie, who's as white as milk, just as nervous as she can be. *What in the world are she and Swain up to?* He looks back at the arrangements of flowers he brought in this morning. *What a burst of glory those gladiolas are. The nicest ones he has seen this whole season.*

Swain feels a stillness fall over the church all the way up to the back pews of the balcony. They know now this is not a metaphor, not a parable he is telling. His wife, Julie, the back patio—they are listening, staring at him and waiting. Swain feels a trembling deep in his gut. He begins with the lady's slipper and the voice that came over the hill.

He tells them about the word "son" and the windbreaker and his own tears. "I asked myself whether I should bring this to you on a Sunday morning," he says. He looks from face to face in the rows in front of him. *What are they thinking?* He can't look at any one face long enough to tell. The shaking inside him has moved outward to his hands, damp against the wood of the pulpit rail. He doesn't trust his voice.

"When I first heard what I heard, I began to ask myself what I could say to you."

Now Swain looks at Julie. He can see her wrists, before the back of the pew breaks his vision. He knows her hands, out of the range of his sight, are knotted together, moving one against the other.

Out of the corner of her eye, she can catch a glimpse of a few of them. She's almost scared to look around. Bill Bartholomew—her heart sinks—looks as if he just ate the bitter part of a pecan; sitting there in his gray suit and his shiny glasses, he could be made out of nothing but gray metal. DeWitt Chambers, with his finger pressed against his pursed-up lips. He probably watches soap operas all day while he polishes his silver. He doesn't care what happens as long as it's juicy gossip. If they can't listen to anything about God, what are they doing coming to church? What are they here for? She's disgusted with all of them. They don't deserve to hear Swain talk, or God either.

Swain says, "I asked myself whether you would want a pastor who hears voices. Whether you'd think I'd completely taken leave of my senses. Or even whether some of you might come to expect wisdom from me that I don't have."

Bernie Morris rolls his bulletin into a tube and hits it against the pew ahead. What is all this coming out of the blue?

Did he come to me and say, "Bernie, old buddy, I got to tell you what happened to me. Bernie, what do you think, what do I do?"

No, not Swain. No, he gets up there and mouths off and looks like an idiot doing it. Voice of God. What am I doing here anyway? Sitting an hour every Sunday, mainly because of him, I'm up to my eyebrows in this church and I've hardly gotten a nickel's worth of business out of the lot of them, and now he gets up and does this. I should have taken Lynne and the girls to the beach. Bernie beats a fast staccato with his ring against the back of the pew.

Patrice Miles is leaning forward, her hands gripping the edge of the seat. Did he say what I think? She looks over at Joe, but he's obviously paying no attention. When we get in the car, he probably won't know anything happened.

I must have heard wrong. Straight reliable old Swain? She has always wanted to pull his tie loose, or mess up his hair. She smiles. Jakey elbows her. She looks down at him. He whispers, "What's so funny?"

272

"Nothing."

"You were laughing."

She whispers back, "I wasn't."

"You were too."

She rumples his hair. Nine years old and he's in charge of everything.

He pats his hair down and looks around to see if anybody saw. She acts like I'm a baby, he thinks. What's so funny about God talking to somebody? I bet she wouldn't laugh if God started doing stuff in our yard.

Swain is saying, "I don't know what to expect from you. Neither do I know what to expect from God. What I heard is not what I ever would have hoped or expected to hear. It hasn't given me any wisdom or any peace. But I will listen and pray to understand more." He steps back, hearing as he does so the first note of the organ.

Gladys Henby is still sitting with her hands clasped on her purse just as they were when this sermon began. She is so startled she hasn't even moved. Now she pats one gloved hand gently against the other. This quiet sensible young man is saying that God has spoken out loud to him in his own backyard? She wants to turn and find Walter beside her and see whatever to think about such a thing. She does the math again: eleven years and three months since he died. If Dr. Hammond can hear God, then maybe it's all true. The life everlasting. The tears well up in her eyes.

Around her people are rising, hymnbooks in hand.

Swain looks out at them, standing, now singing the closing hymn, as if nothing has happened. No one has leaped up from a pew to challenge him. It's as if he had never spoken at all.

He takes his place as usual on the front steps to shake hands and greet people. Going on as if it's all ordinary, the sun heating up his black robe. People filing past him and shaking his hand. It's stunning … weird. How can they do this? How can I …? Three out of all of them tell him that the Lord works in wondrous ways, or something to that effect. Mrs. Frances Eastwood squeezes his elbow and tells him to trust. Ed Fitzgerald lays one hand on his shoulder, close to his collar, and says, "I like what you did here today." Bill Bartholomew shakes his hand and nods curtly, hurries past. He's the one who'll call the elders into session to talk about it. He's the ticking bomb. Gladys Henby peers up at him as if she has cataracts and can't quite see. Maybe she does and hasn't told him. She stares at his face as if she's trying to memorize it, but she doesn't say a word about the sermon. Not a word. DeWitt stops and stares at him as if he's slightly amused. "My, my," he says, shakes Swain's hand and goes on.

On the way home, Swain is quiet in the car. Julie sits closer to him than usual, with her hand first resting on his shoulder, then his leg. "They just sat there like zombies," Swain says.

He wriggles his foot inside his shoe. He itches all over. His feet itch, his scalp feels as if he needs to stop the car and scratch every inch of it with both hands. "They give me the creeps," he says. "I get up there and I tell them, and all they can do is stare at me. I can't believe it."

"They need time to think about it," Julie says.

During the afternoon at home, the phone rings twice. One man calls to congratulate him for speaking out. But the guy was just a visitor, not even a member. Swain doesn't recognize his name. He hears nothing from Bernie. Nothing from Patrice or Joe Miles. Nothing from Ed Fitzgerald, or any of the ones who mean the most to him.

Coming back into the kitchen, where Julie is cleaning out drawers to keep busy, he says, "It's the ones who don't call … They're not calling me, they're calling each other.…"

THE HOUSE

The table, son, is laid
with the quiet whiteness of cream,
and on four walls ceramics
gleam blue, glint light.
Here is the salt, here the oil,
in the center, bread that almost speaks.
Gold more lovely than gold of bread
is not in broom plant or fruit,
and its scent of wheat and oven
gives unfailing joy.
We break bread, little son, together
with our hard fingers, our soft palms,
while you stare in astonishment
that black earth brings forth a white flower.

Gabriela Mistral, born Lucila Godoy y Alcayaga in Vicuña, Chile, in 1889, became a village schoolteacher and a poet as well as an active contributor to educational systems in Mexico and Chile. As Mistral's acclaim grew, she took teaching positions in Spanish literature at Columbia University, Middlebury College, Vassar College, and the University of Puerto Rico. In 1945, Mistral became the first female Latin American poet to receive the Nobel Prize for Literature. She died in 1957. This poem was translated by Doris Dana.

Lower your hand that reaches for food
as your mother also lowers hers.
Wheat, my son, is of air,
of sunlight and hoe;
but this bread, called "the face of God,"*
is not set on every table.
And if other children do not have it,
better, my son, that you not touch it,
better that you not take it
with ashamed hands.

My son, Hunger with his grimaced face
in eddies circles the unthrashed wheat.
They search and never find each other,
bread and hunchbacked Hunger.
So that he find it if he should enter now,
we'll leave the bread until tomorrow.
Let the blazing fire mark the door
that the Quechuan Indian never closed,
and we will watch Hunger eat
to sleep with body and soul.

علم

*In Chile, the people call bread "the face of God."(G. M.)

Abraham Lincoln

PROCLAMATION OF A
NATIONAL FAST-DAY

August 12, 1861
By the President of the United States of America:
A Proclamation.

Whereas a joint Committee of both Houses of Congress has waited on the President of the United States, and requested him to "recommend a day of public humiliation, prayer and fasting, to be observed by the people of the United States with religious solemnities, and the offering of fervent supplications to Almighty God for the safety and welfare of these States, His blessings on their arms, and a speedy restoration of peace:"—

And whereas it is fit and becoming in all people, at all times, to acknowledge and revere the Supreme Government of God; to bow in humble submission to His chastisements; to confess and deplore their sins and transgressions in the full conviction that the fear of the Lord is the beginning of wisdom; and to pray, with all fervency and

---

Abraham Lincoln was born in 1809 to a frontier family in Kentucky and went on to serve as the sixteenth president of the United States of America. On the heels of the surprising defeat of the Grand Army at Bull Run on July 21, 1861, Lincoln and many others realized that the Civil War would not end quickly or easily. It was in response to this increasing sense of alarm that Lincoln issued the proclamation below. Lincoln was assassinated in 1865, almost two and a half years after he issued the Emancipation Proclamation.

contrition, for the pardon of their past offences, and for a blessing upon their present and prospective action:

And whereas, when our own beloved Country, once, by the blessing of God, united, prosperous and happy, is now afflicted with faction and civil war, it is peculiarly fit for us to recognize the hand of God in this terrible visitation, and in sorrowful remembrance of our own faults and crimes as a nation and as individuals, to humble ourselves before Him, and to pray for His mercy,—to pray that we may be spared further punishment, though most justly deserved; that our arms may be blessed and made effectual for the re-establishment of law, order and peace, throughout the wide extent of our country; and that the inestimable boon of civil and religious liberty, earned under His guidance and blessing, by the labors and sufferings of our fathers, may be restored in all its original excellence:—

Therefore, I, Abraham Lincoln, President of the United States, do appoint the last Thursday in September next, as a day of humiliation, prayer and fasting for all the people of the nation. And I do earnestly recommend to all the People, and especially to all ministers and teachers of religion of all denominations, and to all heads of families, to observe and keep that day according to their several creeds and modes of worship, in all humility and with all religious solemnity, to the end that the united prayer of the nation may ascend to the Throne of Grace and bring down plentiful blessings upon our Country.

In testimony whereof, I have hereunto set my hand, and caused the Seal

of the United States to be affixed, this 12th day of August A.D.

1861, and of the Independence of the United States of America the 86th.

[L. S.]

By the President: ABRAHAM LINCOLN.

WILLIAM H. SEWARD, Secretary of State.

Kabir

THE YOGI DYES HIS GARMENTS

The Yogi dyes his garments, instead of dyeing his mind in
    the colours of love:
He sits within the temple of the Lord, leaving Brahma to
    worship a stone.
He pierces holes in his ears, he has a great beard and
    matted locks, he looks like a goat:
He goes forth into the wilderness, killing all his desires,
    and turns himself into an eunuch:
He shaves his head and dyes his garments; he reads the
    Gîtâ and becomes a mighty talker.
Kabîr says: "You are going to the doors of death, bound
    hand and foot!"

Kabir was born in Varanasi (Benares), India, most likely in 1398. His birth and death are surrounded by legends and little is known about him. Raised by Muslim parents, Kabir later became a disciple of the Hindu bhakti saint Ramananda at a time when it was unusual for a Hindu teacher to take on a Muslim student. One of India's most revered poets and mystics, Kabir's life and teachings are spiritually significant to Hindus, Muslims, and Sikhs alike. He did not claim to be Muslim, Hindu, or Sikh and rather claimed that he was "at once the child of Allah and of Râm." His compositions figure largely in Sikh scripture, the *Guru Granth Sahib,* making up the largest contributions to the text. This poem was translated by Rabindranath Tagore.

Anne Lamott

WHY I MAKE SAM GO TO CHURCH

from *Traveling Mercies: Some Thoughts on Faith*

Sam is the only kid he knows who goes to church—who is made to go to church two or three times a month. He rarely wants to. This is not exactly true: the truth is he *never* wants to go. What young boy would rather be in church on the weekends than hanging out with a friend? It does not help him to be reminded that once he's there he enjoys himself, that he gets to spend the time drawing in the little room outside the sanctuary, that he only actually has to sit still and listen during the short children's sermon. It does not help that I always pack some snacks, some Legos, his art supplies, and bring along any friend of his whom we can lure into our churchy web. It does not help that he genuinely cares for the people there. All that matters to him is that he alone among his colleagues is forced to spend Sunday morning in church.

You might think, noting the bitterness, the resignation, that he was being made to sit through a six-hour Latin mass. Or you might wonder why I make this strapping, exuberant boy come with me most weeks, and if you were to ask, this is what I would say.

Anne Lamott, born in San Francisco in 1954, is a best-selling author and a political activist as well as a columnist for *Salon* magazine. Lamott has received a Guggenheim Fellowship and numerous other awards. The selection below is drawn from her 1999 book, *Traveling Mercies: Some Thoughts on Faith*. Lamott currently lives in Northern California with her son, Sam.

I make him because I can. I outweigh him by nearly seventy-five pounds.

But that is only part of it. The main reason is that I want to give him what I found in the world, which is to say a path and a little light to see by. Most of the people I know who have what I want—which is to say, purpose, heart, balance, gratitude, joy—are people with a deep sense of spirituality. They are people in community, who pray, or practice their faith; they are Buddhists, Jews, Christians—people banding together to work on themselves and for human rights. They follow a brighter light than the glimmer of their own candle; they are part of something beautiful. I saw something once from the Jewish Theological Seminary that said, "A human life is like a single letter of the alphabet. It can be meaningless. Or it can be a part of a great meaning." Our funky little church is filled with people who are working for peace and freedom, who are out there on the streets and inside praying, and they are home writing letters, and they are at the shelters with giant platters of food.

When I was at the end of my rope, the people at St. Andrew tied a knot in it for me and helped me hold on. The church became my home in the old meaning of *home*—that it's where, when you show up, they have to let you in. They let me in. They even said, "You come back now."

My relatives all live in the Bay Area and I adore them, but they are all as skittishly self-obsessed as I am, which I certainly mean in the nicest possible way. Let's just say that I do not leave family gatherings with the feeling that I have just received some kind of spiritual chemotherapy. But I do when I leave St. Andrew.

"Let's go, baby," I say cheerfully to Sam when it is time to leave for church, and he looks up at me like a puppy eyeing the vet who is standing there with the needle.

Sam was welcomed and prayed for at St. Andrew seven months before he was born. When I announced during worship that I was pregnant, people cheered. All these old people, raised in Bible-thumping homes in the Deep South, clapped. Even the women whose grown-up boys had been or were dong time in jails or prisons rejoiced for me. And then almost immediately they set about providing for us. They brought clothes, they brought me casseroles to keep in the freezer, they brought me assurance that this baby was going to be a part of the family. And they began slipping me money.

Now, a number of the older black women live pretty close to the bone financially on small Social Security checks. But routinely they sidled up to me and stuffed bills in my pocket—tens and twenties. It was always done so stealthily that you might have thought they were slipping me bindles of cocaine. One of the most consistent donors was a very old woman named Mary Williams, who is in her mid-eighties now, so beautiful with her crushed hats and hallelujahs; she always brought me plastic Baggies full of dimes, noosed with little wire twists.

I was usually filled with a sense of something like shame until I'd remember that wonderful line of Blake's—that we are here to learn to endure the beams of love—and I would take a long deep breath and force these words out of my strangulated throat: "Thank you."

I first brought Sam to church when he was five days old. Then women there very politely pretended to care how I was doing but were mostly killing time until it was their turn to hold Sam again. They called him "our baby" or sometimes "my baby." "Bring me my baby!" they'd insist. "Bring me that baby now!" "Hey, you're hogging that baby."

I believe that they came to see me as Sam's driver, hired to bring him and his gear back to them every Sunday.

Mary Williams always sits in the very back by the door. She is one of those unusually beautiful women—beautiful like a river. She has dark skin, a long broad nose, sweet full lips, and what the theologian Howard Thurman calls "quiet eyes." She raised five children as a single mother, but one of her boys drowned when he was young, and she has the softness and generosity and toughness of someone who has endured great loss. During the service she praises God in a nonstop burble, a glistening dark brook. She says, "Oh, yes.... Uh-huh.... My sweet Lord. Thank you, thank you."

Sam loves her, and she loves him, and she still brings us Baggies full of dimes even though I'm doing so much better now. Every Sunday I nudge Sam in her direction, and he walks to where she is sitting and hugs her. She smells him behind his ears, where he most smells like sweet unwashed new potatoes. This is in fact what I think God may smell like, a young child's slightly dirty neck. Then Sam leaves the sanctuary and returns to his drawings, his monsters, dinosaurs, birds. I watch Mary Williams pray sometimes. She clutches her hands together tightly and closes her eyes most of the way so that she looks blind; because she is so unself-conscious, you get to see someone in a deeply interior pose. You get to see all that intimate resting. She looks as if she's holding the whole earth together, or making the biggest wish in the world. Oh, yes, Lord. Uh-huh.

It's funny: I always imagined when I was a kid that adults had some kind of inner toolbox, full of shiny tools: the saw of discernment, the hammer of wisdom, the sandpaper of patience. But then when I grew up I found that life handed you these rusty bent old tools—friendships, prayer, conscience, honesty—and said, Do the best you can with these, they will have to do. And mostly, against all odds, they're enough.

Not long ago I was driving Sam and his friend Josh over to Josh's house where the boys were going to spend the night. But out of the blue, Josh changed his mind about wanting Sam to stay over. "I'm tired," he said suddenly, "and I want to have a quiet night with my mom." Sam's face went white and blank; he has so little armor. He started crying. I tried to manipulate Josh into changing his mind, and I even sort of vaguely threatened him, hinting that Sam or I might cancel a date with *him* sometime, but he stayed firm. After a while Sam said he wished we'd all get hit by a car, and Josh stared out the window nonchalantly. I thought he might be about to start humming. It was one of those times when you wish you were armed so you could attack the kid who has hurt your own child's feelings.

"Sam?" I asked. "Can I help in any way? Shall we pray?"

"I just wish I'd never been born."

But after a moment, he said yes, I should pray. To myself.

So I prayed that God would help me figure out how to stop living in the problem and to move into the solution. That was all. We drove along for a while. I waited for a sign of improvement. Sam said, "I guess Josh wishes I had never been born."

Josh stared out the window: dum de dum.

I kept asking God for help, and after a while I realized something—that Josh was not enjoying this either. He was just trying to take care of himself, and I made the radical decision to let him off the hook. I imagined gently lifting him off the hook of my judgment and setting him back on the ground.

And a moment later, he changed his mind. Now, maybe this was the result of prayer, or forgiveness; maybe it was a coincidence. I will never know. But even before Josh changed his mind, I did know one thing for sure, and this was that Sam and I would be going to church the next morning. Mary Williams would be sitting in the back near the door, in a crumpled hat. Sam would hug her; she would close her eyes and smell the soft skin of his neck, just below his ears.

What I didn't know was that Josh would want to come with us too. I didn't know that when I stopped by his house to pick up Sam the next morning, he would eagerly run out ahead of Sam to ask if he could come. And another thing I didn't know was that Mary Williams was going to bring us another bag of dimes. It had been a little while since her last dime drop, but just when I think we've all grown out of the ritual, she brings us another stash. Mostly I give them to street people. Some sit like tchotchkes on bookshelves around the house. Mary doesn't know that professionally I'm doing much better now; she doesn't know that I no longer really need people to slip me money. But what's so dazzling to me, what's so painful and poignant, is that she doesn't bother with what I think she knows or doesn't know about my financial life. She just knows we need another bag of dimes, and that is why I make Sam go to church.

TOWARD ACTION

The Interfaith Youth Core Model for Interfaith Reflection and Service

The great rabbi Abraham Joshua Heschel, whose work appears in this anthology, once said, "First we begin in sound and then we must move to deed." The readings compiled in this book offer a powerful call to action. They call us to our better selves individually as well as to our better (religious) communities, nation, and world. Yet without action, their full potential for social change remains unrealized.

Perhaps, however, Rabbi Heschel draws too stark a dichotomy between sound and deed. As stated in the introduction, the first premise behind *Hearing the Call across Traditions: Readings on Faith and Service* is that it is good for people within and across religious and philosophical traditions to reflect on and discuss connections between faith and service. Is not this process of reflection and self-examination around the nature of service a form of action in itself? Moreover, in a world too often characterized by internecine conflict between the world's religious and philosophical traditions, is not the process of identifying and examining shared and nuanced values of service across traditions a symbolic yet powerful act? We suggest that discussing the myriad and varied readings collected in this volume does constitute action and an invaluable form of service.

We believe this is especially the case when the discussion deliberately brings together individuals from different religious and philosophical backgrounds for interfaith dialogue. Interfaith dialogue is a special form of communication between people of distinct religious or philosophical perspectives with the intention of discussing the commonalities and nuances of their shared values. Interfaith dialogue can be a one-time event or a series of conversations; it might span hours, months, years, or a lifetime; it might be structured or unstructured; facilitated by a third party or non-facilitated; intentional or organic. What characterizes interfaith dialogue is the intention of its participants to better understand one another's different religious or philosophical perspectives rather than convincing one another of a particular viewpoint.

We believe that the readings assembled in this anthology provide rich fodder for deep and meaningful interfaith dialogue. It is our hope that this book be read not only within congregations or classrooms, but also in civic spaces where people from different religious and philosophical backgrounds sit down together to reflect on their understanding of and commitment to service across their traditions. We believe that such a discourse will not only deepen understandings of service but also help create interfaith relationships that are harmonious, cooperative, respectful, and mutually beneficial.

This discourse is necessary, but perhaps not sufficient, however, to address the problem of interreligious conflict and the challenge of religious diversity. For us to build societies of religious pluralism founded on mutual respect and inspiration, our collaboration across lines of difference must include more concrete and tangible forms of service in addition to interfaith dialogue. Too often religious communities believe that the weight of addressing the world's many ills falls on their shoulders alone. By engaging with others to build the common good together through common action, we can demonstrate that some of our best partners in realizing the world-as-it-might-be are the other communities in our neighborhood that may pray in a different language but nonetheless share our hope for society. When we couple this action with rich, text-based reflection on our motivation for and understanding of service, we give ourselves the best chance of developing real interfaith relationships defined by respect and loyalty.

It is our hope, therefore, that this book can serve as a catalyst not just for deepened reflection but also for interfaith service for the betterment of our communities and world. Interfaith service is a medium for creating bridges across the chasms of our religious differences. It generates pathways for developing trust, changing old habits of thought and action, and trying new behaviors. This appendix offers one model of utilizing these readings toward this end. It is a model based on the grassroots interfaith organizing experience of the Interfaith Youth Core and is meant to help you understand, envision, plan, and lead interfaith reflection and service projects. We hope that the readings contained within this volume inspire you to take on such projects and that this appendix makes it as easy as possible.

A MODEL FOR INTERFAITH REFLECTION AND SERVICE

The Interfaith Youth Core model for interfaith reflection and service uses a methodology based on storytelling, shared values, and common action—all of which are described below—to advance three main goals:

1. To encourage participants to deepen their own religious or philosophical identity, particularly to help them understand and articulate the connection between their perspective and their inspiration to serve others. Learning to speak publicly about personal identity, as well as listening to others' experiences, helps participants deepen personal understanding and respect the identities of others.

2. To help participants discover shared values across different religious and philosophical perspectives, particularly to realize that the connection between their perspective and inspiration to serve exists in other perspectives as well. Through personal storytelling, participants can begin to develop mutually enriching relationships and be inspired to work for the common good.

3. To build a sense of cooperation and collaboration among religiously diverse people and inspire them to work for the common good. Dialogue should always lead to action.

Storytelling

After spending decades teaching, a wise and venerable professor was once asked by a younger professor, "How do you keep your students' attention, class after class, year after year?" The wise professor answered, "If you want your students' attention, tell them a story. If you want their rapt attention, tell them three stories. If you want them to become your friend, tell them your story. And if you want them to follow you for life, help them draw out their own story." Stories form the foundation of human identity and relationships. We learn about others by asking them, "What's your story?" We come to understand who we are by answering the same question.

Stories are also a nonthreatening way to open interfaith dialogue because, rather than focus on exclusive truth claims, they allow participants to share from their personal life experiences. In contrast to a theological or political dialogue, storytelling about individual experiences helps create safe space because it is nonconfrontational, is nonthreatening, and is not divisive, thereby allowing for a mutually appreciative encounter. Exchanging stories with another person also allows for a personal exchange of experience and identity that gives rise to familiarity and, thus, comfort in relationships.

Shared Values

The world's religious and philosophical perspectives, among their beautiful diversity, also all articulate a variety of certain shared values. These are grand values such as compassion, justice, and service, as well as more tangible values such as hospitality, care of the environment, and charity. These deeply held, widely shared beliefs provide a platform upon which people who may hold many other widely disparate opinions can come together in agreement. The Interfaith Youth Core therefore frames interfaith dialogue around these shared values so that the dialogue can progress in a positive direction and pull out the nuances and differences between how each religious or philosophical perspective understands and defines a given shared value.

Directing the interaction toward differences or divisions among various religious or philosophical perspectives can lead to conflict. Instead, we start by talking about our commonality of values and reinforce the idea of acting out those values together through service. For example, a Christian and a Buddhist may not agree on what happens to a person after he or she dies, but they can agree that both their perspectives have a strong value of hospitality. In addition to identifying that value through dialogue, they can volunteer together at a refugee resettlement agency, reinforcing their understanding that they both work to be hospitable to those in their community. Focusing on common ground makes for a fruitful discussion and leads more easily toward the transition from conversation to action.

Common Action

Alongside identifying the shared values they have in common, we strongly encourage participants to put those values to work through cooperative projects that serve the common good. While common action has many different varieties, one of the most concrete and beneficial forms it can take is when people from different backgrounds come together to serve their communities directly. These types of community service programs are most effective when they abide by the best practices of "service-learning." Service-learning is a methodology of experiential learning that combines meaningful social service with education and reflection into one comprehensive experience.

When we come together with people from different religious and philosophical perspectives and work on common action for the common good, we are providing an opportunity to create deeper connections between individuals and our call to service, as well as among individuals from different religious or philosophical backgrounds. We are putting our inspiration and our shared values into concrete action to create positive change. We are also making real the connection between our perspectives and values and those of our peers.

ORGANIZING AN INTERFAITH REFLECTION AND SERVICE PROJECT

Based on this methodology, we organize interfaith service-learning projects to create spaces where people from different religious or philosophical perspectives can come together and learn about other perspectives in a way that is enriching rather than negative. This appendix will guide you as you think through the key elements of your interfaith reflection and service project, which are:

- Assembling a Diverse Group of Core Leaders

- Preparing for Interfaith Logistical Challenges

- Planning Effective Service

- Creating Effective Reflection

- Joining the Movement

Assembling a Diverse Group of Core Leaders

Assembling a diverse group of core leaders is your first step toward creating a successful project. The core group's role will be to plan and run the event, so that you do not have to do it all on your own. The best way to plan interfaith common action is to have people from diverse religious and philosophical perspectives working together from the start. This may prevent problems from arising down the line by ensuring that every stage of planning reflects different religious and philosophical perspectives' sensibilities. However, depending upon the community where you are, this may not always be possible. If you live in a more religiously homogenous community, make a concerted effort to have as diverse a group as possible organize the event, but do not focus excessive amounts of energy around getting the right people just to get started. How do you put together your core group of leaders?

- Inspire and recruit other leaders: Inspiring others to join the cause requires one-on-one meetings and relationship building. When seeking others to join your core group of leaders, think about the busiest people you know; even though it may seem counterintuitive, they tend to be the ones most engaged and susceptible to new exciting ideas. Take the time to form relationships with these people and sell them on the idea of religious pluralism.

- Build cohesiveness among your core group: Even after individuals have agreed to help organize the interfaith event, continue to provide opportunities for them to build relationships among each other. Your core group of leaders should be a microcosm of the experience you are creating for the participants of your interfaith reflection and service project. Make relationship building and dialogue a priority in your meetings; you can consider having a few smaller dialogues with just the leaders. One great idea is to consider having your core group read *Hearing the Call across Traditions: Readings on Faith and Service* together as you plan, as it will help deepen your conversation about faith and service.

- Establish communication with the community: Even if not every religious or philosophical community is represented in the organizational group, try to receive input and achieve buy-in from multiple religious and philosophical groups in the community through other means (giving regular updates concerning planning, checking in prior to important decisions, and so on). The goal is for your project to be a true collaborative effort among communities, not one community planning everything and hosting it for the others.

- Identify a liaison to the service-learning or event site: It is also a good idea, once a service-learning project or the type of event has been decided upon, to have a person who works at that service-learning or event site act as a partner in planning the event. This way, you are working with community members and not just for community members.

As you think about whom you will ask to be in your group, map out the various local religious institutions and organizations in the community. Whenever possible, recruit through people with whom you already have a personal connection, such as your own religious leader or a professor. Meet face to face with each potential core group member. Organizing an interfaith event can be a sizable time commitment and sensitive work, so it is important to find the right people.

Preparing for Interfaith Logistical Challenges

Logistical planning can often be one of the hardest parts of doing interfaith work. It is helpful to have some religious literacy when planning an interfaith event. When we talk about religious literacy, we are referring to a basic knowledge of the practices and observances of different religious and philosophical perspectives. A few key logistical questions for your core group to ask as you plan your event are listed below.

- When is your event going to be held? Check to make sure that it does not conflict with any religious holidays or weekly observances.

- Will you be having food at your event? What are the different dietary guidelines for the communities with which you are working that you need to consider?

- Are you having both genders work on a project together? What are the considerations around gender interactions that are appropriate and not appropriate for the different communities with which you are working?

- If you are doing a service-learning project, what kind of service-learning work will you be doing? Will this offend the purity and cleanliness concerns of any of your communities?

- What are the different prayer needs of the different religious communities who will be attending? If the event will take place during communities' prayer times, will they have a place to wash and pray?

Remember that you are not expected to have the answers to all of these questions. However, you should know how to find them.

Common action for the common good is most effective when it follows the best practices of the service-learning movement. The advantage of doing a service-learning project as your common action is that the experience is made unique for the participants both by the interfaith nature of the service and by the knowledge gained through the service-learning itself. These are the best, the most effective, and consequently often the most labor-intensive types of common action projects to organize.

If you choose to do a service-learning project, which we strongly encourage you to do, then be sure to follow the best practices of the service-learning movement. For a vast collection of excellent service-learning resources, check out Learn and Serve America's National Service-Learning Clearinghouse at www.servicelearning.org. We include a few of those best practices for making your service project meaningful (with inspiration from P. L. Benson and E. C. Roehlkepartain, *Beyond Leaf Raking: Learning to Serve/Serving to Learn,* Nashville: Abingdon, 1993):

- Set the intention to learn at the outset of the project and offer adequate reflection time for participants to process what they have seen and heard. In order for participants to gain the most from the service project, they must be conscious of the "big picture" of their service experience. Are they serving at a soup kitchen? Start the day with a presentation and discussion about the impact of hunger in your community. Build in reflection times throughout the day that allow participants to grapple with the larger social issue that they are addressing through their service.

- Balance having enough to do to keep everyone busy with achieving completion of the project. Make sure each service site can handle the number of participants you are sending and err on the conservative side—you do not want participants who volunteered to serve sitting around with nothing to do! Conversely, you do not want to leave participants feeling discouraged if you tell them they will be painting an entire house and they only get through the living room. Ask

Hopefully, you have recruited or know a diverse group of peers who are willing and able to answer your questions. If you do not know what a particular community needs to ready itself for prayer, for example, you can ask the person you know in that community. If you are not acquainted with anyone from that religious or philosophical perspective, there are several other places you can go to find these answers:

- www.interfaithcalendar.org
  Interfaith Calendar provides detailed information on religious holidays that shift dates from year to year.

- www.religionfacts.com
  Religion Facts provides a basic overview of the beliefs and practices of most of the world's religions.

- www.religioustolerance.org
  Religious Tolerance gives a basic overview of most of the world's religions and also includes sections on Atheism, Agnosticism, and Humanism.

- www.beliefnet.com
  Beliefnet has a variety of resources—articles, quizzes, devotionals, sacred text searches, message boards, prayer circles, and photo galleries—to help you find information on different religious and philosophical perspectives.

- http://uwacadweb.uwyo.edu/religionet/er/
  This website is sponsored by the University of Wyoming Religious Studies Program and gives a good basic overview of Buddhism, Christianity, Hinduism, Islam, and Judaism, as well as their beliefs, practices, and history.

Planning Effective Service

Once a group of leaders has committed to work together, start brainstorming about possible events or service-learning project the service site coordinator to have a couple of stopping points prepared so that (s)he can guide the group to an intermediate stage of completion, at the least, if the group cannot finish the entire project.

- Be generous with post-service reflection. Interfaith reflection is when all the pieces of the event come together: the shared value of service, interfaith understanding, and personal trans-formation. Make sure that you schedule plenty of time for reflection following the service project to allow the group to debrief both the actual service that they did and the inter-faith encounters that they had. The power of the interfaith component to the day of service is realized when partici-pants learn to see members of diverse religious communities as partners in healing the world.

- Show participants that they are working in partnership with their broader community to build the common good and not just offering a service to someone. Invite speakers from vari-ous service organizations and religious and philosophical insti-tutions in your area to remark on the responsibility of all sectors within the community to work together to address the issues facing society. Focus specifically on the ways in which diverse religious and philosophical communities can enhance the impact of their service efforts by working together.

- Adequately prepare participants for effective service. Is the service site a Habitat for Humanity build? Do participants have experience swinging a hammer? Is the service site a tutoring center? Do participants feel comfortable tutoring children in a variety of subjects? Make sure that participants are aware of the service project before they arrive at the site and that they feel prepared and qualified to contribute in a positive way.

- Celebrate with participants when the project is completed. It is important to affirm young people's service work and celebrate their contributions to building a better world. At the end of the service project, be sure to report to the group the tangible result of their service. Encourage participants to feel proud of the work they have done and to recognize and appreciate their involvement in a broader movement.

Creating Effective Reflection

With this book in your hands, the opportunities for creating effective and deep reflection are boundless. The amount of time you have for reflection in the given interfaith service project you are planning will determine many of your choices. No matter how much time you have and what format you use, however, you want to try to achieve two things through interfaith reflection:

1. Help strengthen the connection between the service work you have just performed or are about to perform and the readings that ground you in the why, who, and how of that service.

2. Help deepen individuals' understanding of the similarities and differences of their call to, understanding of, and reasons for service across different religious and philosophical traditions.

Additionally, before all else it is essential to intentionally set a safe space for interfaith work. Safe space exists when a group of people come together and agree to have interactions in which identity is respected, their experiences will be genuinely listened to by others, and people are collaboratively committed to serving the common good. Creating such a space lets participants in interfaith work know that their religious identities are valued and will not be called into question or challenged by another participant in the group. Having this level of comfort and safety allows for deeper sharing and, in turn, deeper dialogue, better common action, and stronger relationships.

Safe space is, by definition, not a concrete thing; it is a sense that you want participants in your interfaith work to feel. Consequently, it is not something that you can just do and say, "Now I've created safe space." It requires setting a tone for interaction and then defending that tone against anything that might disrupt it. Every action of everyone in a group, but especially you as the leader, contributes to either reinforcing or disrupting safe space. It is therefore critical that you be conscious of your own and others' behavior while leading a group, constantly asking yourself, "Is this helping the other people feel more at ease or less at ease?"

Even though you cannot check off "Setting Safe Space," there are some things you can do to set the correct tone right off the bat. These activities are particularly useful when working with a new group of people who do not necessarily know each other or at least have never interacted in an intentionally interfaith context before.

We have included a sample curriculum below that offers one way of drawing on the readings in this volume to enhance a day of interfaith service and reflection.

SETTING SAFE SPACE

- Make sure everyone has gotten a chance to introduce herself or himself. If working with a younger group, rather than go around in a circle, play an icebreaker game or think of some other creative way to start pushing people out of their defensive postures. With a slightly older group, go around the circle, but make sure that you ask participants to say something that invests them in the conversation in addition to their name: Why are you here? What kind of interfaith work have you done before? If you are working with a group that you do not already know, make sure you have a piece of paper handy to write down people's names as they introduce themselves. Calling people by their names as the dialogue moves forward will help build safe space and better relationships.

- Introduce the kind of interactions you will be having. Tell the participants, "Today, you will be asked to talk about and act on your religious or philosophical perspective and values with others who do not necessarily share your beliefs and ways of life."

- Introduce the concept of "safe space" and brainstorm guidelines for maintaining it. After you introduce the concept, ask them, "What do you need from yourself and others in order to feel safe having these kinds of interactions? What are some suggested guidelines that might help us maintain safe space?" Take notes on your group's responses and then read the responses aloud to conclude the discussion. If possible, write them on a large piece of paper or overhead projector so that everyone can read them.

- If you notice that members of the group are providing general terms for guidelines, ask them to specify what they mean. For example, if a person offers "respect" as a guideline, ask: "What does 'respect' mean for you in the context of this conversation?" The goal of this brainstorming activity is that the participants end with a list of specific guidelines that have an actual bearing on how they converse and interact.

- Here is a list of sample safe space guidelines. If your group is having a hard time coming up with ideas, suggest one or two of these to get them thinking in the right direction:

  - Listen actively at all times and participate fully in the service-learning work going on.

  - Remember the importance of the other person's religious or philosophical perspective in his or her own life.

  - Assume others have no knowledge about your own perspective and take the time to explain everything.

  - Seek clarification if you don't understand something someone else is saying.

  - Everything said should remain in the room.

  - Suspend your judgment.

  - Every question is encouraged.

  - Everyone has the right to pass.

- Ask everyone to commit to these guidelines. The guidelines should be ones by which the entire group feels comfortable abiding. Tell participants to take a moment and think about which guidelines they anticipate having trouble following. Then ask everyone in the group to commit to abiding by the guidelines for the duration of your time together. If possible, leave them where everyone can see them and refer back to them if you feel the safe space being disrupted.

READINGS ON FAITH AND SERVICE

Consider selecting a few readings from *Hearing the Call across Traditions: Readings on Faith and Service* that you have asked participants to read ahead of time. You can try to choose one or two readings from each of the three parts, or just focus on one of the overarching questions that define the parts and pick readings from that part. Either way, try to make sure that you have a good diversity of readings from different religious and philosophical backgrounds. For help in selecting readings and maintaining this diversity, see appendix III.

In addition to the questions found in appendix II that correspond to the readings you have selected, discuss the following questions as well:

- Did any of the readings particularly resonate with you? Why?

- Was the reading that did resonate with you from your own religious or philosophical perspective? If not, were you surprised that you found the reading of another religious or philosophical perspective compelling?

- Did you hear anything from the readings that you found particularly challenging? What was challenging for you and why?

DIALOGUE THROUGH SHARING STORIES

Sharing stories from our own experience is a powerful way to affirm our unique identity while building community with those who hear our stories. An exchange of ideas, experience, and trust occurs each time we tell or hear a story.

Ask and discuss the following questions:

- Talk about an experience of service that was particularly meaningful for you. It does not necessarily have to be related to your religious or philosophical community. Why was the experience so meaningful?

- Reflect on what inspired you to do this particular service work. What was your inspiration? Was it something from your religious or philosophical perspective? If not, where did this inspiration come from?

- Does anyone else's story help you think of or remember a story from your experience? How do you feel they connect or overlap?

- Are you hearing anything from the other participants' stories that makes you think about service differently or in a new way?

RETURNING TO THE READINGS

After everyone who wishes has shared a story, ask participants to think about the readings again and to consider the following questions:

- Did any of the stories you heard remind you of something from one of the readings?

- Do you have any new insights into the readings based on the stories we just shared with one another?

- Do you see the themes of these readings in the stories we just shared?

- Do you see the source of your inspiration to serve in any of these readings? Which one or ones?

CONCLUDING THE DIALOGUE

Thank everyone for their time and participation. Go around the group and ask for closing reflections, reactions, or comments from each person. If you would like, reflect back some ideas or comments that you think are particularly beneficial for the group to remember as your discussion comes to a close. Encourage the group to organize and facilitate a dialogue of their own with friends, classmates, or members of their religious communities or interfaith groups. Suggest that they plan some sort of service event together as part of putting the idea of religious pluralism, which they just demonstrated in their dialogue, into action. If the group is interested, take a few moments to brainstorm what that action might be.

Joining the Movement

One important aspect of organizing interfaith action and reflection is remembering to register your project so that the rest of the interfaith movement knows what you are doing and how they can get involved.

Interfaith Youth Core runs a website that tracks different interfaith projects that the movement is putting on year-round. It is called the Bridge-builder's Network and it can be accessed here:

- http://bridge-builders.ning.com

In addition to registering your project, you can meet other members of the movement, see what they are working on, post questions or challenges, respond to discussion threads, and receive exclusive resources on how to better plan and run projects.

Additionally, consider attending the next National Conference on Interfaith Youth Work in Chicago. The conference will connect you to others doing interfaith work, help you consider ways to deepen this work in your area, and generate ideas for the future of the movement. To find out more about the National Conference, please visit:

- www.ifyc.org/events/conference

For more information on interfaith organizing and the interfaith youth movement, please visit the Interfaith Youth Core's website:

- www.ifyc.org

QUESTIONS FOR DISCUSSION

MARTIN LUTHER KING JR., "THE DRUM MAJOR INSTINCT"

- According to King, what is "the drum major instinct"? How does King see this instinct illustrated in the story of James and John from Mark 10?

- What are the "destructive" and "distorted" effects that King believes the drum major instinct can have on the personality if not "harnessed"?

- In King's view, what is the relationship between the drum major instinct and "forces of classism and exclusivism"? Why is this a particular problem for King when it comes to churches?

- How does the drum major instinct explain why poor white people, in King's view, can be led to support their own oppressors?

- Why does King find Jesus's reply to his disciples so interesting and surprising? What does King mean when he says that Jesus "reordered priorities" and gives a "new definition of greatness"? What is the new definition?

- What does King mean when he says "the great issue of life is to harness the drum major instinct"? How does harnessing the drum major instinct relate to what King calls Jesus's "new definition of greatness"?

- How does King draw parallels between the story of Jesus that he tells at the end of the essay and some of the activities of the civil rights movement? What do you make of these parallels?

- Toward the end of the essay, King lists things that he would like somebody to say about him at his funeral. To what extent does this exercise—imagining what will be said at your funeral—strike you as productive?

- King says that "everybody can be great because everybody can serve." Do you have experiences of feeling great through service?

- According to the "new definition of greatness" that King offers, how do you think the drum major instinct can be harnessed to address personal and social challenges that we face in our time?

"Why the Buddha Had Good Digestion," from *Avadānaśataka*

- What does the Blessed One mean when he says, "the acts that a person performs, whether pure or impure, bear fruit in the body and mind that he receives"?

- Does your tradition similarly attest to a relation between acts and fruits received? Does your experience attest to this?

- Why does the Blessed One respond to his interlocutors by telling a story?

- What do you make of the king's actions and his vow in response to the illness among his people? Why does he "sacrifice his own cherished life"? What makes such a sacrifice possible?

- Why does the fish/king announce himself to the people when he cures them?

- In your view, does this story culminate in the lesson the Blessed One draws from it?

- What do you find to be the relation between your service and your own well-being, physical and otherwise?

"In Praise of Generosity," from the Rig Veda

- How is it that "the riches of the man who gives fully do not run out"?

- What is the relationship between friendship and sympathy in this piece, and in your life?

- What does it mean to say that "the man who eats alone brings trouble on himself alone"?

- It appears to be difficult to argue with the concluding sentence, "two kinsmen do not give with the same generosity." Why don't they? Why are we likely to give with different—and different amounts of—generosity?

- Would it be desirable for all of us to give with the same generosity?

Abraham Joshua Heschel, "Solidarity, Reciprocity, and Sanctity," three Selections from *Who Is Man?*

- What does Heschel mean by "genuine solitude is not discarding but distilling humanity"?

- How could solitude be "a search for genuine solidarity"?

- Why does Heschel declare that "for man *to be* means *to be with* other human beings"?

- What does Heschel mean by "I become a person when I begin to reciprocate"? How do we learn to reciprocate?

- In what sense is "what I am" "not mine"?

Tayeb Salih, "A Handful of Dates," in *The Wedding of Zein and Other Stories*

- What accounts for the narrator's fond memories of his grandfather and the grandfather's apparent affection for the narrator?

- What does the narrator's grandfather think of Masood, and why?

- How does the narrator feel about his grandfather's explanation of what indolence is?

- What happens, literally, after Masood's dates have been harvested?

- Why does the narrator, at the conclusion of the story, disregard his grandfather's call?

- How does the narrator interpret his grandfather's request for the recitation of the "Chapter of the Merciful"?

- What is the relationship between the grandfather's and the narrator's understandings of the religion they have in common?

JANE ADDAMS, "THE SUBJECTIVE NECESSITY OF SOCIAL SETTLEMENTS," IN *TWENTY YEARS AT HULL-HOUSE*

- When Addams refers to the sentiment of universal brotherhood, she distinguishes between an emotion and a motive. What is the difference between the two, and why does Addams highlight this difference?

- In what sense is universal brotherhood a *democratic* ideal?

- What is the "forlorn feeling" Addams describes in the second paragraph of the speech? Have you felt this? When and why?

- What kinds of "destitution" is Addams interested in addressing here?

- Addams refers to "a certain renaissance going forward in Christianity." What does she mean by this, and what makes her think such a renaissance is occurring?

- How might religion "seek a simple and natural expression in the social organism itself"?

- Why does Addams put her hopes on settlement specifically?

- On what kind of action, with the democratic ideal in mind, do you put your hopes?

CHUANG-TZU, "ACTION AND NON-ACTION"

• What is "non-action"? How is it different from inaction?

• In the first part of the poem Chuang-Tzu compares "the sage," who has mastered non-action, with "still water." How are they similar?

• "Still water is like glass. / You can look in it and see the bristles on your chin." In this passage, water becomes a reflecting mirror. Do you see yourself reflected in this poem? What does it show you?

• What relationship does the second part of the poem assert between non-action and action? In what sense is non-action "the root" of action?

• Does this poem confirm or challenge your own ways of thinking about action, as someone engaged specifically in acts of service?

• What is the relationship between non-action and joy? When, if ever, do you experience joy in your service?

• If you were to put this poet's meditation on non-action *into* action—i.e., if you were to begin looking at the world as he does—how would your life change?

ISAIAH 58:2–12

• What is the complaint that motivates Isaiah's response in these verses?

• What kind of fast, according to this passage, ought to be chosen?

• What is meant by the claim "your light shall break forth like the dawn"?

• What explains the need for some or all of us to become "the repairer of the breach"?

• What do you make of the rewards offered toward the end of this passage?

SHIH TE, THREE POEMS

• What is the life the narrator can't enjoy, and why can't he enjoy it?

• What makes him uneasy?

• Why does the narrator discourage the study of "fine-bound books"?

• Why can't the narrator help thinking of the people in the world?

• How would you finish the sentence, "If you want to be happy …"?

LUKE 10:25–37

• What do you make of the lawyer's opening question to Jesus?

• Why does Jesus respond to the lawyer's second question with a story?

• What explains the fact that, in Jesus's story, the priest and the Levite walk past the man lying in the street?

• Why does the Samaritan stop to help this man?

• Are there other reasons why someone might stop to help in such a situation?

HAMZA YUSUF, "MISERLINESS," FROM *PURIFICATION OF THE HEART*

• In what sense is miserliness a "disease," to use Hamza Yusuf's term? What is the treatment for such a disease?

• What is the link between giving charity and being valorous or manly?

• When, according to Yusuf, should debts be forgiven, and why?

• What role does an awareness of death play in the counsel from Imām Mawlūd that Yusuf cites here?

• Yusuf's chapter concludes with the claim that misers are hated and even hate each other. How does this claim fit into the larger treatment of miserliness?

• What might we learn about generosity by thinking about miserliness in this way?

Flannery O'Connor, "The River," in *A Good Man Is Hard to Find and Other Stories*

- Why does Mrs. Connin look after Harry, and why does she take him to see the Reverend Bevel Summers?

- Why does Harry steal the book about Jesus?

- How does Harry/Bevel come to realize "that this was not a joke," and what does this mean?

- How does Mrs. Connin's refusal of money affect your sense of her?

- Why does Harry go back to the river? What is he looking for, and how does he hope to find it?

The Dalai Lama, "Compassion," from *The Essential Dalai Lama: His Important Teachings*

- Why does the Dalai Lama believe that "the individual is the key to all the rest"?

- What does the Dalai Lama understand compassion to be, and how is it different from attachment?

- Why does the Dalai Lama see a link between compassion and a positive or pleasant atmosphere? Do you agree that this link exists?

- How, according to the Dalai Lama, can we develop compassion?

- What, in your view, is the relationship between compassion and service?

Friedrich Nietzsche, "The Joy of Giving Joy," from *On the Genealogy of Morality*

- What does Nietzsche mean by "the happiness of the 'smallest superiority'"?

- Does this happiness necessarily accompany "all doing good," as Nietzsche suggests?

- Are there explanations—other than those offered by Nietzsche—for "the joy of giving joy"?

- What is the role of the priest in the development of the phenomena Nietzsche describes?

- Do you feel any connection between your own "will to power" and engaging in service?

"Selfless Service," from the Bhagavad Gita

- What does Krishna mean by "selfless service" or karma yoga?

- Why is there, according to Krishna, no rest, only work?

- How can one "work unselfishly for the good of all the world"?

- What does Krishna mean by his claim, "I have no work to do.... And yet I work." Why does he continue to act?

- What do you make of Krishna's answer to Arjuna's question about the power that drives man to act sinfully?

- Do you strive to do selfless service? Why or why not?

Surahs 93 and 107, from the Qur'an

- Why, according to this passage, should one neither treat the orphan with harshness nor repulse the petitioner?

- What is the relation between the goodness of the Lord and the treatment of the orphan?

- Who are those who are "neglectful" in their prayer?

- How do you recognize the needs of your neighbors?

- How do you decide whether to try and meet these needs?

Tim O'Brien, "Church," in *The Things They Carried*

- Why does Kiowa say, "You don't mess with churches"?

- What accounts for the relationship between Henry Dobbins and the two monks?

- Why does Dobbins consider taking the pledge after the war?

- What do you think the washing motion means?

- What do you make of the words Dobbins speaks at the end of the story? Why does the story end this way?

- What is the relationship in this story between the discussion about religion and the context in which it takes place?

- What kind of service do Dobbins and Kiowa and their colleagues provide? How is their service related to their religious or spiritual beliefs?

Rabindranath Tagore, Section 50, from *Gitanjali: Song Offerings*

- Why, when the narrator sees the chariot appear, does he think his "evil days were at an end"?

- Why does the narrator think alms will be given without him having to ask for them?

- What causes the narrator to characterize the charioteer's action as "a kingly jest"?

- How does the narrator move beyond his initially indecisive response?

- What do you make of the narrator's feelings—and his bitter tears—at the end of this poem?

- How do you decide how much to give to those who ask or seem to need?

Harold M. Schulweis, "Between"

- Think about a moment in which you felt you came to know God better. Were you, at that moment, in relationship? To what or whom?

- What does Schulweis mean when he says that God is "between" us?

- How does knowing God help us know/love/hear others?

- Why does Schulweis contrast mediation, insight, and feeling with claims, obligations, and commandments?

- Do you agree that we most seek God in connection, rather than in separateness? If so, why would that be? If not, why?

- What is truest, for you, of the claims Schulweis makes? What, if anything, does not ring true?

WALT WHITMAN, "THE BASE OF ALL METAPHYSICS," IN *LEAVES OF GRASS*

- What is the speaker's tone here?

- Who is speaking, and to whom?

- What does the speaker mean by the repeated word *underneath*?

- Why would the "dear love" named here stand beneath—and be common to—all the philosophy and religion this speaker has studied?

- Why end a course with this claim?

- Is there "dear love" between cities or between lands, and how does it appear as such?

- Where else do you see such "dear love"? What are its signs?

LAO-TZU, "A GOOD TRAVELER HAS NO FIXED PLANS," IN THE *TAO TE CHING*

- What, for the narrator, does "embodying the light" mean?

- What is the relationship between "a good traveler" and "a good man"? Do they proceed through the world in the same way? Are they good in the same way?

- Does this poem shed any light on what it is to be a bad man?

- What exactly is the "great secret" Lao-Tzu invokes at the end of the poem? Why is it a secret?

- How does this poem push us to conduct ourselves in the world, if it pushes us any particular way?

DOROTHY DAY, "THE FACES OF POVERTY," IN *LOAVES AND FISHES*

• Why does Day begin this chapter by stating that "poverty is a strange and elusive thing"? In what way is poverty strange and elusive and even paradoxical?

• What are the different faces of poverty that Day identifies?

• What does Day mean when she writes, "I am sure that God did not intend that there be so many poor"?

• What "sins against the poor" does Day describe? Do you agree with her formulation that these are sins against the poor? Are there other sins against the poor that Day does not name?

• What is "characteristically American" about the response to poverty that Day describes?

• How might we not fall short in our care for others?

HAFIZ, "THE DIFFERENCE BETWEEN"

• Why does the visiting prince choose to meet with representatives of the spiritual leaders rather than the leaders themselves?

• What do you think of the competition the prince establishes?

• Why does the saint choose Ramjoo as his representative?

• Why does the Perfect One choose Yasamin, and why does he make this choice without needing any consultation?

• Why does Yasamin's time with the prince make her so happy?

• What do you make of the prince's dream and his actions in its aftermath?

• How would you, following Hafiz's suggestion, "end this tale / In a way that will most / Uplift your heart"?

Leslie Marmon Silko, "The Man to Send Rain Clouds"

- Why, in the beginning of the story, don't Leon and Ken tell Father Paul that Teofilo has died?

- What moves Leon to ask Father Paul to bring his holy water to the graveyard? Is this an easy request to make, and how does Leon go ahead and make it?

- Why does Father Paul change his mind about participating in the funeral for Teofilo?

- Does Father Paul provide the kind of service he is there to provide?

- Why does Leon feel good at the end of the story? Do you feel good when the story ends? Why or why not?

I. L. Peretz, "If Not Higher"

- What kind of a person is the Litvak in this story? What is the significance of the distinction between a person who thinks of the holy books and a person who stuffs himself with the Talmud and the law?

- Why is the Litvak afraid when he finds himself alone with the rabbi?

- Why does the rabbi dress himself in "peasant clothes" for the activity ahead of him?

- What is the rabbi's mysterious business?

- Why does seeing the rabbi's activity lead the Litvak to become a disciple?

Anna Swir, "The Same Inside," in *Talking to My Body*

- Why does the narrator take the beggar's hand?

- How does the narrator come to know that the beggar is "the same inside"? How is she the same?

- What do you think the beggar wants from the narrator? What does the narrator want from the beggar?

- In what way is the narrator "close" to the beggar?

- Why does the narrator end up unsure about the initial reasons for her walk?

- When do you feel close to those you are trying to serve?

JOHN OSKISON, "THE PROBLEM OF OLD HARJO"

- Why does Miss Evans stammer and feel it is "hard to state the case" to Harjo after meeting his wives?

- What is the "humor" of the situation that finally "burst upon" Miss Evans? What does she understand about the "human aspect" that she didn't appreciate before? What does she understand when the text says that "she began to understand why Mrs. Rowell had said that the old Indians were hopeless"?

- How is Harjo Miss Evans' "creation"?

- What causes even Mrs. Rowell, a missionary, to feel that "it is a grievous misfortune that old Harjo should wish to unite with the church"?

- What is "the problem" of Old Harjo? Whose problem is it?

- Is "the problem of Old Harjo" a problem for those who engage in faith-based acts of service? When or when not?

- What is the "perplexity" that Miss Evans cannot "run away from"? How would you describe, in your own words, the central tension Miss Evans feels in this story? Have you ever felt a similar tension in your life? How did you handle it?

- What do either the "obligations of humanity" or the obligations of your tradition say about living with perplexity?

- How would you answer the question posed in the final line of the story: "And meanwhile, what?"

THICH NHAT HANH, "MEDITATION ON COMPASSION" AND "NOT TWO," FROM *PEACE IS EVERY STEP*

- Why does Hanh describe compassion as "a mind that removes the suffering that is present in the other"? Do you think of compassion as a *mind*?

- How is it possible to "become one with the object of our observation"?

- What gives Hanh confidence that compassionate observation "will naturally transform into some kind of action"?

- Hanh suggests that firm and authentic compassion will lead first to more ease in the person feeling the compassion, and then also to benefits for the object of compassion. What do you make of these effects and the order of their arrival?

- Why is it that, in Hanh's view, "Anyone who has made us suffer is undoubtedly suffering too"?

- In "Not Two," Hanh describes how he would look at the pictures of the children whose applications he used to translate. By doing this, Hanh writes, he "became the child and he or she became me, and together we did the translation." How does this process work, and what do you make of it?

"THE LEGEND OF THE LOWLY DEVOTEE," IN *THE TIRUVAÇAGAM*

- Why does the king "release" Paranjotiyar from military service?

- Why does Shiva disguise himself as he does?

- What do you make of Shiva's request and the way in which he reveals its full extent?

- What does Shiva mean when he indicates that it must be a "sacrifice willingly offered"?

- Why do we learn that the mother shares in demonstrating "unflinching devotion"?

• How can an act be "right in its motive, though forbidden in itself"? Does Paranjotiyar's act fit into this category? Can you think of other examples of these kinds of acts?

• What, in your understanding, does it mean to be a saint?

• What should we be ready to give up, and what should we give it up for?

RUTH 1–4:22

• Why, in your view, does Ruth stay with Naomi?

• What does Ruth give up and what does Ruth gain by this choice?

• Why does Boaz direct Ruth to glean from his fields?

• What do you make of Naomi's instructions to Ruth in the third section?

• How does Boaz interpret Ruth's presence at his feet?

• At what points throughout this text do characters choose to look after other characters? Why are these choices made?

CESAR CHAVEZ, "THE MEXICAN-AMERICAN AND THE CHURCH"

• What does Chavez mean by "spiritual guidance"? Why does he suggest that spiritual advice must be given by a friend?

• Why don't food baskets strike Chavez as an appropriate response from the Church to the needy?

• What kinds of beliefs is Chavez challenging with this speech? How does he navigate the challenges?

• What is the difference between paternalism and servanthood, as Chavez sees it?

CHITRA BANERJEE DIVAKARUNI, "THE WALK," FROM *LEAVING YUBA CITY*

- What do you notice about the world described in this poem?

- How does it feel for the narrator to walk this hill? How does she feel about the children? About the nuns? About herself?

- Why was the narrator "trained" not to talk to the kids she walked past?

- What would have been the problem had she talked with them?

- Why, after the walk, were the narrator and her peers unable to drink their tea?

- Do you believe that there are some people you ought not to talk to? What do you see as the dangers of such talk?

LINDA GREGG, "THE SHOPPING-BAG LADY," IN *ALMA*

- Why does the narrator say that she would not guess at the contents of the shopping-bag lady's bags?

- What, if found in these bags, could prove the shopping-bag lady was "happy more or less"?

- To whom is the narrator speaking, and what is the tone of the conversation?

- What does the narrator mean by "if there was disgrace, it was God's"?

- What is the narrator referring to at the end of the poem when she speaks of "the most important place we have yet devised"? What place is this?

BIDPAI, "THE CAMEL DRIVER AND THE ADDER"

- Why does the Camel Driver save the adder?

- What do you make of the Camel Driver's request as he releases the adder?

- Why might the adder be determined to sting the Camel Driver?

- What does the adder mean when he says that it is the custom of man to return evil for good?

- Why does the fox assist the Camel Driver?

- With this fable in mind, what would you say about the relationship between service and gratitude?

VALERIE MARTIN, "A RICH YOUNG MAN ON THE ROAD," FROM *SALVATION: SCENES FROM THE LIFE OF ST. FRANCIS*

- How would you characterize Francesco's first encounter with the two peasants on the road? What explains the way the two parties react to each other?

- What do you make of Francesco's actions at the tomb of Pietro? What inspires him to act this way?

- Why does Francesco exchange clothes with the young man on the church steps?

- What do you make of Francesco's day with the beggars? What do the beggars make of it, and what does Francesco make of it? Why does Francesco leave at the end of the day?

- Why, when Francesco comes across the leper on the road, does he stop rather than ride past?

- What is Francesco waiting for, in this encounter and in a larger sense?

- Why does the leper's extended hand free something in Francesco?

- What is the content of Francesco's realization "that this world is gone from him now, that there is no turning back"?

RUMI, "SAY YES QUICKLY"

- What "life" is Rumi telling us to forget? How is forgetting this life connected to saying "God is great"?

- What kind of street is it where people ask, "How are you," but no one asks, "How aren't you"?

- What does it mean to be "here unfaithfully with us" and why would it cause terrible damage?

- What is Rumi saying that he asks us to acknowledge is true? And why say yes quickly? Why the urgency?

- What is the "it" we were to have known "from before the beginning of the universe"?

- Why is it that the first thing Rumi asks us to do when we "get up" is pray?

- How does Rumi see us helping people? He asks us to pray first thing, then suggests that if we've opened ourselves to God's love, we're helping people we don't know and have never seen. Who are these people? And how exactly are we helping them?

MIKHAIL NAIMY, "HIS GRACE"

- Why is Abu 'Assaf so astonished to learn that the narrator and his friend do not know the bey?

- What accounts for how Sheik As'ad carries himself—at home and in New York?

- How does the restaurant-keeper treat the bey, and why?

- Whose "grace" is named in the story's title, and what form does this grace take?

- What does the narrator make of the way the restaurant-keeper treats the bey? What do you make of it?

- Is the bey worthy of the service the restaurant-keeper provides?

GERARD MANLEY HOPKINS, "GOD'S GRANDEUR"

- What does Hopkins mean by "the world is charged with the grandeur of God"?

- How would you answer Hopkins's question, "Why do men then now not reck His rod?"

• What does the poem's last image suggest to you?

• What does this poem say about the capacity of human action to impact the world?

• How does Hopkins reconcile his sense that "all is seared with trade" with what appears to be his hope?

• Is Hopkins hopeful, and why?

• As you look at the world around you and consider your capacity to impact it, where do you find hope?

Swami Vivekananda, "The Secret of Work," in The Complete Works, I:3

• Why does Vivekananda assert that "the gift of knowledge is a far higher gift than that of food and clothes"?

• In what sense is physical help "the last" and "the least" kind of help we can give?

• Why, in Vivekananda's view, must *every* work necessarily be a mixture of good and evil? Do you agree that this is the case?

• How can we work incessantly without being attached to that work?

• Why does Vivekananda turn from discussing work to discussing character?

• How can we "work like a master and not as a slave"? Why is this desirable?

• What do you make of Vivekananda's exhortation to "invariably take the position of a giver"?

• What does Vivekananda mean when he writes, "God is unattached because He loves"?

• What is the significance of Vivekananda's story about the gold and brown mongoose?

- Do you agree with Vivekananda's sense of how the world is changing and the causes of this change?

SHOLOM ALEICHEM, "REB YOZIFL AND THE CONTRACTOR," IN *INSIDE KASRILEVKE*

- How does Reb Yozifl decide what his town most needs? Why a home for the aged and not, as the narrator says, a hospital?

- If Aleichem had continued with the parable Reb Yozifl used in his sermon, how might it have gone?

- What does Reb Yozifl mean by "messengers of a good deed ... can suffer no injury"?

- How does Reb Yozifl go about securing the funding to implement his plan?

- What do you make of Reb Yozifl's response to the slap? Why is it that "what happened next can't be told"?

- What is the connection between what finally became of the home for the aged and the way it was conceived?

- Does the work of service put us in the way of getting slapped, literally or figuratively? Why? How should we respond?

- What are the long-term impacts of Reb Yozifl's endeavor and Poliakov's gift?

- Who decides what your community's needs are and how those needs are met?

RYOKAN, "FIRST DAYS OF SPRING"

- How would you describe the narrator's mood? How does the narrator spend his day?

- In what ways does the narrator seem like a monk or a beggar?

- Why do passersby upbraid the narrator for being a fool?

- Why does the narrator choose not to answer those who criticize him?

- What is in fact in the narrator's heart? Why does he choose to answer this question—what's in his heart—given that nobody seems to have asked?

- What does "just this" refer to? Just what?

WILLIAM TREVOR, "SITTING WITH THE DEAD," IN *A BIT ON THE SIDE*

- Why do the Geraghty sisters come to sit with the dying?

- In what way, if at all, is their company a help to Emily?

- What does Norah mean by her comment, "You're Protestant here, but that never made a difference yet"? Is she right in this instance?

- What was so strange, so different, about this visit by the sisters?

- How should the dead be served, and why?

UMAR FARUQ ABD-ALLAH, "MERCY: THE STAMP OF CREATION"

- What, according to Abd-Allah, does mercy consist of? What is the difference between proactive and retroactive mercy?

- What, if anything, should place limits on mercy? Are there any beings to which or to whom we should not feel mercy, and if so, why not?

- How does a merciful nature, as Abd-Allah put it, establish authority?

- What is the relationship between love or affection and mercy?

- What is the relationship between justice and mercy?

- How important is it, in your service, to feel that you are acting with mercy?

Mahatma Gandhi, "Yajna, Welfare, and Service," from a letter to Narandas Gandhi, October 28, 1930

- What does Gandhi mean by "renunciation"? How is it that, in Gandhi's words, "For human beings, renunciation itself is enjoyment"?

- What binds all of us, in Gandhi's view, to "place our resources at the disposal of humanity"?

- When Gandhi writes of the sacrificial merchant, he claims that "the type ceases to be imaginary as soon as even one living specimen can be found to answer to it." What are the implications of this claim?

- What does Gandhi mean when he says, "Yajna is not yajna if one feels it to be burdensome or annoying"?

- How much do the feelings behind service matter, and why?

- Gandhi seems to imply at the end of the fifth paragraph that a person is either a servant or a tyrant—is this indeed Gandhi's implication, and is he right?

- How comfortable are you with Gandhi's assertion that voluntary service "must take precedence over service of self"? Do your beliefs make the same strong claim?

George Orwell, "Reflections on Gandhi," from the *Partisan Review*

- Can you think of a time when you have had to make a clear choice between loving humanity as a whole and loving a particular human being? If so, what guided your choice?

- What is the choice "between God and Man" that Orwell lays out? What would it mean to choose God—and why, according to Orwell, does Gandhi favor this option? What would it mean to choose humanity—and why does Orwell favor this option?

- Is there, as Gandhi claims, "some limit to what we will do in order to remain alive"? What is that limit? Where does it come from?

- Is it the essence of human beings not to seek perfection, as Orwell claims? If so, what makes this our essence? (Do we even have an essence?)

- In what way is Orwell's argument relevant for those who do service? If we accept his argument, how would we serve?

MAIMONIDES, "LEVELS OF GIVING," IN *MISHNEH TORAH*

- How would you explain the order of giving that Maimonides lays out? Are there guiding principles that explain his ranking?

- Why is anonymity so important in a few of the higher stages of giving?

- What exactly do you see happening at the highest stage, and do you agree that this should be considered the highest kind of giving?

- Why does Maimonides call attention to the identity of the recipient only at the highest level?

- Could you design your own ranking of kinds of giving or service?

- Is it useful, in your view, to rank different kinds of giving in this way? If so, under what circumstances might it be especially useful?

MARY OLIVER, "THE BUDDHA'S LAST INSTRUCTION," IN *HOUSE OF LIGHT*

- What is the import of the Buddha's last instruction? What does it mean to make of yourself a light?

- What does the narrator observe about the sun, as a light?

- What does the narrator mean by "clearly I'm not needed," and how does this square with the feeling of becoming valuable?

- Why are the faces surrounding the Buddha frightened?

- Could you really think every morning of making of yourself a light? Would this be a good thing?

- What sort of light should you try to be?

Mark Helprin, "North Light—A Recollection in the Present Tense," in *Ellis Island and Other Stories*

• What does the narrator mean when he says, "No one wants this"?

• What makes the men in the story so angry? Is anger useful for the activity ahead of them?

• Why is it so difficult for these men to wait?

• Is this a story about service?

Rumi, "Come Out and Give Something"

• What does Rumi mean by "every prophet is a beggar"? Would Rumi say that the reverse is also true, that every beggar is a prophet?

• Why do prophets, to whom all the doors of heaven are open, beg for pieces of bread?

• Why does Rumi move between prophets and teachers as if there is no difference between them?

• What is the "alchemy" that happens inside us?

• How does every experience beg us to come out and give something? What should we give, and to whom?

Peggy Payne, "The Pure in Heart," in *Revelation*

• What is the difference between being "called" to do something and, as Swain would have it, knowing "that it would be so"?

• Why are Swain and his wife so thrown by Swain's having heard God talk to him?

• Why does Swain end up telling his congregation what has happened? Do you agree that Swain should have gone ahead and said all this?

- What does Swain mean when he says, toward the end of the story, "What I heard is not what I ever would have hoped or expected to hear"?

- To what extent are you comfortable discussing your beliefs—and your feelings around these beliefs—with your colleagues and with those you serve?

GABRIELA MISTRAL, "THE HOUSE"

- What is "bread that almost speaks"?

- Why does the speaker encourage the little son to lower his hand that reaches for food?

- What are the "ashamed hands" the narrator refers to, and what causes them?

- Why do they leave the bread "until tomorrow"?

- How does the poem's concluding image leave you feeling?

ABRAHAM LINCOLN, "PROCLAMATION OF A NATIONAL FAST-DAY"

- What does Lincoln intend to accomplish by establishing a day of "humiliation, prayer, and fasting"?

- Does Lincoln succeed, in this short proclamation, in establishing a connection between the state of the nation and the conduct of individuals?

- What specific kinds of conduct does he push his countrymen toward, if any?

- Toward the end of the proclamation, Lincoln explicitly appeals to countrymen of all religions; does this appeal in fact speak to such a potentially wide array of people?

- What good might national fasting serve, in Lincoln's view? In yours?

- What would be the effect of—and the reaction to—such a proclamation today?

KABIR, "THE YOGI DYES HIS GARMENTS"

• Why does the yogi dye his robes?

• What does Kabir think the yogi should do differently?

• In what sense is the yogi shackled?

• How might Kabir think a person could enter the gates of death freed?

• What is a mind dyed in the colors of love?

ANNE LAMOTT, "WHY I MAKE SAM GO TO CHURCH," FROM *TRAVELING MERCIES: SOME THOUGHTS ON FAITH*

• What link does Lamott see between practicing your faith and having "purpose, heart, balance, gratitude, joy"? Do you see a similar link?

• What do you think Lamott means by "spiritual chemotherapy"?

• Why do Lamott's fellow churchgoers rejoice and then provide for Lamott and her family? Why do they *stealthily* stuff bills into her pocket?

• Why does Lamott feel shame at these moments, and how does she handle this feeling of shame?

• Why do you think Josh changes his mind in the back of Lamott's car, and what do you make of Lamott's behavior throughout the whole episode?

• What, in Lamott's view, is the relationship between Mary Williams and why Lamott makes Sam go to church?

GUIDE TO READINGS BY FAITH
TRADITION AND GENRE

Our hope for *Hearing the Call across Traditions: Readings on Faith and Service* is that the book will be of service to people as they talk within and across religious and philosophical traditions. The readings in this book were selected because we believe they can be put to good use in fostering meaningful conversations.

As we thought about how different individuals and groups might use this book, we imagined that some might want to select specific types of texts for certain gatherings or conversations. A group might want to select texts representing each of the major religious traditions. For example, a Christian group may want to organize a series of conversations around Islam and may want to select only texts by Muslim authors. Another group may want to mix up the texts so that they include essays, stories, and poems. And another group, pressed for time in its gatherings, may want to select pieces that are short and that do not need to be read in advance.

In order to help people more readily find the kinds of readings they seek, this appendix organizes the readings according to the faith tradition they represent and according to their genre or format.

A note about how we have categorized the readings by faith tradition: In general, readings were "assigned" to a particular faith category when the faith tradition of the writer was clear or a particular faith is clearly referenced in the text. This means that a number of texts in the anthology are not categorized here and that some of the categorical decisions we have made here might be disputed. We recognize that the list below is far from perfect, but hope that it can be helpful.

READINGS BY FAITH TRADITION

(Please note that titles are listed in order of appearance.)

BUDDHIST

"Why the Buddha Had Good Digestion," from *Avadānaśataka*

Shih Te, Three Poems

The Dalai Lama, "Compassion," from *The Essential Dalai Lama: His Important Teachings*

Thich Nhat Hanh, "Meditation on Compassion" and "Not Two," from *Peace Is Every Step*

Ryokan, "First Days of Spring"

Mary Oliver, "The Buddha's Last Instruction," in *House of Light*

CHRISTIAN

Martin Luther King Jr., "The Drum Major Instinct"

Jane Addams, "The Subjective Necessity of Social Settlements," in *Twenty Years at Hull-House*

Isaiah 58:2–12

Luke 10:25–37

Flannery O'Connor, "The River," in *A Good Man Is Hard to Find and Other Stories*

Dorothy Day, "The Faces of Poverty," in *Loaves and fishes*

Leslie Marmon Silko, "The Man to Send Rain Clouds"

Ruth 1–4:22

Cesar Chavez, "The Mexican-American and the Church"

Valerie Martin, "A Rich Young Man on the Road," from *Salvation: Scenes from the Life of St. Frances*

Gerard Manley Hopkins, "God's Grandeur"

William Trevor, "Sitting with the Dead," in *A Bit on the Side*

Peggy Payne, "The Pure in Heart," in *Revelation*

Anne Lamott, "Why I Make Sam Go to Church," from *Traveling Mercies: Some Thoughts on Faith*

HINDU

"In Praise of Generosity," from the Rig Veda

"Selfless Service," from the Bhagavad Gita

Rabindranath Tagore, Section 50, from *Gitanjali: Song Offerings*

"The Legend of the Lowly Devotee," in *The Tiruvaçagam*

Swami Vivekananda, "The Secret of Work," in *The Complete Works*, I:3

Mahatma Gandhi, "Yajna, Welfare, and Service," from a letter to Narandas Gandhi, October 28, 1930

JEWISH

Abraham Joshua Heschel, "Solidarity, Reciprocity, and Sanctity," three selections from *Who Is Man?*

Isaiah 58:2–12

Harold M. Schulweis, "Between"

I. L. Peretz, "If Not Higher"

Ruth 1–4:22

Sholom Aleichem, "Reb Yozifl and the Contractor," in *Inside Kasrilevke*

Maimonides, "Levels of Giving," in *Mishneh Torah*

Mark Helprin, "North Light—A Recollection in the Present Tense," in *Ellis Island and Other Stories*

MUSLIM

Tayeb Salih, "A Handful of Dates," in *The Wedding of Zein and Other Stories*

Hamza Yusuf, "Miserliness," from *Purification of the Heart*

Surahs 93 and 107, from the Qur'an

Hafiz, "The Difference Between"

Rumi, "Say Yes Quickly"

Mikhail Naimy, "His Grace"

Umar Faruq Abd-Allah, "Mercy: The Stamp of Creation"

Rumi, "Come Out and Give Something"

TAOIST

Chuang-Tzu, "Action and Non-Action"

Lao-Tzu, "A Good Traveler Has No Fixed Plans," in the *Tao Te Ching*

READINGS BY GENRE

ESSAYS, SERMONS, MEMOIRS, AND SPEECHES

Martin Luther King Jr., "The Drum Major Instinct"

"In Praise of Generosity," from the Rig Veda

Abraham Joshua Heschel, "Solidarity, Reciprocity, and Sanctity," three selections from *Who Is Man?*

Jane Addams, "The Subjective Necessity of Social Settlements," in *Twenty Years at Hull-House*

Hamza Yusuf, "Miserliness," from *Purification of the Heart*

The Dalai Lama, "Compassion," from *The Essential Dalai Lama: His Important Teachings*

Friedrich Nietzsche, "The Joy of Giving Joy," from *On the Genealogy of Morality*

Dorothy Day, "The Faces of Poverty," in *Loaves and Fishes*

Thich Nhat Hanh, "Meditation on Compassion" and "Not Two," from *Peace Is Every Step*

Cesar Chavez, "The Mexican-American and the Church"

Swami Vivekananda, "The Secret of Work," in *The Complete Works,* I:3

Umar Faruq Abd-Allah, "Mercy: The Stamp of Creation"

Mahatma Gandhi, "Yajna, Welfare, and Service," from a letter to Narandas Gandhi, October 28, 1930

George Orwell, "Reflections on Gandhi," from the *Partisan Review*

Maimonides, "Levels of Giving," in *Mishneh Torah*

Abraham Lincoln, "Proclamation of a National Fast-Day"

Anne Lamott, "Why I Make Sam Go to Church," from *Traveling Mercies: Some Thoughts on Faith*

STORIES, FABLES, PARABLES, AND MYTHS

"Why the Buddha Had Good Digestion," from *Avadānaśataka*

Tayeb Salih, "A Handful of Dates," in *The Wedding of Zein and Other Stories*

Flannery O'Connor, "The River," in *A Good Man Is Hard to Find and Other Stories*

Tim O'Brien, "Church," in *The Things They Carried*

Rabindranath Tagore, Section 50, from *Gitanjali: Song Offerings*

Leslie Marmon Silko, "The Man to Send Rain Clouds"

I. L. Peretz, "If Not Higher"

John Oskison, "The Problem of Old Harjo"

"The Legend of the Lowly Devotee," in *The Tiruvaçagam*

Bidpai, "The Camel Driver and the Adder"

Valerie Martin, "A Rich Young Man on the Road," from *Salvation: Scenes from the Life of St. Fancis*

Mikhail Naimy, "His Grace"

Sholom Aleichem, "Reb Yozifl and the Contractor," in *Inside Kasrilevke*

William Trevor, "Sitting with the Dead," in *A Bit on the Side*

Mark Helprin, "North Light—A Recollection in the Present Tense," in *Ellis Island and Other Stories*

Peggy Payne, "The Pure in Heart," in *Revelation*

POEMS

Chuang-Tzu, "Action and Non-Action"

Shih Te, Three Poems

Harold M. Schulweis, "Between"

Walt Whitman, "The Base of All Metaphysics," in *Leaves of Grass*

Lao-Tzu, "A Good Traveler Has No Fixed Plans," in the *Tao Te Ching*

Hafiz, "The Difference Between"

Anna Swir, "The Same Inside," in *Talking to My Body*

Chitra Banerjee Divakaruni, "The Walk," from *Leaving Yuba City*

Linda Gregg, "The Shopping-Bag
Lady," in *Alma*

Rumi, "Say Yes Quickly"

Gerard Manley Hopkins, "God's
Grandeur"

Ryokan, "First Days of Spring"

Mary Oliver, "The Buddha's Last
Instruction," in *House of Light*

Rumi, "Come Out and Give
Something"

Gabriela Mistral, "The House"

Kabir, "The Yogi Dyes His Garments"

SACRED TEXTS

Luke 10:25–37

"In Praise of Generosity," from the Rig
Veda

"Selfless Service," from the Bhagavad
Gita

Isaiah 58:2–12

Ruth 1–4:22

Surahs 93 and 107, from the Qur'an

SHORT TEXTS THAT CAN BE
READ AT THE DISCUSSION

"Why the Buddha Had Good
Digestion," from *Avadānaśataka*

"In Praise of Generosity" from the Rig
Veda

Chuang-Tzu, "Action and Non-
Action"

Isaiah 58:2–12

Shih Te, Three Poems

Luke 10:25–37

Friedrich Nietzsche, "The Joy of Giving
Joy," from *On the Genealogy of Morality*

"Selfless Service," from the Bhagavad
Gita

Surahs 93 and 107, from the Qur'an

Rabindranath Tagore, Section 50, from
Gitanjali: Song Offerings

Harold M. Schulweis, "Between"

Walt Whitman, "The Base of All
Metaphysics," in *Leaves of Grass*

Lao-Tzu, "A Good Traveler Has No
Fixed Plans," in the *Tao Te Ching*

Hafiz, "The Difference Between"

Anna Swir, "The Same Inside," in
Talking to My Body

Thich Nhat Hanh, "Meditation on
Compassion" and "Not Two," from
Peace Is Every Step

"The Legend of the Lowly Devotee," in
The Tiruvaçagam

Ruth 1–4:22

Chitra Banerjee Divakaruni, "The
Walk," from *Leaving Yuba City*

Linda Gregg, "The Shopping-Bag
Lady," in *Alma*

Bidpai, "The Camel Driver and the
Adder"

Rumi, "Say Yes Quickly"

Gerard Manley Hopkins, "God's
Grandeur"

Ryokan, "First Days of Spring"

Mahatma Gandhi, "Yajna, Welfare, and
Service," from a letter to Narandas
Gandhi, October 28, 1930

George Orwell, "Reflections on
Gandhi," from the *Partisan Review*

Maimonides, "Levels of Giving," in
Mishneh Torah

Mary Oliver, "The Buddha's Last
Instruction," in *House of Light*

Rumi, "Come Out and Give
Something"

Gabriela Mistral, "The House"

Abraham Lincoln, "Proclamation of a
National Fast-Day"

Kabir, "The Yogi Dyes His Garments"

ABOUT THE SUPPORTING ORGANIZATIONS

The Illinois Humanities Council (IHC) is an educational organization dedicated to strengthening civic life by bringing people together to reflect, think critically, and actively exchange ideas. The IHC promotes greater understanding of, appreciation for, and involvement in the humanities by all Illinoisans, regardless of their economic resources, cultural background, or geographic location. The Illinois Humanities Council's programs and grants offer Illinois residents the opportunity to experience the humanities through a rich variety of formats, including small discussion groups in neighborhood coffee shops, lectures and performances at cultural venues, and reading and reflection seminars in hospitals across the state. The IHC seeks to broaden public involvement in civic dialogue, deepen the quality of community conversation and reflection, increase public access to the humanities by lowering barriers to participation, and expand humanities activities in unexpected places. Organized as a state affiliate of the National Endowment for the Humanities (NEH) in 1973, the IHC is now a private nonprofit (501 [c] 3) organization funded by contributions from individuals, corporations, and foundations; by the Illinois General Assembly through the Illinois Arts Council, a state agency; and by the NEH. For more information about the IHC, please visit www.prairie.org.

The Interfaith Youth Core (IFYC) is a Chicago-based international nonprofit striving to build a global movement of religious pluralism among young people from diverse religious and philosophical perspectives by empowering them to work together to serve others.

These religiously diverse young people number in the millions across the world and they are interacting with greater frequency. That interaction tends toward either conflict or cooperation. Where so many of these interactions tend toward conflict, IFYC believes it is critical to shape a positive response to interreligious interaction. IFYC envisions a world in which young people from diverse religious and philosophical perspectives interact peacefully to create understanding and collaboration, thereby strengthening civil society and stabilizing global politics. Instead of focusing interfaith dialogue on political or theological differences, we build relationships on the values that we share—such as hospitality and caring for the Earth—and how we can live out those values together to contribute to the betterment of our community. IFYC is catalyzing and growing this movement by spreading the idea of religious pluralism with young people as its builders; training young people and their allies with the framework, knowledge base, and skill sets to build religious pluralism; and nurturing and networking leaders who have made a sustained commitment to building religious pluralism. For more information about IFYC, please visit www.ifyc.org.

The Project on Civic Reflection (PCR) helps civic groups build capacity, commitment, and community through programs of reading and discussion. By reflecting on their values and choices, people who are civically active can work more effectively together and respond more imaginatively to those they serve. The Project on Civic Reflection was established at Valparaiso University in 1998, with support from Lilly Endowment Inc., by Elizabeth Lynn. Begun as a local experiment in northwest Indiana, the Project has evolved into a national presence with a reputation for excellence and expertise in civic reading and conversation. Among the resources that the Project on Civic Reflection offers are an extensive electronic resource library; an online forum in which facilitators share their experiences; expert training in facilitation; individual consultation with Project staff; partnerships with service and philanthropic networks; and anthologies of readings that inspire rich conversation about civic engagement. For more information about the Project on Civic Reflection, contact us at (219) 464-6767 or visit our website at www.civicreflection.org.

PERMISSIONS

Global Spiritual Perspectives

Spiritual Perspectives on America's Role as Superpower
by the Editors at SkyLight Paths

Are we the world's good neighbor or a global bully? From a spiritual perspective, what are America's responsibilities as the only remaining superpower? Contributors:

Dr. Beatrice Bruteau • Dr. Joan Brown Campbell • Tony Campolo • Rev. Forrest Church • Lama Surya Das • Matthew Fox • Kabir Helminski • Thich Nhat Hanh • Eboo Patel • Abbot M. Basil Pennington, ocso • Dennis Prager • Rosemary Radford Ruether • Wayne Teasdale • Rev. William McD. Tully • Rabbi Arthur Waskow • John Wilson

5½ x 8½, 256 pp, Quality PB, 978-1-893361-81-2 **$16.95**

Spiritual Perspectives on Globalization, 2nd Edition
Making Sense of Economic and Cultural Upheaval
by Ira Rifkin; Foreword by Dr. David Little, Harvard Divinity School

What is globalization? Surveys the religious landscape. Includes a new Discussion Guide designed for group use.

5½ x 8½, 256 pp, Quality PB, 978-1-59473-045-0 **$16.99**

Religious Etiquette / Reference

How to Be a Perfect Stranger, 4th Edition
The Essential Religious Etiquette Handbook
Edited by Stuart M. Matlins and Arthur J. Magida

The indispensable guidebook to help the well meaning guest when visiting other people's religious ceremonies. A straightforward guide to the rituals and celebrations of the major religions and denominations in the United States and Canada from the perspective of an interested guest of any other faith, based on information obtained from authorities of each religion. Belongs in every living room, library and office. Covers:

African American Methodist Churches • Assemblies of God • Bahá'í • Baptist • Buddhist • Christian Church (Disciples of Christ) • Christian Science (Church of Christ, Scientist) • Churches of Christ • Episcopalian and Anglican • Hindu • Islam • Jehovah's Witnesses • Jewish • Lutheran • Mennonite/Amish • Methodist • Mormon (Church of Jesus Christ of Latter-day Saints) • Native American/First Nations • Orthodox Churches • Pentecostal Church of God • Presbyterian • Quaker (Religious Society of Friends) • Reformed Church in America/Canada • Roman Catholic • Seventh-day Adventist • Sikh • Unitarian Universalist • United Church of Canada • United Church of Christ

6 x 9, 432 pp, Quality PB, 978-1-59473-140-2 **$19.99**

The Perfect Stranger's Guide to Funerals and Grieving Practices
A Guide to Etiquette in Other People's Religious Ceremonies
Edited by Stuart M. Matlins
6 x 9, 240 pp, Quality PB, 978-1-893361-20-1 **$16.95**

The Perfect Stranger's Guide to Wedding Ceremonies
A Guide to Etiquette in Other People's Religious Ceremonies
Edited by Stuart M. Matlins
6 x 9, 208 pp, Quality PB, 978-1-893361-19-5 **$16.95**

Judaism / Christianity / Interfaith

Talking about God: Exploring the Meaning of Religious Life with Kierkegaard, Buber, Tillich and Heschel *by Daniel F. Polish, PhD*
Examines the meaning of the human religious experience with the greatest theologians of modern times.   6 x 9, 176 pp, HC, 978-1-59473-230-0 **$21.99**

Interactive Faith: The Essential Interreligious Community-Building Handbook *Edited by Rev. Bud Heckman with Rori Picker Neiss* A guide to the key methods and resources of the interfaith movement.   6 x 9, 304 pp, HC, 978-1-59473-237-9 **$40.00**

The Jewish Approach to Repairing the World (*Tikkun Olam*)
A Brief Introduction for Christians *by Rabbi Elliot N. Dorff, PhD, with Reverend Cory Willson*
A window into the Jewish idea of responsibility to care for the world.
5½ x 8½, 256 pp, Quality PB, 978-1-58023-349-1 **$16.99** *(A book from Jewish Lights, SkyLight Paths' sister imprint)*

Modern Jews Engage the New Testament: Enhancing Jewish Well-Being in a Christian Environment *by Rabbi Michael J. Cook, PhD*
A look at the dynamics of the New Testament.   6 x 9, 416 pp, HC, 978-1-58023-313-2 **$29.99**
(A book from Jewish Lights, SkyLight Paths' sister imprint)

Disaster Spiritual Care: Practical Clergy Responses to Community, Regional and National Tragedy *Edited by Rabbi Stephen B. Roberts, BCJC, & Rev. Willard W.C. Ashley, Sr., DMin, DH* The definitive reference for pastoral caregivers of all faiths involved in disaster response.   6 x 9, 384 pp, Hardcover, 978-1-59473-240-9 **$40.00**

The Changing Christian World: A Brief Introduction for Jews
by Rabbi Leonard A. Schoolman 5½ x 8½, 176 pp, Quality PB, 978-1-58023-344-6 **$16.99**
(A book from Jewish Lights, SkyLight Paths' sister imprint)

The Jewish Connection to Israel, the Promised Land: A Brief Introduction for Christians *by Rabbi Eugene Korn, PhD* 5½ x 8½, 192 pp, Quality PB, 978-1-58023-318-7 **$14.99**
(A book from Jewish Lights, SkyLight Paths' sister imprint)

Christians and Jews in Dialogue: Learning in the Presence of the Other
by Mary C. Boys and Sara S. Lee; Foreword by Dorothy C. Bass Inspires renewed commitment to dialogue between religious traditions.   6 x 9, 240 pp, Quality PB, 978-1-59473-254-6 **$18.99**; HC, 978-1-59473-144-0 **$21.99**

Healing the Jewish-Christian Rift: Growing Beyond Our Wounded History
by Ron Miller and Laura Bernstein; Foreword by Dr. Beatrice Bruteau
6 x 9, 288 pp, Quality PB, 978-1-59473-139-6 **$18.99**

Introducing My Faith and My Community: The Jewish Outreach Institute Guide for the Christian in a Jewish Interfaith Relationship *by Rabbi Kerry M. Olitzky* 6 x 9, 176 pp, Quality PB, 978-1-58023-192-3 **$16.99** *(A book from Jewish Lights, SkyLight Paths' sister imprint)*

The Jewish Approach to God: A Brief Introduction for Christians *by Rabbi Neil Gillman*
5½ x 8½, 192 pp, Quality PB, 978-1-58023-190-9 **$16.95** *(A book from Jewish Lights, SkyLight Paths' sister imprint)*

Jewish Holidays: A Brief Introduction for Christians *by Rabbi Kerry M. Olitzky and Rabbi Daniel Judson* 5½ x 8½, 176 pp, Quality PB, 978-1-58023-302-6 **$16.99**
(A book from Jewish Lights, SkyLight Paths' sister imprint)

Jewish Ritual: A Brief Introduction for Christians
by Rabbi Kerry M. Olitzky and Rabbi Daniel Judson 5½ x 8½, 144 pp, Quality PB, 978-1-58023-210-4 **$14.99**
(A book from Jewish Lights, SkyLight Paths' sister imprint)

Jewish Spirituality: A Brief Introduction for Christians *by Rabbi Lawrence Kushner*
5½ x 8½, 112 pp, Quality PB, 978-1-58023-150-3 **$12.95** *(A book from Jewish Lights, SkyLight Paths' sister imprint)*

A Jewish Understanding of the New Testament *by Rabbi Samuel Sandmel;*
new Preface by Rabbi David Sandmel 5½ x 8½, 368 pp, Quality PB, 978-1-59473-048-1 **$19.99**

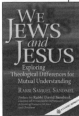

We Jews and Jesus: Exploring Theological Differences for Mutual Understanding
by Rabbi Samuel Sandmel; new Preface by Rabbi David Sandmel A Classic Reprint
6 x 9, 192 pp, Quality PB, 978-1-59473-208-9 **$16.99**

Show Me Your Way: The Complete Guide to Exploring Interfaith Spiritual Direction
by Howard A. Addison 5½ x 8½, 240 pp, Quality PB, 978-1-893361-41-6 **$16.95**

About SKYLIGHT PATHS Publishing

SkyLight Paths Publishing is creating a place where people of different spiritual traditions come together for challenge and inspiration, a place where we can help each other understand the mystery that lies at the heart of our existence.

Through spirituality, our religious beliefs are increasingly becoming a part of our lives—rather than *apart* from our lives. While many of us may be more interested than ever in spiritual growth, we may be less firmly planted in traditional religion. Yet, we do want to deepen our relationship to the sacred, to learn from our own as well as from other faith traditions, and to practice in new ways.

SkyLight Paths sees both believers and seekers as a community that increasingly transcends traditional boundaries of religion and denomination—people wanting to learn from each other, *walking together, finding the way.*

For your information and convenience, at the back of this book we have provided a list of other SkyLight Paths books you might find interesting and useful. They cover the following subjects:

Buddhism / Zen	Global Spiritual	Monasticism
Catholicism	Perspectives	Mysticism
Children's Books	Gnosticism	Poetry
Christianity	Hinduism /	Prayer
Comparative	Vedanta	Religious Etiquette
Religion	Inspiration	Retirement
Current Events	Islam / Sufism	Spiritual Biography
Earth-Based	Judaism	Spiritual Direction
Spirituality	Kabbalah	Spirituality
Enneagram	Meditation	Women's Interest
	Midrash Fiction	Worship

Or phone, fax, mail or e-mail to: SKYLIGHT PATHS Publishing
Sunset Farm Offices, Route 4 • P.O. Box 237 • Woodstock, Vermont 05091
Tel: (802) 457-4000 • Fax: (802) 457-4004 • www.skylightpaths.com
Credit card orders: (800) 962-4544 (8:30AM–5:30PM ET Monday–Friday)
Generous discounts on quantity orders. SATISFACTION GUARANTEED. Prices subject to change.

For more information about each book, visit our website at www.skylightpaths.com